Making Software Measurement Work

Building an Effective Measurement Program

The QED Software Evaluation Series

Making Software Measurement Work is the first of a planned series of books on the increasingly critical areas of how to evaluate and measure modern software systems.

The objective of the series is to provide an integrated set of books describing evolving best practice techniques and methods for evaluation, and how they are being effectively used by working practitioners and software managers.

Series development is a joint effort between QED and Software Quality Engineering's Software Practices Research Center. Each book undergoes extensive review to qualify for inclusion in the series and to be considered for the *Best Software Engineering & Software Management Books Catalog* offered by SingleSource™.

Other Books from QED

Systems Development

The Complete Guide to Software Testing
Developing Client/Server Applications
Quality Assurance for Information Systems
User-Interface Screen Design
On Time, Within Budget: Software Project Management Practices and Techniques
Managing Software Projects: Selecting and Using PC-Based Project Management Systems
From Mainframe to Workstations: Offloading Application Development
A Structured Approach to Systems Testing

Rapid Application Prototyping: The Storyboard Approach to User Requirements Analysis
Software Engineering with Formal Metrics

Information Engineering/CASE

Practical Model Management Using CASE Tools
Building the Data Warehouse
Information Systems Architecture: Development in the 90's
Enterprise Architecture Planning: Developing a Blueprint for Data, Applications, and Technology
Data Architecture: The Information Paradigm

Making Software Measurement Work

Building an Effective Measurement Program

Bill Hetzel

QED Publishing Group
Boston • London • Toronto

© 1993 QED Publishing Group
P.O. Box 812070
Wellesley, MA 02181-0013

QED Publishing Group is a division of QED Information Sciences, Inc.

Library of Congress Catalog Number: 93-18965
International Standard Book Number: 0-89435-465-5

Printed in the United States of America
93 94 95 10 9 8 7 6 5 4 3 2 1

Library of Congress Cataloging-In-Publication Data

Hetzel, William C., 1941–
    Making software measurement work : building an effective program / Bill Hetzel
        p.   cm.
    Includes bibliographical references and index.
    ISBN 0-89435-465-5
    1. Computer software—Quality control.   2. Function point analysis.   I. Title.
QA76.76.Q35H48   1993
005. 1'4—dc20   93-18965
                                                             CIP

Contents

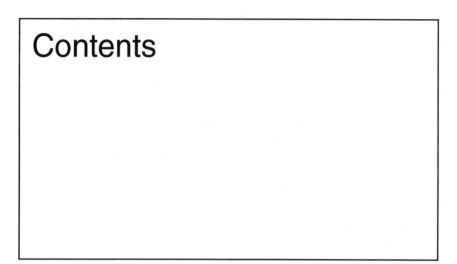

Making Software Measurement Work is divided into three parts:

Most readers (and especially those with substantial software and measurement backgrounds) will find that the three parts of this book, as well as most of the individual chapters, can be read and referenced quite independently.

Part 1 serves as the foundation, and at least Chapters 2 and 3 should be read first in order to understand the basic bottom-up measurement engineering approach and philosophy. Managers may find it best to then skip to Part 3 and return to Part 2 only as needed or appropriate.

In addition to being targeted at software practitioners and managers, the book is also intended to support industrial or college courses in software measurement and metrics. Discussion questions and suggested exercises are included at the end of each chapter. A teaching guide is also available.

For reference and follow-up research, the book also contains three comprehensive appendices. Appendix A lists several hundred software measurement references alphabetically by author. References to the bibliography are noted in the text by enclosing the author's last name and the year of publication in brackets, e.g., [Hetzel 93].

Appendix B is a selected bibliography of major references recommended for supplemental reading. These are annotated with brief descriptions and listed by category to help the reader understand what is available and how to locate or select the materials he or she needs.

Appendix C is a list of major measurement tool vendors with brief descriptions noting their products and services.

For updates to these reference appendices or suggested changes and additions to the text, readers may contact the author at the following address:

Dr. Bill Hetzel
Software Practices Research Center
3000-2 Hartley Rd.
Jacksonville, FL 32257
(904) 268-8639
Fax (904) 268-0733

PART I   SYSTEMATIC MEASUREMENT ENGINEERING

The first three chapters define what measurement is all about and introduce the book's philosophy of systematically designing and engineering a good measurement program around practitioner needs and engineering fundamentals.

Introduction to Software Measurement Practice provides a review of current industry measurement practices and their evolution and a definition of basic measurement terms and concepts.

The Measurement Process introduces a systematic measurement process model and contrasts the major paradigms for selecting measures. Describes the bottom-up IOR Measurement Engineering approach that forms the foundation for the book.

Getting Started outlines a recommended approach for starting or overhauling a software measurement program. This includes establishing a baseline and focusing on the three measurement building block systems (Resource Tracking, Work Product Tracking, and Problem or Defect Tracking).

PART II   PRACTITIONER-BASED MEASUREMENT

The next three chapters survey practitioner-based measurement techniques and present case examples of practical measurements for each major software activity.

Measuring Software Specifications and Designs outlines measures used in the early requirements and design activities.

Measuring Software Code and Implementation describes measures for the coding, implementation, and maintenance activities.

Measuring Software Test and Evaluation describes how to measure reviews, inspections, and testing.

PART III   MEASUREMENT FOR MANAGERS

The final three chapters demonstrate how the bottom-up measurement engineering approach also supports the needs of management and the industry to drive process improvement.

Measuring Projects describes what the project manager needs to measure and how to obtain it from the bottom-up IOR approach.

Measuring Processes outlines how to measure across projects and assess processes.

Measuring Best Processes examines techniques for defining and measuring best processes. Case examples of assessment and benchmarking best processes are presented.

APPENDICES

Foreword

FOREWORD BY NORMAN FENTON

Although papers on software metrics have appeared in research literature for 20 years, it is only in the last 5 years that there has been a widespread awareness of the important role of measurement in software engineering. Prior to this everybody knew there was a problem with inferior software quality and productivity, but few people bothered to quantify the situation, and even fewer still understood the potential of measurement to improve things. As the serious ramifications of *not* performing proper measurement have dawned on the software industry, the status of software metrics as a key subject in its own right has been elevated. The commercial desire to learn more about software measurement and compare best practices is immense. This is reflected in an explosion of activity.

Bill Hetzel, through the activities of Software Quality Engineering and the Annual International Conference on Software Measurement, has done more than anybody to promote awareness and technology transfer of software measurement. Bill has been a catalyst in the metrics revolution. It is therefore fitting that he should write this book. Apart from being a superb and extensive introduction to the subject, I believe this is the first book to give a truly broad picture of what is going on in practice in software measurement.

The book is radical in its approach to software measurement. Bill does not settle for the popular (but generally unvalidated) notion that all software measurement activities must start with high-level goals. He explains clearly the problems with this and proposes a bottom-up approach. Unlike some authors' writings on the subject, Bill has no particular axe to grind, model to promote, or tool to sell. His treatment of the subject is clear and objective, and he makes a very powerful argument for using measurement. The examples throughout are excellent. If you want to get started on a measurement program, small or large, then this book will explain the necessary practical steps.

While no introductory text can provide complete coverage of the subject area, Bill always provides pointers to where further details can be found. The result is that the book is a definitive source of information as well as a practical handbook.

I believe this book will prove to be a very significant milestone in software engineering. I am delighted to be a small part of it!

Preface

This book will tell you how to make software measurement work in your organization. A strong measurement program is a goal many of us seek, but few have found. We will explore the reasons for this and outline what you must do to engineer an effective program for your project, your division, or your company.

The book is also about getting working software practitioners and managers to use measurements routinely and to enthusiastically embrace measurement as a way of life. In most programs there is poor support—particularly at the engineering level. Measurement programs have failed to sufficiently recognize and target the practitioner. My aim is to demonstrate that good engineering and good management are intertwined and inseparable from good measurement. I see measurement as an integral part of all software (indeed all engineering) activity and hope to induce every reader to require good measurements as a basis for all important product, process, or project decisions.

Finally, this book is about getting all of us to take more professional responsibility in presenting measurement data. The good news is that many more measured results are making their way into various company reports and the published software literature. The bad news is that much of what we see lacks the elementary basics of good science and really cannot or should not be used as a basis for judgment or action. As an industry we must raise our standards and demand more measures of the measurements. Published results require validation, and all of us need to get better at making sure we don't make claims we can't support.

Some readers will sense a sort of missionary zeal in what I have written. If so, I make no apologies. I am personally arriving late to the measurement field, having traveled for many years in and about the testing discipline. For a long time I have been working to shape and develop better testing methods, and one of the key issues we still struggle with is how to measure its effectiveness. This brought me to the broader topic of overall software measurement, led to the organization of an annual international conference and an industry workshop on measurement applications and finally to this book. I have found the challenge of this new field to be immensely satisfying and hope this book will help convert and influence others so that together we can bring good measurement into the mainstream of engineering practice.

Bill Hetzel
Jacksonville, Florida

Acknowledgments

There are many people to whom I owe special thanks for making this book possible.

My biggest collective debt is to the thousands of students who have attended my seminars and lectures over the past ten years. Their questions, suggestions, ideas and discussions often centered on measurement issues and sharpened my interest and awareness of the importance of the field. It was to meet student needs that we first began measuring and tracking industry practices. Students eagerly devoured the data that we gathered and their skepticism and questions in response to everything we presented helped convince me how little we really understood about the job of properly and systematically measuring.

A special debt is also owed to those individuals who had a significant influence on my thinking.

First to Dave Gelperin, my partner at Software Quality Engineering, for the many stimulating (and sometimes seemingly endless!) details and discussions we've shared over the years. Dave's influence on testing methodology and practice has been profound and his impact on the field, as well as on my thinking and the book, has been major.

Secondly, to Bill Silver, my colleague in the development of our Software Measurement seminar and the editor of *Software*

Quality World. Bill and I spent an intensive couple of months in early 1990 honing our ideas about software measurement and researching the field. Much of the foundation thinking about measurement engineering and the practitioner paradigm that the book is built on was the result of this work, and a number of the illustrations and examples are taken directly from the seminar materials that were produced.

Thirdly to the authors of all of the recent measurement books that have done so much to help me and the industry better understand the field. Many good measurement books are now available. (See Appendix B for an annotated bibliography.) Of particular importance were Bob Grady's two books; *Practical Software Metrics for Project Management & Process Improvement* and *Software Metrics: Establishing a Company Wide Program,* and Norm Fenton's *Software Metrics—A Rigorous Approach.* Their impact on the measurement field has been very significant and their influence is felt throughout my book. I also drew significant material for Chapter 7 from David Youll's *Making Software Development Visible.*

Finally, to my friends and colleagues who agreed to serve as early reviewers and so patiently offered suggestions and improvements to the early versions of the text. I would especially note the contributions from Bob Glass and Norm Fenton. Ed Kit, Dave Gelperin and a number of my students also read portions of the draft and offered many helpful improvements.

My family and my company should also be singled out for making this possible. To Nancy, Andy and Ben who again suffered as I went from on the road to into my office and onto my computer, thanks for your enduring love and understanding. And to Software Quality Engineering and its leading edge clients I am truly indebted. The experience and knowledge gained in practical, real world measurement through my consulting, major conference and seminar engagements is immeasurable (even for a newly converted measurement fanatic!) and the opportunity to work on a labor of love like this book has been a special and wonderful privilege.

PART I

Systematic Measurement Engineering

"To measure is to know."
James Clark Maxwell

"You cannot control what you can't measure."
Tom DeMarco

"Invisible targets are usually hard to hit."
Tom Gilb

Introduction to Software Measurement Practice

"There is no other industry that knows so little about itself in a quantitative way."

Jerold Grochow

WHAT IS SOFTWARE MEASUREMENT?

Software Measure

A dimension, attribute, or amount of any aspect of a software product, process, or project.

A quantified observation.

From the first program written and the first project completed (or not completed) on time programmers, analysts, and managers alike have been concerned with the ideas and application of measurement.

The project manager wants to know where the project stands, how much time or effort has been spent, how much is left to do, and what will make the customer happy. The analyst wants to know what parts of the design are complete, how well it fulfills the requirements, and what will make the manager happy. The programmer wants to know what has and has not been coded and tested, what is left to do, and what will make everyone else happy. And everyone wants to know all of the outstanding issues and problems affecting the project or their particular area of responsibility.

"Knowing" the answers to such questions depends (at least in part) on the measurement of the properties of individual programs, systems, and projects. What we mean by a "measurement" is a *quantified observation* on some attribute or aspect of the software product, process, or project.

The observation may range from very simple counts (for example, pages of design documentation, lines of code, number of interfaces, number of hours worked, and so forth) to much more complex computed or derived measures of "fuzzy" properties like functional complexity, test thoroughness, quality, productivity, or effectiveness.

USEFUL MEASUREMENTS

While any measurement provides us with some additional knowledge, what ultimately distinguishes the relatively small number of "useful" measurements from the vast array of possible measurements is the degree of insight obtained and the usefulness of the information balanced against the cost and effort of obtaining it.

Useful Software Measure

Useful measures are those that support effective analysis and decision making and that can be obtained relatively easily.

We want measures that we can use to help us make decisions more effectively and to support our engineering efforts. The number and scope of potential software measurements is limited only by imagination and practical feasibility. Any quantified attribute on any aspect of a software product, process, or project could be a potentially useful measurement—even measurements on measurements, such as how accurate or valid they are or how much they are used! As in all engineering endeavors, some of the measures we wish we had are impractical to obtain while those that are available have various limitations and problems that restrain their effectiveness. Balancing this tradeoff and selecting the "right" mix of measures is what this book is all about.

Measures, Metrics, and Meters

What we care about most is being able to use measures to help us engineer and manage the software effort more successfully. "Use" of a measurement ranges from simply extending our knowledge and insight to directly influencing or controlling project or process actions and everyday engineering or management decisions. In this book *metric* and *meter* signify measures being *used* in an organization to guide and shape decision making or affect the software process.

Any measurement used to *compare* software projects or to *estimate* or predict project outcomes is a metric. Any measurement used to *control* or regulate a process is a meter. Note that any measurement has the potential to become a metric or meter or both. What makes it one in a given organization is the *act* of using it for comparative or predictive or control purposes. Such an act normally implies that an organization has sufficient experience and confidence with the measure and that they have been able to demonstrate its usefulness in support of decision making. This is an example of the important task of measuring our measurements—what we'll be discussing in the next chapter under the topic of *validation*.

Software Metrics

Measurements used to compare software processes and projects or predict software outcomes.

Software Meters

Measurements used to control or regulate a software activity or process.

These metric and meter notions are not standardized, but we believe the distinction is helpful and that this terminology will find increasing acceptance. An example of a predictive metric is the use of the number of *function points* taken at design time as a predictor for the effort required to build and implement the design. Examples of meters might include using the number of problems found during a code inspection to regulate the thoroughness of unit testing or using a design complexity measure such as *McCabe Complexity* to trigger the use of more rigorous design analysis techniques. The metering control action could be applied automatically (for example by invoking a special analysis tool when some measure reaches a threshold value), or it could serve as a manual signal to the engineer or manager that some action is required.[1]

THE STATE OF THE PRACTICE—A SURVEY PERSPECTIVE

The use of measurement to support software development and engineering is far short of what the casual observer or even the seasoned software manager might infer. A quick scan of current literature or attendance at various industry seminars and conferences leaves one with the impression that the use of measurement is extensive and mature. Recently published industry surveys (measurements of actual practice patterns), however, tell a much different story.

Baseline Measurement Practices Survey

In 1990 Software Quality Engineering conducted a large-scale survey aimed at measuring how industry was using software measurements and to *benchmark* what best companies and projects were doing. (I'll have more to say about the benchmark results in Chapter 9. In this chapter our concern is with typical or average practices, not the best or leading edge practices.)

The survey was distributed to eight hundred software organizations around the world. Respondents were asked to report their organization's degree of usage of a representative list of selected software measures. Company practices were highly variable. A very small percentage of companies reported regular use of most of the measures. Another one-third to one-half used none of the measures!

---

[1]Function points, defect density, and McCabe Complexity are measurements described in more detail in Part II of this book.

	Percent Reporting Common Use
Number of defects found after release	61%
Number of changes or change requests	55%
User or customer satisfaction	52%
Number of defects found during development	50%
Documentation completeness and accuracy	42%
Time to identify and correct defects	40%
Defect distributions by type or class	37%
Effort by major function or feature	32%
Test coverage of specifications	31%
Test coverage of code	31%
Defect density	27%
Module or design complexity	24%
Number of source lines delivered	22%
Documentation size and complexity	20%
Number of reused source lines	16%
Number of function points	10%

Figure 1.1.   Use of selected measurements in industry.

Overall usage of the measures surveyed was low. As shown in Figure 1.1 none of the measures were found to be in regular use by more than two-thirds of the responding companies. The trade press would have you believe that almost everyone is out counting lines of code or function points. The reality is far from it, with most companies (78 percent) not counting lines of code and an even greater percentage (90 percent) not using function points. Other seldom used measurements (by more than 70 percent) included defect density, test coverage, and complexity.

Most organizations also reported general dissatisfaction with their current measurement program. Over half rated the support and acceptance of their measurement program as "Non-existent" or "Poor." The baseline survey confirmed that most measurement programs are in their early stages. Use of measurements tends to lag behind the use of other software development technology. Over 60 percent felt usage was "Somewhat Systematic" compared to just 25 percent for the use of software measurements.

International Measurement Conference Survey

Attendees at the 1991 Applications of Software Measurement Conference (ASM91) were surveyed on the use of 65 commonly cited measurements. The measures in the survey included anything appearing in the literature as a recommended or suggested measurement, and were judged to be a comprehensive list covering all phases of the software life cycle from planning to maintenance.[2] The purpose of the survey was to determine software measurement usage and perceptions of value from experienced and knowledgeable organizations and individuals.

Most of the ASM91 attendees were professionally involved in measurement and were employees of companies progressive enough to recognize and fund their attendance at the conference. I suspect they typify the top quartile or decile of measurement practices. Yet, despite this obvious bias, the conference respondents were even harsher in their judgments about the state of current measurement programs than was apparent in the general industry baseline survey (see Figure 1.2).

When asked to rate their current program maturity 64 percent chose "in infancy"; only 15 percent indicated "established" and none selected "highly developed." (The remaining 21 percent indicated they had no measurement program.) When asked to rate their current program effectiveness, 66 percent chose "poor" and only 6 percent chose "good" or "excellent." Perhaps these knowledgeable measurement respondents are just overly critical of their own programs because they expect so much more from

---

[2]Most of the measures surveyed were fairly specific and defined clearly enough that the respondent had a good idea of how it might be collected (e.g., pages or lines of documentation, number of times tests are rerun, etc.). A few were more general (e.g., Customer Satisfaction or Design Coverage of Requirements). It is unclear how this impacts the responses. Some people might have valued "Customer Satisfaction" highly (gave it a 3). However, if asked to value Customer Satisfaction measured by the median value of a subjective survey, they might have scored that considerably lower (a 2 or perhaps even a 1 or a 0).

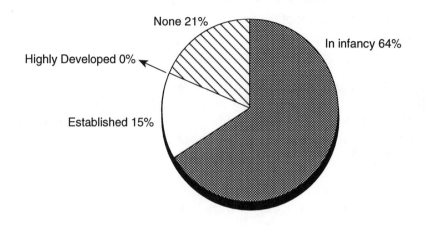

Maturity

None 21%

In infancy 64%

Highly Developed 0%

Established 15%

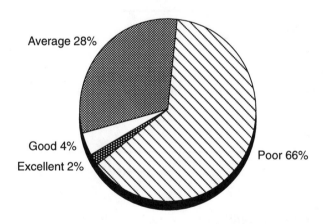

Effectiveness

Average 28%

Good 4%

Excellent 2%

Poor 66%

Figure 1.2.   Measurement program maturity and effectiveness.

them, however, I suspect the reality is that practitioners within the companies would be even harsher.

Respondents were also asked to indicate the usage and perceived value for each of the 65 measurements with the following 0 to 3 scale.

Usage Scale	Value Scale
0 Not in Use	0 Unimportant—a waste of time
1 Infrequent Use—some of the time	1 Limited—would be nice
2 Common Use—most of the time	2 Significant—recommended
3 Standard Use—routinely	3 Critical—should be standard

Industry use for almost all of the measurements was low. Sixty-two of the 65 measures had average "usage scores" (the arithmetic mean of the 0 to 3 usage responses)[3] of 1.5 or lower. Forty-four had means below 1.0. The lack of use was not due to a lack of perceived value. In contrast to the low reported usage, most of the measures received rather high "value scores" (the arithmetic mean of the 0 to 3 value responses). None of the value means were below 1.0; only 4 were below 1.5; and 36 were above 2.0 (see Figure 1.3).

The only 3 measures with mean usage scores above 1.5 were in

MEAN SCORE	USAGE	VALUE
Above 2.0	0	36
1.5–2.0	3	25
1.0–1.5	18	4
Below 1.0	44	0
	65	65

Figure 1.3. Usage and value of 65 selected measurements.

---

[3]*Note:* From a measurement theory point of view the study should have used *median* values, not means. (The median is the proper averaging statistic because the ordered response scale does not imply that the "difference" between a rating of 0 and a rating of 1 is the same as the "difference" between a rating of 1 and 2 or 2 and 3.) Converting to the median does not change any of the findings. For example, 62 of the 65 usage medians were 1 or less (implying that over half the respondents reported no use or infrequent use). Sixty of the 65 value medians were either a 2 or a 3 (implying that over half the respondents considered the measure to have significant value or critical value).

the project management area (plan versus actual budget and schedule, plan versus actual tasks, and plan or schedule changes), and none of these had means above 2.0. Included in the list of infrequently used measures were such oft-publicized ones as defect density, productivity, requirements problems and changes, complexity of designs and code, test coverage, function points, and reuse. The least-used measure of all was function point counting, which had a usage mean of only .3 (see Figure 1.4).

The measurement with the highest perceived value (perhaps not unexpectedly) was customer satisfaction, which scored 2.68. Several other highly valued measures were more of a surprise: for example, measuring the usage and value of measurements, compliance with process steps and test coverage, test effectiveness, and reliability. Seventeen of the measurements had value scores over 2.25 (see Figure 1.5).

The difference or *gap* between the value and usage scores was also analyzed. All of the 65 measurements surveyed had positive gaps, with most as large as 1.0. The 8 largest (those with gaps greater than 1.5) are listed in Figure 1.6. These are the measures with the biggest difference between perceived value and actual use. They should be the ones we are most motivated to use regularly.

It is interesting to me that the meta-measurement of measuring the use and value of measurements made this list. Throughout this book my emphasis will be on getting measurements *used*. Unless you measure how your measurements are used you won't really know how you are doing! Indeed, when we actually go out and measure the use of software measurements in industry, we find out how little industry progress and impact has been achieved and how much of a challenge lies ahead.

THE STATE OF THE PRACTICE—A HISTORICAL PERSPECTIVE

The last section examined the current state of software measurement practice with a review of industry survey data. Another perspective is gained through a look back at how the field has developed during the past three decades.

As little as 20 years ago there was only a trace of literature about the field and not a single prominent book on the subject.

Project Management
Effort or cost spent on
  measurement
Project or organization productivity
Individual productivity and
  schedule performance
The accuracy/validity of
  measurement information
The use and value of
  measurement information

Requirements
Effort or cost to review and inspect
Effort or cost to rework or correct
Amount (pages or lines) of
  documentation
Requirements problems (defects)
Requirements changes
Number of requirements
Requirements review effectiveness
Time spent by requirement or
  feature

Design
Effort or cost to review and inspect
Amount (pages or lines) of design
  documentation
Number of function or feature
  points
Design or system complexity
Reuse (percentage or amount)
Design coverage of requirements
Use of design automation tools
Design review effectiveness

Testing
Test execution code coverage
Requirements and design
  coverage
Test effectiveness
Reliability based on tests results
Use of test automation
Number of times tests are rerun

Coding
Effort or cost to review and inspect
Effort or cost to rework and fix
Lines of modified or changed
  source code
Number of function points
  delivered
Module or program complexity
Code inspection or review
  effectiveness
Coding problems during
  development
Number of source code compiles
Number of source code changes
Defects by phase introduced

Maintenance
Defect density
Impact of bad requirements or
  designs (cost or time)
Number of new defects per fix
Time to identify and correct defects
Defects by phase introduced
Defect detection efficiency
Maintainability

NEARLY ALL OF THE MEASURES SURVEYED!!

Figure 1.4.   Measurements with little usage
(mean usage score of 1.0 or lower).

Project Management
Actual vs. plan budget & schedule
Use and value of measurement
  information
Actual vs. plan task performance
Compliance with process steps &
  methods

Requirements
Requirements changes
Requirements problems (defects)

Design
Open issues or defects
Effort or cost to complete
Design changes

Coding
Effort or cost to complete

Testing
Requirements & design coverage
  of tests run
Test effectiveness
Testing problems (defects)

Maintenance
Customer or user satisfaction
Effort or cost to maintain
Number of defects found after
  release
Operational reliability

Figure 1.5. Most valued measurements (mean value score above 2.25).

	Gap
Test effectiveness	1.63
Maintainability	1.61
Impact of bad requirements or designs	1.60
Reuse	1.55
Requirements changes	1.55
Use and value of measurement information	1.52
Function points delivered	1.51
Defects by phase introduced	1.50

Figure 1.6. Measurements with the largest value—usage gaps.

Only two measures (counting lines of code and bugs or errors) were discussed frequently and then only on a very superficial level. What to do with the counts or how to interpret the measures was not covered.

Purists might also want to acknowledge the fuss made over various special issues of the time such as counting the number of GO TO's. For those readers too young to remember (or so old that they've forgotten) it may be helpful to point out that there was indeed a program statement called a GO TO that branched to any desired location in a program. A very active debate was waged over how harmful the GO TO's were and how to measure them. Despite the few lively flurries sparked by such matters, the early literature on measurement is rather sparse. All the attention at the time was on development methods and very little serious coverage of measurement experiences or ideas can be found.

1970s

The field began to take off in the 1970s, and in 1976 the first book was published, *Software Metrics* by Tom Gilb [Gilb 76], followed a year later by Maurice Halstead's *Elements of Software Science* [Halstead 77] and a spate of papers on various early attempts to measure complexity and quality.

The 1970s were the decade in which automated code analysis tools began to appear (reflecting the work of McCabe and Halstead), and the basic primitive measures of lines of code and error or bug counting came into more widespread use. Special topics such as design coupling and cohesion and computer system performance analysis and modeling also emerged and helped shape the literature of the period, but they had little effect on the practicing engineer or typical software process.

The 1970s saw the publication of several classic books like Fred Brooks' *Mythical Man Month* [Brooks 75] and Gerry Weinberg's *Psychology of Computer Programming* [Weinberg 71]. While certainly not measurement books, such texts did begin to emphasize the importance of good measurements to a project. For example, it was Brook's book that gave us the wonderful and oft used analogy that "you can't make a baby in 1 month by putting 9 people on the task!"

1980s

During the 1980s the field matured significantly. In 1981 Barry Boehm published his pioneering book *Software Economics* [Boehm 81], which helped popularize the emergence of project-estimating models and tools just a few years later. The general emphasis on software management was also reflected in books like Tom DeMarco's *Controlling Software Projects* [DeMarco 82] and the continuing popularity of classics published in the 1970s such as the *Mythical Man Month*.

Prominent measures of the period (besides just collecting and tracking project management data) included function points and test coverage. Function point counting drew enough interest to see the formation of a special users group (the International Function Point Users Group—IFPUG) that now holds annual conferences and serves as the focal point for the function-point-counting community. It was also during this decade that we began to see measurement groups forming as functional units or significant elements embedded within some other function, such as a Project Management Support Office or Quality Assurance.

Other evidence of progress and interest is reflected in the series of fine books that appeared in the late 1980s including Grady and Caswell's *Software Metrics: Establishing a Companywide Program* [Grady 87] (the story of Hewlett Packard's Corporate Metrics Council and the effort to establish a minimum set of corporatewide metrics); Musa, Iannino, and Okumoto's *Software Reliability: Measurement, Prediction, Application* [Musa 87] (provides a firm foundation for the reliability engineering practice that we have begun to see in the 1990s), and Watts Humphrey's *Managing the Software Process* [Humphrey 89] (provides the software process maturity model and sets the stage for the current emphasis on process measurement and assessment).

Frustration over lack of progress with measurement also was evident. For example, the NASA/Goddard Software Engineering Lab reported "that the two biggest disappointments of the decade were metrics and management."

1990s

The 1990s have opened with a flurry of measurement activity and interest. Throughout the U.S., Europe and the Far East many special projects have been launched focused on better software measurement and metrics. The ESPRIT programme (ESPRIT is a cooperative effort supported by DGXIII of the Commission of the European Communities aimed at promoting the use of measurement in software development) alone has spent more than 200 million ECU's on projects concerned with metrics. This includes the development of educational aids (such as METKIT—Metrics Educational Toolkit) and a new project called AMI—Application of Metrics in Industry which has developed and published a "how to do it" handbook. The handbook is based on the experiences of a consortium of leading European companies and contains guidelines and templates drawn from past ESPRIT projects as well as worldwide best practices. In 1990 Software Quality Engineering launched an annual international conference devoted to the applications of software measurement and attracted nearly 400 practitioners. This was followed in early 1991 with a new public industry seminar on Software Measurement, and other proprietary seminars and conferences on measurement have begun to dot the landscape.

One special characteristic of the decade is the emphasis on process measurement and software capability evaluation. Triggered by Watts Humphrey's book in 1989 and the support of the Software Engineering Institute, process assessment and practices baselining and benchmarking have become hot topics. As this book goes to press several hundred software organizations have been formally "assessed" by outside assessment companies, with hundreds (and possibly thousands) more conducting informal assessments themselves. The assessment involves a survey measurement of current practices and an on-site visit focused on identifying software process strengths and weaknesses and establishing a plan for improvement (See Chapters 8 and 9 for a full discussion of assessments and benchmarking and how they should be used in support of the overall measurement program.)

The second significant feature that began in the 1980s and continues unabated today is the proliferation of automated measurement tools and support that have become available. Consultants and software package vendors have found the measurement area to be fertile ground and now offer a broad range of products and services to help companies launch or improve their measurement programs. They fall into several broad categories: (1) Project management estimating and tracking aids (tools that produce project budgets, schedules, and task plans, and provide ongoing project status as well as a corporate history and project data repository); (2) Static measurement and analysis aids (tools that take source designs and code as input and measure or analyze various attributes such as size, complexity, structure, and so on); (3) Dynamic measurement and analysis aids (tools that take source code and trace or analyze dynamic properties during execution such as test coverage or data flow); and (4) Measurement system aids (tools that support the building block systems for tracking resource usage, source and document configurations, and defects or open issues, and help provide an integrated reporting and analysis capability).

Most of these tools will be covered and described in subsequent chapters. Use of measurement tools (as well as overall measurement maturity) is in its infancy. The 1990s, however, will bring us a wide range of choices and should result in significant penetration of automated measurement support throughout the industry. In addition to the tool offerings, many vendors also offer specialized measurement and metrics consulting. This includes help in baselining current practices and performing process assessments, helping the organization define and implement basic metrics, and specialized assistance to support and improve established programs.

World-wide interest in total quality management and customer satisfaction programs, along with the European Community push toward ISO9001[4] certification and registration of quality management systems and capabilities, has heightened management's interest in measurement in general and software measurement in particular. That interest is reflected in the number of books on the subject (including this one) that have been published recently. This includes Card and Glass's *Measuring Software Design Quality* [Card 90] (the first software measure-

---

[4]ISO9001 Quality Systems—Model for Quality Assurance in Design/Development, Production, Installation, and Servicing has become a prime international standard for assessing overall quality systems. It is supported by ISO9000-3 Guidelines for the Application of ISO9001 to the Development, Supply, and Maintenance of Software.

ment book focused on design activity); Capers Jones's *Applied Software Measurement* [Jones 91] (an ambitious effort to recast the software industry and project management experience in function point terms); Bob Grady's *Practical Software Metrics for Project Management and Process Improvement* [Grady 92] (expanding on Hewlett Packard's experience); and Putnam and Myers's *Measures for Excellence: Reliable Software on Time, Within Budget* [Putnam 92] (showing how to use industry trend data and statistics to quantify and measure the software activity).

A host of other specialized measurement books reflecting the active research going on in the field have also been published in the past year or two. (See the Bibliography in Appendix B.) I see no slackening of this interest and activity as the decade progresses. By the year 2000 it is expected that all or nearly all software organizations will have visible product and process metrics that are regularly tracked and analyzed; that most will regularly track and analyze customer and client satisfaction; and that a large number will have obtained some formal certification or registration for their quality and measurement reporting systems.

Moving to this measurement-based software world of the future will indeed test the mettle of many organizations. Much of what this book aims to do is pave the way and help make the transition easier and faster.

THE SOFTWARE MEASUREMENT CHALLENGE

Over the past few years, it has become fashionable for companies to establish quality goals and targets. Top management has emphasized the need to measure (and improve) quality in virtually every major U.S. industry. Motorola has become famous for its Six Sigma Initiative,[5] and it is clear that ambitious quality goals and initiatives are spreading. In 1990 IBM chairman John Akers

---

[5]Six Sigma is the name for a level of quality that allows less than four defects per million opportunities. Such a target for quality may be hard for some readers to appreciate. Companies that are perfect 99 percent of the time are producing 10,000 defects per million! At Six Sigma you must be perfect 99.99966 percent of the time. In the case of service businesses like a restaurant, you must have no more than three mistakes or three unhappy customers per million meals served.

told his managers that Six Sigma "must permeate our entire enterprise" and set goals for a tenfold reduction in defects in all IBM products by 1992, another tenfold reduction by 1993, and attainment of Six Sigma quality by 1994. Many other companies have put forward equally challenging quality goals and objectives. Motorola has shared and taught their methods to more than a thousand organizations, and virtually every major corporation has jumped aboard the quality bandwagon.

The good news is that we have management's interest and attention. Measurement is in the limelight, and it is a hot topic. Given these very public and objective targets, the casual observer might be led to conclude that there is in place an effective mechanism for measuring quality, that companies know where they stand today and can measure improvement so as to report to top management how they are doing toward achieving these goals. For those of us in the trenches, we know the reality to be otherwise. In many respects it is as though some great illusion is being created. We simply don't have the capability to measure effectively, and many of our most distinguished experts would also argue that we don't have the capacity to improve software quality by anything even close to several orders of magnitude.

In 1987 the Defense Science Board Task Force released its now rather famous report on the state of software in the military. The task force, a group of the best software experts that could be assembled and chaired by Fred Brooks, concluded that the "day of the dramatic breakthrough in software was basically behind us." They took the position that building software is hard and always will be, and no magic bullets existed to produce tenfold or even twofold improvements. The report also offered some especially pertinent things to say about measurement itself. They felt that the "current metrics for things like source and object code quality or documentation quality were ineffective or unavailable" and stressed an urgent need to work on better development process and product quality and completeness measures.

The Pressure to Report Success

So, we seem to be caught squarely in a box. Management is expecting us to measure and to bring home evidence of dramatic tenfold improvements. The best gurus in the land have told us our measures aren't very useful and the best we can hope for is a modest incremental improvement of perhaps 10 to 20 percent a year.

The pressure to claim success on these high-visibility upper-management initiatives is strong. No one wants to tell the CEO that they either don't know *how* to measure their progress, or that they failed to achieve a tenfold improvement. Despite the pressure, those of us in the measurement business have one clear responsibility—to measure accurately. That requires reporting what we don't know or aren't very confident of and, fundamentally, to measure what *is*—not what we or someone else (including our bosses) want it to *be*.

Lack of Practitioner Support

When I raise the subject of measurement with high-level managers or researchers, I see lots of enthusiasm (and often a fair dose of unrealistic expectations!). When I talk with first-level software managers, there is still lots of interest and positive attitudes, but there is some skepticism and frustration about what can and can't be achieved in real world projects. Such generally positive attitudes are in stark contrast to the feelings of most practitioners doing the work.

Practitioners' attitudes tend to range from barely neutral to outright antagonistic. It is rare to find the practitioner who really thinks of measurement as a useful and indispensable tool for good software work. Most feel that they get back very little from the measurement activity, and if management would only leave them alone they could get their work done just fine! They do not see it as a means of better performance or as a necessary adjunct to engineering efforts.

The psychological dislike and distrust our practitioners have about measurement is a significant challenge facing us. From my perspective, we've been pretty unsuccessful in serving working engineers and practitioners. This must change in the next decade if measurement is to come close to fulfilling its potential.

One industry survey in which I was involved asked respondents to categorize the level of acceptance and support for measurement within their companies. Over half viewed it as negative, and only 2 percent of the practitioners reported positive feelings about their measurement activity. One took the trouble to write us a note suggesting that we had worded the survey incorrectly. Instead of asking about the level of support he felt we should have asked about the level of rejection. That, he said, was enthusiastic! Such survey data is telling. Why haven't we attracted the working software developer or engineer? My answer is that we have overemphasized the management and control aspects of measurement and underemphasized the basic role measurement plays in all good engineering and scientific endeavors.

There is a fundamental clash between the notions of measurement that suggest control—big brother is watching you—and performance evaluation and the service notions of direct support and feedback for basic engineering. When measurement is thought of as an object of management control, it is bound to be resisted. The situation presents two goals in direct conflict: We all want facts and accuracy to help us achieve excellence, and no one likes to be evaluated and found lacking. But it is especially frustrating when the factors with which we are measured are faulty.

A Vision and Personal Challenge

I am convinced that our main use of measurement should be in service—not in management. I look forward to the day when the software practitioner values measurement as the doctor does diagnostic tests—as an indispensable source of information to get an effective job done, confident that it's been done well.

Doctors use basic measurements like body temperature and blood pressure to guide each patient interaction and evaluate the "results" of their treatment. Hospitals and clinics use measurements to evaluate or manage doctor performance. The use of measurement in medical research and experimental evaluation is pervasive and fundamental. Very high standards are imposed on what medical findings get published. Experimental results are expected to be confirmed and reviewed by outside, unbiased observers, and they are viewed with healthy skepticism until proven valid. Nonfindings (proof that certain treatments don't work) as well as positive findings of what is effective are published, and there is a fair and proper dampening of miracle cures and the next great idea. Few treatments are considered legitimate without experimental results that support them.

Comparing our practice of software to medicine, we differ sharply in that we emphasize measurement as a means of management much more, and we see far less measurement at the practitioner level. Examples abound from the unsubstantiated claims made about "miracle" software tools and methods to our excessive focus on status and project evaluation. This must change. Measurement should be a natural by-product of software activity at every step and not considered a threat or project overhead that keeps the manager happy.

In other words, we must reach down to the micro level and accommodate our engineers, not foster distrust and disdain. We must put basic tools and measurement devices into the hands of every software professional (like the carpenter's ruler or the doctor's thermometer). We need to place more value on the human dimension. Remember, one of the few things we have been able to convincingly measure is people—the single biggest influence on software costs, schedule, or quality. We need engineers who are measurement enthusiasts and who regularly use and depend on measurements to perform their duties. This will not be achieved by touting control, elegance, or theory. Measurement must be a convincing source of accuracy and helpful information.

To meet that challenge measurements must be relevant and readily used by practitioners and managers alike. As we will see, software measurement is not yet playing a pervasive role in the engineering process or in decision making. Everyone clamors for more measurements and more metrics but, few seem interested in using their measurements more. We all agree that the reason we measure is to help people make decisions and to improve their understanding and insight. Yet, few in the industry really seem to depend on measurement to support their important actions. If our measurements aren't used, if people don't really care about them or don't consider them to be vital to doing their job better, then we have to conclude that our effort is failing.

My goal—and one I hope every reader will adopt—is to make software measurement data as important and as commonly used in our software decision making as financial data is in corporate decision making. Financial data is often incomplete and based on assumptions and uncertainties, but no one makes important decisions without at least evaluating how it will impact financial results. This is the attitude we want software managers and practitioners to have toward software measurements—an important element in any decision and vital and useful for everyone in the software community.

SUMMARY

It is clear that the current state of software measurement practice is very immature. Both surveys we discussed reinforce the lack of use of measurements.

Such nonuse emphasizes for me how formidable a challenge we face. We agree that measurements help people make decisions and improve their understanding and insight. Yet, few in the industry really seem to depend on measurement to support their important actions. Even within the few organizations that have implemented comprehensive measurement programs, there is often poor support and credibility, and the measures that are collected are often ignored or are poorly defined and too unreliable to use effectively for decision making.

So, we indeed have a long way to travel. We have also, however, come a long way, and I am optimistic that measurement's time has arrived. The past couple of decades have seen very significant development in the field and the emergence of at least a small number of progressive, leading edge organizations that rely on measurement as a foundation element behind most decisions. I expect to see continuing progress in industry use of measurements and toward making hard objective data a vital and key ingredient for all decision making.

CHAPTER 1 EXERCISES AND DISCUSSION POINTS

1. List 10 examples of what you consider to be useful software measurements.
2. Explain the difference between a product, process and project measure.

3. Provide an example of some aspect of a software product or process that is *not* a measure. Why isn't it?

4. Explain the difference between measurements, metrics and meters, and give an example of each.

5. Contrast the state of measurement maturity in the software field with any other field or discipline you are familiar with. Identify similarities and differences.

6. Identify at least three reasons why establishing effective software measurement programs is difficult.

7. True or False—Good measurement is essential for the development of modern, complex software? Defend your position.

8. True or False—The number of potentially useful software measurements is unbounded? Explain.

9. Can a measurement be a metric and a meter at the same time?

10. Do you have to define the software process before you can measure it? Why or why not?

2

The Measurement Process

"Each measurement must have a linkage to a need."
   Howard Rubin

"Measurement must be focused, based upon goals and models."
   Vic Basili

"If we had management that knew what the right goals and questions to ask were, we wouldn't need better measurement nearly as badly as we do!"
   Bill Hetzel

MEASUREMENT PARADIGMS

We emphasized in Chapter 1 that the number of potential software measures is very large and greater than any organization's resources to systematically collect, present, and use effectively. That requires us to prioritize and identify a rather small subset to work on at any one time.

Accepting this basic fact has been a hard pill to swallow in most organizations. Management thinks it can launch a measurement effort, define everything they'll ever want or need to collect, and then just go forward and implement! That is almost as wishful as expecting your systems group to somehow develop and implement all the software systems you'll ever want or need.

Since we can't do everything at once, we need some practical guides for prioritizing and selecting the measures we will provide. In general, we have two basic approaches: *top-down* and *bottom-up*. The top-down approach starts with high-level goals and needs and derives the measures needed to support them. The bottom-up approach starts with measurable engineering observations and reality points and builds up to management objectives and goals.

THE TOP-DOWN PARADIGMS

Much has been published about systematic top-down approaches to defining a measurement program. Two of the most visible and active contributors to the field of software measurement, Vic Basili and Howard Rubin, are prominent proponents. Their basic idea is that the measurement program should be built top-down and focused around clearly defined goals. The best known top-down model is Basili's GQM approach. Figure 2.1 illustrates the basic steps involved.

GQM starts with an identified set of desires or needs. A set of measurements to be collected is derived top-down from these needs by first identifying or listing a set of questions that if answered would establish whether the goals had been met or not. Measurements are then selected to provide answers or insight about each question.

Software goals often start out with a set of "quality factors": reliability, usability, maintainability, and so on. These factors were initially identified by Barry Boehm and the Rome Air Development Center in the 1970s as "components" of quality. To quantify the fuzzy notion of software quality, they tried to break down quality into a series of factors and subfactors (called criteria) and then identify specific metrics for each. The aim was to end up with a metrics set that collectively served to "measure" overall quality. I call this top-down approach the ILITY paradigm from the fact that most of the quality factors end in "ility."

Many folks got involved with the ILITY effort, and a lot was published about it. At one point a major technical report from

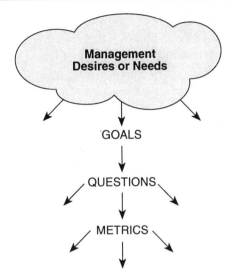

1. *Development of **goals*** (The goals may be at a corporate, divisional, or project level and usually will address both productivity and quality concerns.)

2. *Generation of **questions** that define the goals* (A list of questions that need answers in order to know whether the goals have been met.)

3. *Identification of **metrics** (measures) that answer the questions* (A list of measures to be collected or tracked to answer the generated questions.)

Figure 2.1.   Goal, Question, Metric steps.

Rome was published that had broken down over a dozen quality factors, more than two dozen subfactors, and over 200 specific measures. It included tables and forms to measure the 200+ items and a scheme to roll up all the results into one quality score or "figure of merit." The full ILITY model proved rather unwieldy and impractical to apply in the real world, but it has influenced and impacted many organizations and made its way into the draft *IEEE Standard for a Software Quality Metrics Methodology (P1061)* as the recommended approach for defining a set of quality metrics.

Many adaptations of GQM and the ILITY model have been made, and sufficient experience has been gained to demonstrate that a systematic top-down approach is far superior to no approach or the informal, ad hoc, shotgun approaches that many organizations have tried. However, there are also some fundamental flaws and problems that must be recognized. The basic problem with any top-down method (whether for measurement, system development, or anything else) is who gets to define the top. The experience in many companies (especially the bigger ones), is that no one knows (or they are unable to agree) what the *right* set of goals should be. Companies often desperately need good measurement in order to *set* their goals! The GQM approach fails to recognize this, and it may not collect the measures needed to reshape the organization's goals or raise new and interesting questions. If management always knew the right goals to set and questions to ask, better measurements would not be so critical.

Top-down methods have also suffered from a lack of support and enthusiasm from the practitioners who must implement them. Some goals and questions are fairly easy to set but extremely difficult to measure effectively. Practitioners quickly recognize that the measures only address a small part of the goal and worry that managers will not interpret the metric information properly.

Yet another problem I've personally experienced with GQM is the tendency to "manipulate" the measured data. With the goals determined, there is a strong pressure for measurements that indicate or "show" progress. This may lead to "managing the news" or "finagling" the results to make management a little happier (after all, no one likes to set a goal and then see no progress). One wag went so far as to tag the approach "GAF" or "*G*oal, *A*nswer, *F*inagle," suggesting that more than a few organizations have abused their measurement program in the mistaken "service" of their management masters! Such practices are diametrically opposed to the true purpose of any really effective measurement activity. As Sophocles has told us "None love the bearer of bad news.", and Fred Brooks adds, "No one enjoys bearing bad news either, so it gets softened without real intent to deceive."

THE BOTTOM-UP MEASUREMENT ENGINEERING PARADIGM

In early 1991 Bill Silver and I collaborated on the design and introduction of an industry seminar on software measurement.

As a part of that effort we conceived a new model built on the premise that the right place to start defining the set of needed measurements is at the engineering level integral with the software engineering process itself.

The approach is bottom-up and methodology based. It focuses on the basic *objects* that make up the core of all software engineering work: *work products* and the *people* who produce and use them. As software is specified and developed or enhanced, the people doing the job produce a series of work products. (The work products include such familiar items as feasibility studies, requirements documents, design specifications, code modules and components, test plans, tests and test reports, and user documents.) These work products are used in turn (sometimes by the same people who created them and sometimes by others) to produce new and changed work products. Eventually the work product created is a complete system for use by end users and customers.

The bottom-up measurement engineering paradigm specifies a base set of measurements to be collected on every work product developed and used (see Figure 2.2).

We need measures about the *inputs* (the resources, activities, and other work products that have been expended or used in completing the work product); the *outputs* (measures that describe and quantify the work item or items produced, such as their size and complexity); and the *results* (measures that quan-

---

1. **Input Measures**

   Information about the resources (people, computers, tools, other work products, etc.) applied and the process steps or activities carried out.

2. **Output Measures**

   Information about the deliverables and work products that are created.

3. **Results Measures**

   Information about the usage and effectiveness (perceived and actual) of the deliverables and work products in fulfilling their requirements.

Figure 2.2.   Fundamental software work product measurements.

tify the experience and satisfaction with the work product and how good it is in terms of satisfying the people using it).

The point to stress is that these fundamental measures are required to answer just about *any* interesting question and are quite independent of what any organization's particular management goals and questions might be. This is true even if we are very familiar with our goals and can count on them not changing for a few months (or years) while we got our measurement program in place. This is not to say that it isn't important to know what your top-down goals are or that knowledge of such goals won't influence your selection of measures. It will and it should, but most of what we can really measure effectively is determined at the bottom, and we will argue that is the place where you should start.

The underlying principle behind the bottom-up measurement engineering model is that measurement's primary role is to support the engineering activity. In contrast to the top-down GQM approach, one might describe the model as a "MQG spiral." The important point to stress is that *measurements come first, not last.* The purpose of measurement is to stimulate questions and help provide knowledge and insight about the engineering activity. From such knowledge comes the ability to set goals and targets and to improve or change the process. Such changes, along with the natural forces for change brought on by new technology and various external influences, stimulate the need for new or modified measures that in turn raise new questions and so on around the MQG spiral (see Figure 2.3).

Rather than start by asking managers what their goals are, we start by analyzing and modeling the software engineering activity to identify the fundamental measurements that all good projects should use. These measures are integrated into the engineering process and provided as a natural by-product of all software work.

When the bottom-up approach is used and measurements are defined (and engineered) as part of the engineering process, we obtain much more practitioner involvement and support. Practitioners correctly come to see the measurement effort as a basic part of all good technical work and are much less likely to fear and oppose it. We consider that strength a key element—thus the name "practitioner-based" measurement paradigm.

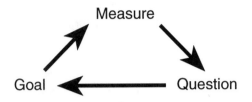

Figure 2.3.   The MQG spiral.

A key concept built into the paradigm from the start was to serve the practitioner first. Note the emphasis here on the word *service*. What the practitioner fears most (often with good reason) about measurement programs is the possibility that his or her performance will be displayed in a poor light or that management will somehow act inappropriately due to incomplete or misunderstood measures. To succeed, this fear of management control and misuse must be replaced with a recognition that the measurement activity is primarily aimed at serving the practitioner and that it is an activity that the practitioner controls and is responsible for— just as any other part of the software process!

Figure 2.4 displays the overall conceptual model. Software engineering is our discipline for the systematic production of a series of software-oriented work products. For each such work product we must define and provide measures that cover the three fundamental measurement needs: inputs (resources and activities that went into or will go into producing the work item), outputs (attributes that define and describe the work item, like its size and complexity), and results (measures that describe how the work item has been used and help assess its effectiveness and value).

Rather than asking management what they want or think they need, we engineer and instrument our processes to provide the basic data we know we can collect and use effectively, doing our best to prepare for the still unasked questions. The data is used by practitioners and first-line managers as meters and metrics to help make decisions and avoid surprises. As it is gathered and analyzed it will trigger new questions and help to set new goals and objectives realistically. This is turn leads to changes in the process (new work

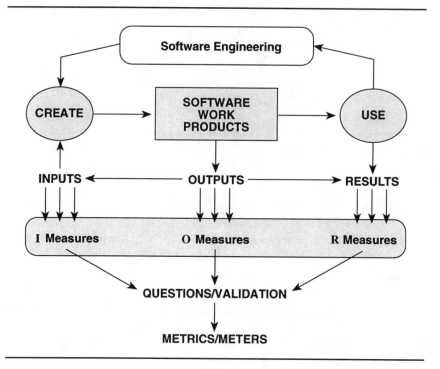

Figure 2.4.   Measurement engineering bottom-up IOR model.

products as well as new measures, meters, and metrics) and so on around our spiral.

A basic goal is to stimulate new and interesting questions and to have the raw data at hand to answer most of the questions that do come up. We have discovered that most of management's needs can be satisfied easily if we've built in a strong, effective measurement program from the ground floor up. Conversely, trying to install measurements top-down does not work as well, especially when it loses or never even gains the strong support of the practitioners who have to implement it. (Of course we must always have the top-level commitment to make bottom-up, or for that matter any kind of measurement program work.)

We now realize that if we want well-run projects, if we want to avoid surprises and bad decisions with costly rework, if we want to learn from the past and engineer our software more and more effectively, then we really have no choice about providing the basic IOR measures. I should stress that such a bottom-up approach to measurement is not something the reader should view as new or surprising. Good measurement is a basic element of all good engineering. Software practices developed historically as an artistic craft (remember we started out *writing* programs!) with little embedded measurement. As software grew in importance and consequence, management sought to impose measurement programs from the top to gain visibility and control. With the wisdom of hindsight we should now understand why this has not met with great success. If we really want to achieve an effective measurement program we must work from the bottom up and engineer measurement in every step of our emerging software engineering discipline.

Measurement Engineering Paradigm Principles

- Focus on the software practitioner and the work products produced.
- Define and build in measures as part of the engineering activity bottom-up.
- Measure the inputs, outputs, and results (IOR) primitives for each work product.
- Use measures to create understanding, which drives questions and enables goal setting.
- Measure perceptions—what people who produce and use the work products think.
- Measure the use and results of the measurements.
- Understand that the measurement system will continuously evolve and change.
- Drive toward establishing validated process metrics and meters.
- Stimulate knowledge and prepare for the next question.
- Educate management to expect and require measurements as inputs to decisions and goal setting.

Some who have experimented with the measurement engineering approach have characterized it as Object-Oriented Measurement (OOM) to distinguish it from the Goal-Oriented Measurement implicit in the top-down approaches. The objects are the individual work products that analysts, developers, and maintainers produce. Each can be viewed as a self-contained item with its collection of input, outputs, and results measures that specify and describe it. People both create and use the objects, and their attributes and perceptions are a basic part of the input and results measurements.

Systematic measurement of each "object" allows for systematic measurement of the whole and turns out to be a most satisfactory philosophy and alternative for introducing and engineering an overall measurement effort. The paradigm provides the foundation philosophy behind this book. Subsequent chapters will flesh it out and illustrate it with various case studies and examples. Part II of the book takes each of the primary types of software work products (specifications, code, and test) and discusses appropriate bottom-up IOR measures in detail. Part III shows how the systematic collection of such measures can also serve the needs of managers (first line and executive) and customers for effective project, process, and product management.

THE BASIC MEASUREMENT PROCESS MODEL

Having introduced the bottom-up measurement engineering philosophy, let us now take a look at the basic process steps involved in any software measurement effort. For any set of measurements we might want to make, it is useful to identify four basic activities: *defining* what we want to measure, *collecting* the defined measures, *presenting* the collected information, and *using* the results to gain insight and take action.

Figure 2.5 displays these basic activities (define, collect, present, and use) as a simple process model that we will employ as a framework for systematic measurement engineering.

It is of primary importance in all activities to ensure that we are accomplishing what we really wanted to. Is the definition precise? Are we collecting what was defined? Are we presenting it accurately? Is it having the effect we expected? This involves a fifth activity to measure the measurements and *validate* their effectiveness. As we will learn, it is surprisingly easy to collect, present, and even use incorrect measures. Validation is a key

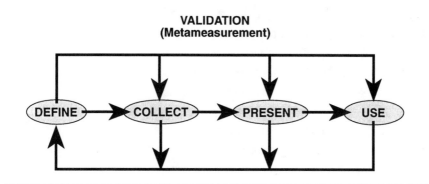

Figure 2.5.   A simplified process model.

and never-ending activity that ensures our measured data is reasonable and our meters and metrics are appropriate.

Most readers will view the define, collect, present, and use activities as sequential steps (obviously we must define something before we collect it, and we have to collect and present it before we can use it). In reality each activity provides feedback and influences the other. For example, we'll often collect some information to observe trends before defining a new measure or discover that just presenting and using a measure for a while leads to new insights and questions that in turn brings about new or revised definitions. The model assumes such interactions are the norm with each of the activities overlapped and cross-feeding each other.

DEFINE

The logical first step in any systematic measurement process is one of *definition* or specification. Once we've identified a potential measure (whether top-down or bottom-up or some combination of both), we've got to define it carefully and make sure everyone understands just what is going to be collected and presented. Lack of careful specification is a common failing in many measurement programs. Most practitioners and managers new to measurement fail to realize how much information is really required to clearly define a new potential measure. Figure 2.6

Handle:	A convenient shorthand name
Description:	Short description of what the measure is and the purpose for collecting
Observation:	How the measure is captured or collected
Frequency:	When the measure is collected
Scale:	Units of the measure
Range:	Minimum and maximum values observed or experienced
History:	What the measure has been like in the past
Expectation:	What the measure is expected to do in the future
Relationship:	How the measure is assumed to relate to the software process
Threshold:	Control or trigger values for metering action
Validation:	Backup data that validates the relationship strength and accuracy

---

Figure 2.6.   Elements of a measurement definition or specification.

lists some typical data elements that should be specified when a measurement is defined.

The specification should include a short description and a *handle* or shorthand name as well as details on how and when the measure is collected and its past and predicted values and value ranges. Additional information must be specified for any measure used or proposed as a candidate metric or meter. The existence of an organization metric or meter implies *use* within the organization for prediction, comparison, estimation, or control purposes. It is important that the usage relationship be fully specified and the validation information be available for anyone interested in using the metric or meter.

Figure 2.7 provides an example of what a definition specification might look like for a lines of code measure in a hypothetical company. Such a definition does not have to be complete before collection (and in some cases even use) of the data can start. Often it will be appropriate to collect loosely specified data on an informal or pilot basis. The data can then be studied and analyzed for patterns that enable us to define it more carefully or simplify the collection procedure. Quite often we will want to

Handle:	KLOC (Pronounced K—LOCK)
Description:	Thousands of lines of delivered new or modified code per project or system
Observation:	Measured by the automated tool KLOC-COUNTER whenever code is provided to integration test. See reference X for a more complete description of the tool.
Frequency:	Any time source code is modified or moved to the integration library
Scale:	Rounded to units of thousands of lines where a "line" is defined as a nonblank source code statement including comment lines, data definition lines, and any executable code.
Experience:	The measure has been used in pilot status for seven months. The range has run from a low of .8 (for a small enhancement project) to a high of 206 for the new billing system project.
Usage:	The measure is being used to support improved project estimation. Estimated KLOC is a required input to the project management estimation tool—ESTIMAN. Measuring actual KLOC delivered will help provide better estimates in the future.
Validation:	The project history database contains effort and KLOC data for a series of over 100 recent projects. A correlation study performed last year (See reference Y) showed a correlation of .82 between actual effort and measured KLOC. Only 12 percent of the projects varied by more than 20 percent over or under predicted effort. This means we should expect 9 out of 10 projects to be accurately estimated provided we can estimate or predict eventual KLOC delivered. It does not mean or imply that KLOC may be used to evaluate individual effort or productivity, only that total KLOC correlates reasonably well to total effort for a project.
Known Problems:	Does not count or help estimate nondeliverable code like testware and drivers.
	Not supported with an automated tool on language A or platform B.
	Does not yet count deleted lines or changed lines on modifications.

Figure 2.7. Sample definition for a Lines of Code measure.

change the definition to meet pragmatic engineering constraints and allow for less costly and more automated collection.

We may also want to consider measures defined for short durations of time or to address very specific issues. Such impromptu measurements may be collected to help analyze or resolve particular questions. Once the issue has been satisfactorily answered, the measure can be set aside or put on the shelf until it is needed again.

COLLECT

The second major step in the systematic process is to *collect* measurement data. Implicit to the measurement engineering paradigm is the goal of seamlessly integrating the collection within or as a direct by-product of other, already existing software process steps. Our goal is to make collection as unobtrusive as possible; it must be efficient and perceived as *not* involving any extra or unnecessary steps.

Practitioners will quite properly resist collection activities that require significant manual effort or added steps. Automating the collection effort is often a critical success factor and should be done as a routine part of the development, testing, and maintenance activities. For example, many companies who measure lines of code call a line-counting tool whenever a module or component is checked in or turned over to integration for final testing and release. The source library and configuration management procedures invoke the tool as part of the check-in procedures and automatically log the result so that no extra effort is required from the practitioner.

As we stressed in the previous section, it is important to have clear definitions that are published and available to everyone on the project for any measures that are being collected. We recommend full disclosure to all involved even when the definition is very loose or fuzzy and the collection is only for a trial or evaluation period. The best way to ensure you are collecting good data is to feed back whatever you collect for review and validation as close to the source as possible. If the practitioners are not aware of what is being collected and don't review all the data you collect, you are almost assured of introducing bad data sooner or later.

Measurement Data Collection Principles

- Unobtrusive
- Automated whenever possible
- Based on clear and unambiguous, published definitions
- Validated as collected (as close to the source as possible)
- Saved as a repository and for future validation or analysis purposes

The bottom-up paradigm assumes and relies on practitioners to be responsible and committed to a successful engineering-based measurement effort. They need to be part of the process and take responsibility to see that what is collected is reasonable and matches their engineering knowledge base. By feeding back any data whenever it is collected, we can avoid surprises and make sure this responsibility is met.

If practitioner action is required to make a measurement or provide data, and you discover that some (or even many) of the practitioners are not cooperating, it is important to analyze the reasons. Ask the individuals involved what is happening. Are they aware of what is expected of them? Is it an education issue? Do they support providing the measure but just do not have the time? Or is it a matter of choosing to not cooperate and a lack of faith in the value or use of the measurement?

Exploring and analyzing why measurements are not collected accurately is a key part of collection. Measurement as a *service* means we must understand our customers and how they feel and work *with* them to achieve desired results.

It is also worthwhile to stress that a little analysis and creativity will often unearth alternative sources that may serve as substitutes for having to collect data at all or provide a much easier and more unobtrusive measure that approximates or highly correlates with the data that you really need.

Astronomers can't see black holes, but they assert their existence and analyze their properties on the basis of movements of visible objects around them. Similarly, we may not be able to directly "observe" certain software attributes because the relevant measures are not available or cost too much to obtain. But we may be able to show (through special analysis or industry research or data taken from other projects) that the attribute we want to look at is highly correlated with something much simpler that is readily available.

Some of the common alternative sources of measurement data include both objective and subjective information drawn from interviews and surveys, third-party databases, shared intra- or inter-company project data, and research or case study data in the published literature and conference proceedings.

PRESENT

Step 3 of the systematic process is to analyze, organize and present the collected data so it can be used effectively. Over the years I have sat through many status meetings where people had good measurements (carefully defined and accurately collected), but failed to get their message across because of poor analysis. There is never a substitute for creative thinking! People need to focus on what the data means, how to interpret it, and what actions are being recommended. The presentation step is much more than just communicating data—it includes a high degree of judgment and creativity and the application of a broad array of analyses and modelling techniques. There are two key goals to be achieved: First, we must tabulate and array the information in a form that can be easily understood. Second, we want to encourage and support questions and conclusions about what the data means. That involves modeling and analysis to develop hypotheses and help understand the underlying relationships and implications.

For both there exists a fairly standard set of data manipulation, tabulation, and analysis techniques that are typically provided by standard spreadsheet software or commercial statistical packages. None of the capabilities are highly sophisticated, nor should they require the talents of a specialized analyst or statistician. What is required is a little training and experience to get comfortable with the package and a good foundation and awareness of basic data analysis techniques.

To illustrate the capabilities of such packages I've created a simple hypothetical example covering a few measurements that we might collect on the modules or program work products within an overall system design and development effort. Figure

2.8 displays a sample spreadsheet that might be produced in such a situation.

Each module is represented as one row in the spreadsheet. As data on additional modules is collected, new rows are added. The columns denote the specific information and measures being collected on each module. Figure 2.8 includes the following information:

1. The initials of the assigned developer
2. The module name or identification
3. The number of days spent working on the module
4. The date work started
5. The date the module was first checked in to integration
6. The number of lines of code
7. A confidence measure reflecting the confidence in the module at check in (high, medium, or low)
8. The number of changes made after check in
9. The number of defects found after check in

Although this is a hypothetical example, the selected measures include at least a couple of each of the basic IOR elements: two **Input** measures (resources and dates), two **Output** measures that describe something about the module as a work product (lines of code and coder confidence), and two **Results** or effectiveness measures (defects and changes that were made after check in). In any actual application other measures such as rework

Resp	Module	Days	Start	Check In	Lines	Confidence	Changes	Test Defects
BH	DD11	21	3/15/92	3/29/92	405	Low	2	3
JB	CA1	8	2/9/92	2/26/92	145	High	0	0
JB	CA4	6	2/9/92	2/13/92	110	High	1	1
RC	UI1	14	2/22/92	3/11/92	245	High	0	0
BH	UI2	22	2/11/92	3/1/92	550	Medium	1	0
AM	UI3	6	3/5/92	4/22/92	401	High	0	0

Figure 2.8.   Example of a measurement spreadsheet.

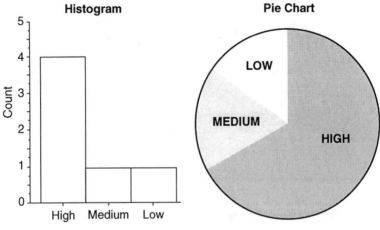

Frequency Table

Element:	Count:	Percent:	
High	4	66.667%	-Mode
Medium	1	16.667%	
Low	1	16.667%	

Figure 2.9.   Displaying discrete measures.

days spent, lines of code changed or reused, code complexity, user defects found, and so forth may need to be added. See Chapter 5 for a more complete discussion on applicable coding phase measurements and techniques.

Once the data is contained in a spreadsheet format it is very easy to view and present. All the packages make it very easy to display various tabulations and descriptive statistics. Figures 2.9, 2.10, and 2.11 show several typical outputs provided by the STATVIEW[1] package on my Macintosh. Each of these required only a few mouse clicks and a minute or two to produce.

---

[1]STATVIEW is a proprietary package marketed by Abacus Concepts of Berkeley, CA. Columns in the spreadsheet file typically denote selected I, O, or R measurements with rows used to enter one related set of observations. Alternatively the rows might be used to record data from different individuals within the same project or periodic observations over time.

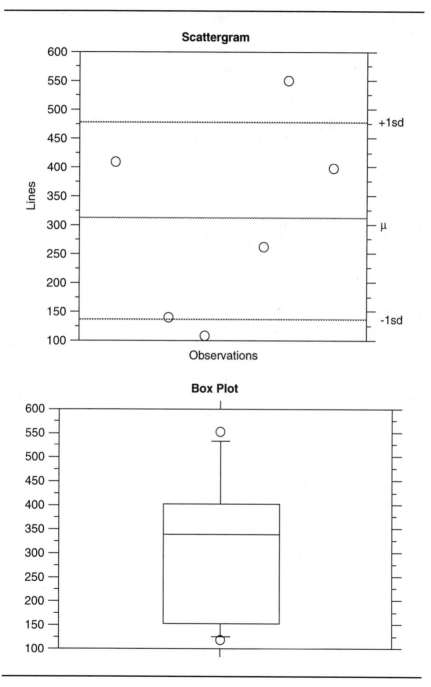

Figure 2.10.   Displaying continuous measures.

The tables and plots in Figure 2.9 provide alternative presentations for column 7—the Coder Confidence measurement. This is a discrete category variable with choices of high, medium, and low. The different forms of presentation (frequency table, histogram, and pie chart) help us visualize the distribution of responses and better understand our data.

For continuous measures we can't use frequency tables (or histograms or pie charts) directly because the observed values are almost all different. What we can do is plot the observed values and try to describe or summarize the resulting distribution with various statistics (percentiles, median, mean, standard deviation). This is illustrated for the Lines of Code measure in our hypothetical example in Figures 2.10 and 2.11.

The first plot in Figure 2.10 is called a *scattergram*. Each of the six observed values for Lines of Code is shown as one point in the plot. The middle line through the plot is the computed average or *mean* value. Also shown are lines at plus and minus one *standard deviation* from the mean.

Below the scattergram is a *box plot*. The box plot is one of a variety of plotting techniques that helps focus attention on the distribution of a set of observed values. The bottom of the box is drawn as a line at the 25th percentile value (145) and the top at the 75th percentile value (405). The box thus contains the middle half of the distribution. The line inside the box is the median or 50th percentile value. The short lines above and below the box (called *whiskers* in statistical texts) help highlight any outer values (shown on the box plot as small circles). Box plots are most useful when comparing the distributions of several measures at once.

Figure 2.11 illustrates some of the common descriptive statistics that almost any presentation package will offer. This includes the mean (309) and standard deviation (171) as well as the minimum, maximum, range, and various percentile values. There is no entry for the mode (most common value) since all values were unique in this small sample set.

Often it is desirable for presentation and analysis purposes to recode or classify a measurement into groups of values, thus converting it from a continuous measure into a discrete category measure. This is done to focus attention on the common groups of

Mean:	Std. Dev.:	Std. Error:	Variance:	Coef. Var.:	Count:
309.333	171.087	69.846	29270.667	55.308	6

Minimum:	Maximum:	Range:	Sum:	Sum of Sqr.:	# Missing:
110	550	440	1856	720476	0

# < 10th %:	10th %:	25th %:	50th %:	75th %:	90th %:
1	113.5	145	323	405	535.5

# > 90th %:	Mode:	Geo. Mean:	Har. Mean:	Kurtosis:	Skewness:
1	•	265.347	223.462	-1.366	.13

Figure 2.11.   Descriptive statistics.

values and is another example of something that is very easy to do with most presentation tools. As an illustration, Figure 2.12 shows a frequency table and a histogram for the Lines of Code measurement recoded into one of five value ranges (0–100, 100–250, 250–500, 500–1000, and over 1000).

Another major benefit of having our measurement data in a spreadsheet or statistical package format is that many "what if" kinds of questions and relationships can be easily explored. The most common analyses performed are simple comparisons of one measure against another. Figure 2.13 gives an example with a scattergram plot of the Lines of Code measure (column 7) versus the Days of Effort measure (column 3).

The points (or in this case, circles) show a general relationship (more lines requiring more effort), except for the 401 line user interface module (UI3), which took just six days. Such plots help us raise questions and "see" underlying relationships that might be present in the data. Once again, producing the scattergram requires only a couple of clicks and can easily be done for any pair of variables we might be interested in displaying.

The "strength" of the linear association between Lines of Code and Days can be measured by a statistic called the correlation coefficient. (The correlation coefficient for this data has a value of .71 reflecting the positive association that we can observe from the plot.) We can also perform a simple *regression analysis* and find the best straight line through the scattergram points (see Figure 2.14).

The line drawn through the data points is the computed "best"

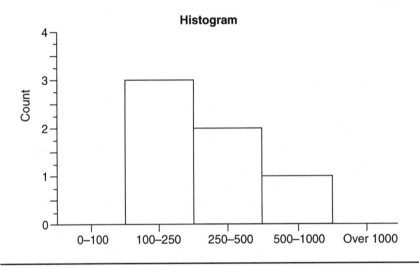

Frequency Table

Element:	Count:	Percent:
0–100	0	0%
100–250	3	50%
250–500	2	33.333%
500–1000	1	16.667%
Over 1000	0	0%

Figure 2.12.   Recoded lines of code.

linear fit. The equation for the line is indicated above the plot and offers a "model" that we can use as a possible predictive metric. Based on our small sample of observations we would "predict" that the average 300-line module would require 12 to 13 days. (.03 × 300 + 3.44 = 12.44)

Your statistical package regression analysis routine will also provide much more information—probably more than you need. In STATVIEW, tables are provided that give the standard error and confidence intervals for the slope and intercept, an analysis of variance and residual statistics if desired. You need not worry about understanding what all this means but it is nice to know it is there and occasionally you may want to take advantage of it.

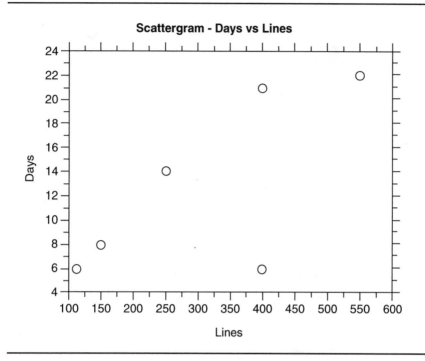

Figure 2.13.   Scattergram of lines of code vs. days of effort.

Regression analysis can't be used on discrete or category measures like Coder Confidence. An alternative commonly employed is to present the data in the form of a contingency table. An example is shown in Figure 2.15.

If there were no relationship between Coder Confidence and the number of changes, the likelihood of falling within any column entry would be equally probable. For example, since three out of the six (half) of the observed number of changes is 0, we would also expect half of each of the Coder Confidence values (high, medium, and low) to have 0 changes. This expected number is what is shown in the expected values table. Differences between the observed and expected table entries can be used to measure or test for a possible relationship between Coder Confidence and changes.

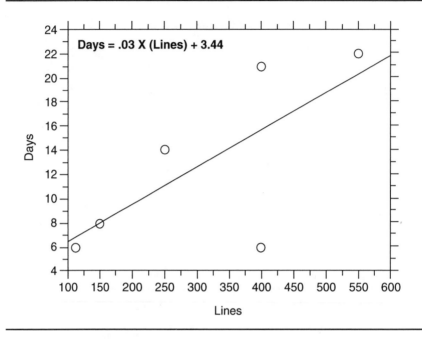

Figure 2.14.   Regression fit for Lines of Code vs. Days of Effort.

This is done by computing the chi-square statistic or a contingency coefficient. As shown in the summary statistics table in Figure 2.15 the coefficient is .76. The chi-square test is significant at the .08 level, which means that statistically speaking the chances of this result occurring if the measures were not related are 8 out of 100.

Don't despair if you feel a little lost with all the statistical jargon. All the illustrations in this section are intended to *help* demonstrate how important having some automated data manipulation and presentation tools are to the successful measurement effort. *You need not (and should not) become bogged down in statistical analysis techniques and methods.* Certainly you can be successful without them. However, it is increasingly evident that most managers and practitioners are familiar with basic package data analysis and presentation techniques and expect them to be employed or at least available.

Observed Frequency Table

	High	Medium	Low	Totals:
0	3	0	0	3
1	1	1	0	2
2	0	0	1	1
Totals:	4	1	1	6

Expected Values

	High	Medium	Low	Totals:
0	2	.5	.5	3
1	1.333	.333	.333	2
2	.667	.167	.167	1
Totals:	4	1	1	6

Summary Statistics

DF:	4	
Total Chi-Square:	8.25	p=.0828
G Statistic:	•	
Contingency Coefficient:	.761	
Cramer's V:	.829	

Figure 2.15.   Contingency table analysis—Coder Confidence vs. changes.

You should take advantage of this and plan on exploiting the power and ease of use of the presentation and analysis tools now available. It really doesn't make too much difference which one you choose—just pick one and take the time to learn and get comfortable with it.

I personally prefer the PC or workstation package approach

that allows and supports a high level of individual hands-on work. As data is captured it should be entered in spreadsheet or standard data file format for easy use and manipulation. Design of the file organization and layout will eventually be required for the long run (especially as file sizes get large), but typically most groups start out experimentally and make many modifications as they go along. A big advantage of nearly all of the standard packages is that they support this flexibility and make later changes, regrouping, or packaging of files easier. Thus, you shouldn't have to study or worry too much about setting things up "right" at the start.[2]

Besides the analytical modeling benefits, the tools will also give you lots of graphical options to help make your reports more colorful and interesting and allow you to get practitioners and managers *personally* involved in the presentation and analysis. This merging of the present and use activities is one of the clear trends in modern engineering measurement and something we'll have much more to say about in later chapters. It may well be the most important of all the many wonderful things the tools do for us!

One final point I'd like to stress again is the importance of viewing the measurement program dynamically and striving for continuous improvements in everything you present. You should make it a point to study and collect good (and bad) examples and save them for future use. I encourage keeping a scrapbook of interesting measurement presentations that you particularly like and dislike and that you encounter at various courses, conferences, or in reference materials such as this book. It is becoming more and more important to convert your data into graphical form to highlight trends and relationships. Any time you see a nice plot or graph, copy it and stick it in your scrapbook as a candidate for future application within your own organization. Better yet, swap scrapbooks with your friends and coworkers. Maybe we could even get some enterprising firm to start a new series of trading cards!

---

[2]*Warning:* For most big projects you need some type of distributed network or server database. It is by no means a simple task to set this up and manage it properly. If your project is large and decentralized it will be important to think ahead carefully. If in doubt, seek out specialized help from others who have had to handle similar problems before.

USE

The fourth step in the process is getting customers to actually *use* the data and measurement information. Use should mean much more than just getting and reviewing a report or a presentation. What we seek is the triggering of new and more interesting questions and the direct use of information to help take action and make decisions. At the very minimum we want our measures to increase practitioner and manager knowledge and to help provide real insight and visibility for what is happening.

You can't *force* use, but you can make sure that information is presented and then measure what it is used for. In the systematic engineered measurement process I believe that everyone should start out measuring the usage of any measurements they collect. You should know who is getting which reports and what they do with them.

What we recommend is a regular periodic survey—perhaps every 6 to 12 months. This is an opportunity to ask what your customers want and need and to determine which reports or measures might be unnecessary or eliminated. Such a survey may be incredibly discouraging (when you find out most of what you collect and present is not being used for much of anything!), but measuring it is the key to helping you understand why and beginning to make changes that may be needed in your program.

To increase use you must be *responsive* and *timely*. This means getting data into the hands and heads of your customers before it is old hat or no longer useful to support decisions. The need for timely response is yet another argument for the kind of presentation tools discussed in the previous section. When employed properly they enable you to quickly create or change a report on demand—to answer the next question as soon as it arises! They also help you translate the raw data into forms that more closely relate to different customer needs and to respond whenever possible in the user's language and problem space. All of that encourages and supports growing usage and happy measurement customers.

Remember from Chapter 1 that use of measurement implies the existence of metrics and meters within the organization. The meters serve to control or trigger decisions, and the metrics support decision making by helping in estimation, prediction, or comparison. Measurements also help communicate and train people throughout the organization and support project and process improvement efforts with before, during, and after baselines. Track and publicize the uses that are working successfully, and strive to understand and improve those that aren't. As long as you can show a small but steady increase in real use of measurements over time, your program is headed in the right direction and will emerge as a success.

VALIDATION

The final step and one that spans and supports each of the others is the basic activity of validation and making sure that what we define, what we collect, what we present, and what we use results in effective products, projects, and processes for our company or organization. Measurement is not a political activity; its first and foremost goal is to portray reality accurately. The validation job is to make sure there is no accidental or deliberate distortion and that the use of measurement is effective in helping the organization to improve.

Validation involves many ongoing actions all aimed at making sure each step of the systematic measurement process is carried out properly. Two broad types of validation activities can be usefully distinguished. One is focused on the accuracy and completeness of data being defined and collected—does the data match reality? Are there any biases introduced? The second is concerned with showing that our measures can reliably be used in some externally beneficial way to make more effective decisions. Both types are important and difficult (time consuming) to conduct.

Shigeo Shingo stresses four principles as underlying the effective control of quality (see Figure 2.16). While these principles grew from Shingo's experience teaching production engineering to a generation of Toyota managers and were meant to be applied on a shop or factory floor, they apply equally well to validation activities and efforts. Good measurement engineering programs will pay heed to these principles and must invest substantial energy in ongoing validation.

It does not take much to distort or kill the effectiveness of an entire program. We have learned through the school of hard knocks that a lot of effort must be invested in validity checking

1. Control upstream, as close to the source of the potential flaw as possible.
2. Establish controls in relation to the severity of the problem.
3. Think smart and small. Strive for the simplest, most efficient, and most economical.
4. Don't delay improvement by overanalyzing.

Figure 2.16. Shingo principles.

and validation. Even with excellent validation programs, it is seldom possible (or necessary) to get data much more accurate than within 10 percent to 20 percent of the "true" reality.

Part of the problem can usually be traced to sloppiness, poor procedures, and lack of communication. Fortunately, this is usually the major part and is generally quite correctable as long as someone is responsible and accountable for working on the problem. Another part lies in the basic human nature to fudge and rationalize personal views of reality. This is especially so when there are negative consequences to be faced and when the person feels it is unlikely that they will be exposed or called to task.

One side of every practitioner and manager knows that good and accurate information will really lead to a better job and better environment for everyone. The other side fears the consequences of any negative news and worries that it may be used in harmful or ill-considered ways. This creates a constant tug of war to get at reality and the truth—particularly when significant doses of bad news are involved.

There are lots of examples of the juggling problem throughout our industry. One classic example is the famous 90 percent complete syndrome where as much as 25 percent or more of the total project effort is required to complete what the project claims is the last 5 percent to 10 percent of the job. Another example is described by Putnam and Ware as "pouring from one pot to another." [Putnam 92 p. 98]

> It is far too easy to allocate some of the actual manmonths to one pot and some to another in order to match what somebody's planning assumptions were a year back. It may be hard to dis-

tort the total number of effort months for the whole organization, but within this total there can be a lot of pouring from one pot to another. A new project, in particular, is regarded as a lady bountiful. The general idea is to transfer folks there as quickly as possible to get billings up. Financial people seem to want a steady cash flow. The actual work, however, may not be ready for these people, so some of these manmonths are wasted. Later in the project when the effort is needed, these manmonths are no longer in the budget. The temptation is to play the same game with the next lady bountiful so as to complete the latest project.

Many more examples will be seen in case studies to come. It is the job of validation to anticipate this kind of fudging distortion and see that appropriate checks and balances are in place to avoid them. Many so-called "validation techniques" are available, but most boil down to careful checking and double-checking and a good dose of common sense.

The most important basic technique is the fundamental idea of feeding back any collected data right at the source or as close to the source as possible. The people supplying measurement data are in the best position to see if it has been captured incorrectly and rigorous source feedback can help breed individual responsibility for data accuracy.

Spot checks and audits that trace selected data to its source should be applied periodically as an overall check on the measurement effort. Outlier analysis focuses on understanding extreme and boundary values to surface special cases and avoid biasing of average results from the inclusion of a few points of bad data. Special calibration studies and sanity checks should be used to assure that results being obtained make sense and are repeatable. Encouraging everyone to look for and propose alternate data interpretations is a great way to avoid jumping to preliminary and wrong conclusions.

None of these techniques requires sophistication or special tools. What they share in common is a recognition that the organization must set aside ongoing effort into making sure that the measurement system is working and that everyone must be expected to be responsible and accountable for data validity and accuracy.

SUMMARY

This chapter has provided a foundation model for the measurement process. The reader should understand and be able to characterize the key features and elements of the bottom-up, practitioner-based measurement engineering paradigm as well as the five-step measurement process model.

We've stressed that the place to start engineering your measurement program is around the *work products* that are produced as a project proceeds, and that for each work product we need measurements of the *inputs*, the *outputs*, and the *results*.

We've also driven home the idea that measurement's primary role is the support of the working practitioner. Measurements should be integrated into all software work, and, fundamentally, measurements come *before* goals, not after.

We've provided a systematic model that can be used to engineer and structure a successful measurement effort. The steps of the model (define, collect, present, use, and validate) have been illustrated and shown to apply straightforwardly to most organizations.

Finally, we've stressed that a good measurement process will always be *changing*. New engineering techniques and new products will continually be forcing us to recalibrate and readjust our program. Even without such influences, we should constantly be raising new questions and striving for new or added insight. That leads to new metrics and meters and produces ongoing evolution and improvement of the process. The one constant we can count on is change, and our measurement program must be built from the start to support it.

Software is no longer a mysterious black art. We understand (even if we don't always do it) what is required to engineer it in an effective fashion. We also understand most of the measurements that need to be collected to support the effort and recognize that they must be built in from the bottom as the work process is defined and evolves. *Software measurements aren't something different or separate from software methodologies and techniques.* You don't first set up a process and *then* implement a measurement program. Good methods require and naturally support good measures, and hence most practical and useful measures should derive bottom-up, not top-down!

CHAPTER 2 EXERCISES AND DISCUSSION POINTS

1. Explain the major differences between the top-down and bottom-up (measurement engineering) approach and highlight at least two advantages and disadvantages of each.
2. Are the top-down and bottom-up approaches mutually exclusive? Explain your answer.
3. Critique the sample Lines of Code definition given in Figure 2.7. Is any information missing that you would want to know? What questions or concerns do you have with this definition?
4. Explain the difference between a continuous and discrete measure and give an example of each.
5. True or False—It makes no sense to use a metric or meter that has not been validated? Defend your answer.
6. What does it mean to say two measures are correlated?
7. Why is measuring the use of measurements important? List and describe at least three reasons.
8. Give at least three examples of common I, O and R measures.
9. Can a measurement be an I measure and an O measure at the same time? Explain.
10. What kind of a measure is productivity? (I, O or R?) Could it be a metric or meter? Explain or provide an example.

Getting Started

"You've got to be very careful if you don't know where you're going, because you might not get there."

Yogi Berra

The hardest steps to implementing a successful measurement program seem to be the first ones so this chapter is all about how to get started. The chapter will make the case that there aren't any quick hit simplistic solutions—companies who want good measurement programs must get on board for the long haul and build upon their existing support framework.

WISHFUL THINKING—THE MAGIC MAN

In Chapter 1 we presented industry survey data that showed most organizations regard their current measurement program as "in its infancy" or "just getting started." Many organizations have set goals to significantly improve their efforts in the near future. Unfortunately, most also assume there is a quick fix, a fairy godmother to sweep in, sprinkle a little magic dust, and PRESTO—a perfectly functioning measurement program!

Unfortunately, a measurement program is not like a new car

that you can go out and buy and simply trade or replace for your old one. It is rather like the plumbing and electrical systems in your house—hard to get at and change and something you are pretty much forced into having to understand and learn to live with. There is just no easy or magical way to replace pipes and wires without getting inside the walls and under the foundation.

Wishful thinking isn't going to go away. Sadly, our industry promotes it. Companies are out there selling lots of magic dust— one promises to "bring in a complete program in just 30 days, satisfaction guaranteed." Well don't count on it. The truth is your company "got started" with software measurement several decades ago with the gradual evolution of early project management and configuration tracking systems. From these early systems have grown a whole complex of procedures, tools, and processes your organization uses to build and maintain its software today. They are your infrastructure, like the plumbing and electrical systems of a house. To improve your measurement program you must understand and build on the basics.[1]

I know of no easy shortcuts. If we really want to be successful we've got to commit and invest for the long term. This chapter is about how to get started—first establishing a baseline inventory of the current effort, secondly assessing that effort and setting a realistic long term vision and finally applying the systematic measurement engineering process described in the last chapter to bring about and manage steady, ongoing improvement.

BASIC MEASUREMENT SYSTEM BUILDING BLOCKS

All software organizations with even limited process maturity have established some basic standards and procedures in each of the following three measurement-related areas:

---

[1] I should stress that a rather large problem for our industry is that there are lots of influential people who are convincing companies that you *can* just "buy-in" a measurement program in the form of some canned tools and consulting expertise. Magic and wishful thinking have always been potent forces!

Foundation Support Systems

1. *Resource Tracking*—estimating and tracking resource use, tasks, deliverables, and milestones.
2. *Work Product Tracking*—tracking and control of source code (and possibly document) versions and changes.
3. *Problem Tracking*—tracking and control of problems, defects, and open issues.

These are the basic building blocks in any bottom-up software measurement effort. They provide the necessary support for systematic measurement engineering. Much of what is practical and useful to measure comes directly from one or more of these building blocks. *Resource Tracking* provides measurements of the input effort and how it gets spent (I measures); *Work Product Tracking* (often called Configuration Management or Version Control) identifies work product versions and changes, and should be used to collect simple size and complexity measures like lines of new or changed code (O measures); and *Problem Tracking* gives us at least a primitive gauge of work effectiveness (R measures) by tracking problems that arise as the work product is used. As such they are the place to start engineering your bottom-up measurement effort. No company can achieve a highly successful measurement effort without them.

Most organizations (even those claiming little or no existing measurement program) have already invested rather substantially in these areas to establish routine procedures and provide for at least basic project tracking and control. Most have also provided at least some degree of automated support and already collected substantial amounts of data. The problem almost all face is that the "systems" were not designed or engineered from an integrated measurement point of view, or even a reasonable systems point of view. Most got started as bootlegged internal projects and were expanded in scope and function over time as the organization evolved. Few ever get the support or resources assigned to be implemented or maintained properly.

It shouldn't surprise us that fairly shoddy, low-quality systems result when you skip requirements definition, design and build the systems in your spare time, and fail to assign needed ongoing support. Trying to engineer good measurement programs into them is tough. Despite the problems and challenges they present, any effort to "get started" with measurement or even to improve existing programs should begin with a close examination of the building blocks. The next three sections survey the characteristics of what these building block systems should look like and what you should expect from them to support the measurement program.

The Resource Tracking Building Block

The Resource Tracking building block provides measurement of the input effort going into each project and major work product or output. The earliest versions of these systems were built in order to produce paychecks and calculate project cost. In many (probably most) companies they are not viewed as part of the "measurement system" at all, but serve merely to tabulate time sheet or time card data. In a mature measurement engineering environment they capture and analyze all effort by activity and support extensive project comparison and predictive metrics analysis.

A basic assumption in bottom-up measurement engineering is that all our software engineering work is broken down into sets of defined "activities" or "tasks" and that the effort (months, weeks, or days) spent on these activities is accumulated at least at a summary or major activity level. The detail of the work breakdown and accounting is not very critical, but tracking input resources and effort by activity is a fundamental requirement of the bottom-up paradigm. You have to understand where your effort is going (even that portion of effort spent on measurement) in order to be able to compare and quantitatively improve processes and answer most of the questions management is likely to raise. As just one example, any question about productivity or efficiency requires a relative comparison between what we get out of an activity and what we put into it—some ratio of output to input. Without basic input resource tracking by major activity we can't begin to answer such questions quantitatively.

What we need then is a breakdown list of standard activities against which to track effort. The *IEEE Standard for Developing*

Software Life Cycle Processes (1074–91) provides one such list. This standard identifies a good set of basic process steps and activities applicable to all projects for the development and support of software. The list contains 65 activities grouped in 5 major categories, as shown in Figure 3.1. (Only 16 of the activities are listed—the others are subcategories of these.) I find these to be an excellent starting point for anyone defining or establishing the effort buckets to be tracked. The standard provides definitions for each of the activities and identifies the outputs that should result. These outputs are the work products that we measure and track in the Work Product Tracking building block system. (See the next section.)

To support the collection of effort data by activity, each practitioner and manager must thoroughly understand the activity categories selected and complete a time sheet for their own effort.

Project Management Processes
Project Initiation
Project Monitoring & Control
Software Quality Management

Pre-Development Processes
Concept Exploration
System Allocation

Development Processes
Requirements
Design
Implementation

Post-Development Processes
Installation
Operation & Support
Maintenance
Retirement

Integral Processes
Verification & Validation
Software Configuration
 Management
Documentation Development
Training

Software Life Cycle: A sequence of defined process steps and activities.

Process: A function to be performed in the software life cycle. (Processes define activities that must be performed.)

Activity: A constituent task or group of tasks within a process.

Task: The smallest unit of work subject to management accountability. (Related tasks are usually grouped to form activities.)

Product: Any output of the software processes and activities.

Figure 3.1.   Standard activity categories and definitions (IEEE 1074).

Most systems collect the time data weekly, but a satisfactory system of effort reporting can also be done biweekly or monthly if the practitioners take it seriously and keep notes of how they actually spend their time throughout the month.

Activity and effort must be separated by project and by major work product. Since it is common for an individual to work on multiple projects, a time sheet in matrix format with activities listed down the left side and columns for each project being worked (plus an additional column for nonproject effort) works best. Many of the better Resource Tracking systems generate the time-reporting forms as turnaround documents or electronic mail messages. These provide feedback reporting to the individual to show what was entered on the last submission and cumulative effort by activity over time. This is a helpful validation mechanism and guards against careless transposition and data entry errors.

The Work Product Tracking Building Block

Output measures are collected to describe and quantify any work products that are created. They typically include some very primitive measures of size (such as lines of code or pages in a document) and complexity (such as the number of decisions in a program). We also like to have information on the number and types of work products produced and the changes and rework applied to them as well as any measures that might be unique or specific to the particular work products. The specific measures to collect and how they are used will be addressed in Part II when we cover each of the major work products.

Many of the simple output measures can and should be collected automatically as an extension of the library or configuration management procedures. The measurement tool is built into the version control procedures and is invoked whenever a new version of a work product is submitted. This provides a record of each change and a history of the output measurements over time.

Figure 2.8 in Chapter 2 gave an example of how such data can be gathered and presented. In that example, a spreadsheet format was employed where each row contained various measures for a particular code module (the work product). The spreadsheet columns contained basic input resource data on the effort expended (provided by the Resource Tracking building block) as well as some simple output measures (lines of code and number of changes). The latter would be provided by what we are defining as our Work Product Tracking building block system. The example also included two result measures (remember that the result or R measures quantify use of the work product and how good it is)—the coders perception or confidence rating as well as the number of defects found in later stages of testing after check-in. If such a perception measure is used, it must be gathered manually. This may be part of the Work Product Tracking building block or a separate measurement activity.

In most companies a measurement-oriented Work Product Tracking system is just beginning to emerge as an outgrowth from the existing library or configuration management systems. Such systems are already a key part of the software engineering infrastructure and can be adapted to provide a wealth of useful measurement information quite easily. We'll see many examples and illustrations of actual product tracking system features later in the book. To get started the reader only needs to understand the key features and measurements we expect to draw from the Work Product Tracking building block and be able to compare that with their existing baseline capability.

The Problem Tracking Building Block

Our third and final building block supports the measurement and tracking of problems or defects. The use of defect counts is common to most measurement programs. A defect is something wrong that needs to be fixed. It seems a simple matter to just count them up.

As it turns out, it is far from simple. Even after counting defects in millions of actual software work products, the industry still doesn't have a very satisfactory handle on just what a defect is, how to objectively count them, or how to interpret the count. Few companies have taken the time or discipline to carefully define what they mean by a defect, and even fewer have reasonably unambiguous and validated collection and counting procedures.

Most companies have implemented some sort of database to record "problems" or "incidents" when they are discovered—especially those reported by end users and customers. Some even have the problem of having too many. (One company I am familiar with had seven different defect tracking "systems"—all in use by different teams and organizations, all working on *one* integrated product line!)

Like the work product or configuration management area, the initial motivation for defect tracking was control, not measurement. Bugs and problems were entered into the database to make sure they didn't get lost or forgotten. Only later did we begin to worry about counting and analyzing them for predictive and comparative purposes or as measures of results and quality. Most of the existing tracking systems are very simple; many are even implemented in something like DBase or Lotus Notes. Whenever a problem is discovered, a problem record is "opened" and basic data about the problem (activity or phase, symptom, suspected cause, type or classification) is recorded. The problem is then "assigned" and analyzed. Additional data about the problem may be recorded that identifies and scopes what is required to fix it. After the fix is "approved," a change is prepared and tested, and the problem can be "closed." Still more data (actual cause, source of the problem, effort to fix) is usually entered upon closing. The Problem Tracking system allows analysis of all this data and provides various reports showing open and closed problems, defects by type or category, and so on.

Considerable effort and time may be required to collect (enter), analyze, and present all the problem data. In a large project it is not uncommon for there to be thousands of problems that must be opened, fixed, and closed. Manual effort has to be expended on each of these problems, and thus the tracking system must be kept as simple as possible. In most cases an entry screen or window is provided for the practitioner to call up whenever required. This entry screen should require no more than a minute or two to be completed. If too much time is required, the practitioner will resist using the system, and the data collected will end up being incomplete or inaccurate.

For organizations just starting out or planning to redesign their Problem Tracking system, *IEEE Standard P1044 for Error, Fault and Failure Classification* (still in draft form at the time of this writing) offers a useful set of guidelines and suggested classification categories for the data items that should be captured in a defect tracking system. The standard identifies four sequential steps involved in every problem report: Recognition, Investigation, Action, and Disposition. Required classifications and data elements that must be captured in each of these steps are provided and described in the standard (see Figure 3.2).

At "Recognition" the current project phase; the activity that was going on when the problem was found; and a classification for the symptom are required. During "Investigation" a cause classification; type of problem classification; and the source for the problem are required. At "Action" the decision is made as to what to do about the problem is made and the resolution is recorded. Finally the problem is "Disposed" which will either close it, defer it or merge it with some other open problem. The standard includes many other optional data elements that an organi-

	Recognition	Investigation	Action	Description
PROJECT ACTIVITY (Analysis, review, inspection . . .)	X			
PROJECT PHASE (Rqmts, design, implementation . . .)	X			
SYMPTOM (Crash, input problem output problem . . .)	X			
ACTUAL CAUSE (Product, test system, user, unknown . . .)		X		
SOURCE (Specifications, code, manuals . . .)		X		
TYPE (Logic, computation, interface,data . . .)		X		
RESOLUTION (Immediate, eventual, deferred)			X	
DISPOSITION (Closed, deferred, merged)				X

Figure 3.2. Defect tracking data elements and classifications (IEEE P1044).

zation might want to consider tracking and provides suggested codes and categories for all of the classifications.

Using the standard helps address one of the problems with our problem tracking systems: what data to collect and how to classify or categorize it. It does not address the sticky issue of the definition of a problem. While in theory it might be nice to track every problem, in practice small issues and problems found and corrected by the work product author before the product is placed under version or configuration control are not included. For measurement and comparative purposes it is important that a definition for problems to include or omit be established and conformed to.

WHAT IS A DEFECT ANYWAY?

Although we have been working hard at it for a decade or two we still have no real industry standard for what a software "problem" is. This is not from lack of trying. Figure 3.3 lists a few of the more prominent published definitions.

The definitions reflect evolution over time in how we think about defects. While we've made progress (For example, the newer definitions make it clear that defects may appear in requirements and specifications as well as code. Note also that each successive definition is measurably longer (at least in the number of words). This is presumably some progress!), the definition of a defect remains fuzzy, and there are still plenty of counting troubles.

It is more difficult than you might expect to establish consistent counting procedures. Some projects rigorously count everything they find; others leave it up to individual judgment. Defects found by the work product producer are sometimes included and sometimes not. Multiple defects are often counted or recorded as one; single defects get counted more than once. On top of the pure counting issues we also have to be concerned with whether and how to weigh the count for severity or failure impact. Some organizations adjust the counts for impact or keep separate counts by impact class. For others the weight is arbitrary or not determined at all.

Certain aspects of the problem in defining what is a problem remain rather subtle and undefined. Most literature views the activities of software evaluation (reviews, inspections, tests, etc.)

A defect is a deviation from the specification.

Bill Hetzel, *Program Test Methods*, 1972

A defect occurs whenever the software does not behave the way the user reasonably expects it to behave.

Glen Myers, *Art of Software Testing*, 1979

A defect includes any deviation from the specification and also errors in the specification. (Once the specification is accepted, any new features added or old features deleted are considered defects.)

Hewlett-Packard, 1989

A defect is something that, if not corrected, will result in an authorized problem analysis report (APAR), or result in a defect condition in a later inspection or test stage or is in noncomformance to a documented specification or requirement.

IBM, Rochester, MN, 1991

Figure 3.3.   Some attempts at a defect definition.

as being performed at discrete points in time over the life of the software project (for example, in a formal review or during the execution of a planned test). Defects are reported as "found" only in these discrete evaluation windows. Other defects found and fixed as a "side effect" of the process are not counted. Yet anyone who has had experience in developing tests early in a project (in parallel with the software design) knows that early test design surfaces many specification issues and discrepancies. Should these be counted as "defects" found by testing, or should they just be viewed as supportive communications that help the project to get clearer specifications?

The potentially even bigger problem is how valid any defect count is as a predictive metric for the underlying work product quality. What we really want to know about is the *defects that remain* (aren't yet found) and *their impact* in terms of *results* or effectiveness. What does knowing that we found a certain number of defects in a certain way tell us about the defects we haven't found and how important they are or might be to our customers?[3] The honest answer right now is that although we see many cases where it provides good insight we still have a lot to learn. The next few sections provide examples of some of the common defect-related measurements that various companies track and report. We'll talk about how to apply these measures in Parts II and III when we cover the measurements for each of the individual software work products.

BASIC DEFECT MEASUREMENTS

There are a variety of defect measurements that are widely used in industry—at least within a small number of leading edge companies. Figure 3.4 lists the more commonly used measurements.

Defect Types—Counts by category of various kinds and classes of defects.

Defect Distributions—Location and distribution of defects throughout the software.

Defect Rate—Plots over time showing defects per unit of time or effort.

Defect Age—Time from introduction to detection.

Defect Response or Fix Times—Time from detection to fix.

Defect Cost—Cost of failure or impact as well as the cost of analyzing and fixing the defect.

Defect Density—Defects detected per unit of work product such as per page of a design specification or per line of code.

Figure 3.4.   Some of the more common defect measures.

---

[3]One study [Adams 84] has been published that *indicates it is quite likely that products which have a large number of defects may fail rarely, if at all!* In an article in the *IBM Journal of Research and Development* Ed Adams reported on an analysis of 9 software products, each with many thousands of years of logged use. Consistently he found that most software faults or defects rarely lead to operational failures, while a small proportion cause the most frequent failures. Adams found over 95 percent of all the detected faults had associated mean times to failure in excess of 50 years of run time. A third were in excess of 5000 years of run time.

Illustrations for each of these measures, along with case experiences and problems to be anticipated, are provided in subsequent sections. The intent is to provide the reader with some perspective on how these measures are gathered and presented and to establish the desired capabilities we want built into our Problem Tracking building block system. We'll visit these measures again and how they are *used* to support decision making and analysis in later chapters.

Defect Type and Classification

Simple frequency tables that categorize defects into classifications by type, severity, and cause may be the most prevalent form of defect measurement we find in the industry. An example showing a breakdown of the causes or origin of all defects found in system level testing of a programmable controller device and interface at Allen Bradley is shown in Figure 3.5.

The data was gathered by collecting and entering the defects reported during system and product testing into a defect tracking database. They were assigned to developers to fix and for classification by "origin" using the categories listed. The two most frequent origin categories that resulted are "Design" (120 defects) and "Code" (89 defects). Since these were the source of the majority of the defects, they were further categorized by "cause" to produce the two additional categories we see.

Note that the most frequent design cause listed is "Misinterpretations of requirements" (39 defects). When I saw this data my first question was whether these should not have been counted as "requirements" defects under the original origin classification. Perhaps it was really an inadequacy in the requirements specification that *caused* the misinterpretation and resulted in a design flaw being made. Similar questions might be posed about the two highest categories of "coding" causes—"Initialization errors" and "Control errors." Is it possible that these are arising because of inadequate design specification? (*Challenge*: The reader should be able to spot a number of other definitional questions and potential inconsistencies. Can you find them? What questions would you have or want answered before you could interpret the data or use it to make decisions?)

Such questions are typical of the kind that arise whenever

Severity		Design Cause	
Critical	23	Misinterpretations of	
Major	211	requirements	39
Minor	97	Oversight	27
Cosmetic	9	Inadequate error traps	15
	340	Initialization error	7
		Full range check	5
Primary Origin		Incompatibility with hardware	5
Bad fixes	7	Synchronization	4
Code	89	Timing problems	4
Design	120	Incompatibility with software	4
Documentation	15	Premature execution	4
Hardware	2	Code entry	3
No problem	37	Computational error	2
Procedural	21	Wrong priorities	1
Requirements	24		120
Suggestion	8		
Data errors	2	**Code Cause**	
Vendor software	2	Initialization error	27
Duplicate	13	Control error	18
	340	Computation error	17
		Silly programming errors	12
		Interface error	8
		Data errors	7
			89

1990 Applications of Software Measurement Conference. Ed Ely presentation.

Figure 3.5.   Example of defect classification by severity and cause.

real data is presented. As emphasized in Part I our measurement goal is to build understanding and be prepared to answer the next unasked question. Actual examples like this emphasize the importance of having careful category definitions and saving the source information about each defect so that deeper analysis can be performed if required.

Distribution of Defects

Many other types of defect classifications and simple analyses of defect results are often presented. Figure 3.6 is an example of a

	Product #1	Product #2
Number of files	244	166
Number of defects	157	234
Number of files with no defects	161	91
Percentage of files with no defects	66%	55%
Number of defects in 5% most defective files	74	98
Percentage of defects in 5% most defective files	47%	42%

Figure 3.6.   Sample defect distribution by source file.

typical report with defects grouped by source file (UNIX source files in this particular case). These distributions are typical. We commonly see a significant number of defect-free files or modules with half or more of all the defects bunched in under 10 percent of the most defective files. This may help focus attention on the right questions to ask and possibly enable us to spot common factors contributing to the defect-prone modules. If this can help us to identify or learn about some common cause, we can significantly improve the process for the future. We shouldn't expect all such measurements to yield useful results. Once again our point is that the measures come first—that spawns questions and insight, which in turn may spawn the need for real changes (goals and new process steps) and the introduction of working meters and metrics.

Defect Rate

Another common way of presenting defect data is in the form of a chart or plot that displays *defect rate*. Figure 3.7 shows several examples. In both plots the horizontal axis is time (weeks) and the vertical axis is the number of defects found. (One plot denotes the number of defects found per week; the other shows a cumulative count over the life of the project.) Although the charts indicate the counts, most companies that produce them are more interested in the *shapes* of the plot trended over time. The intent is to generate interest and questions from managers and practi-

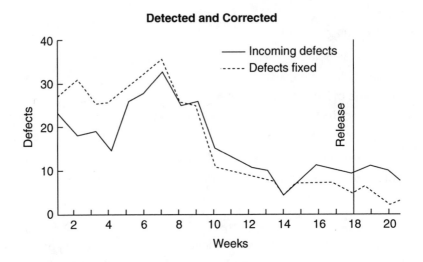

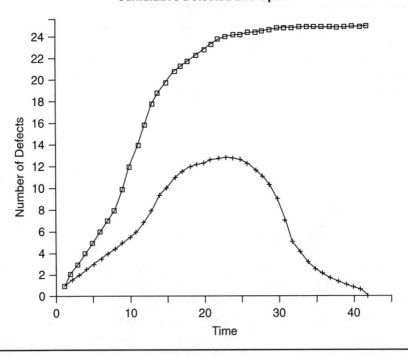

Figure 3.7.   Example of defect rate plots.

tioners and possibly serve as a metric or meter to determine release readiness.

WARNING: Remember that a low detection rate may indicate software that is nearing readiness for release, but it may also be due to ineffective testing or little testing activity. Defect rate is strongly correlated with test activity: Whenever you run more tests, you will likely discover more defects! So be careful not to misinterpret the plot, and be sure to ask other questions and have other measurements in hand before making any conclusions. The quickest way to kick up the defect rate is to kick up the intensity of the test effort!

Defect Age

Another important defect measurement is the time from introduction to detection and correction or the *defect age*. To calculate age we need data on when a problem is found (the date of detection) and when it first was made or introduced (the date of introduction). The date of detection is the easy part. Determining the date that a defect was first made may be much harder and must be done long after the facts and circumstances have been obscured.

Often some simplification may be necessary to achieve a practical age measure. Some companies try to estimate the date a defect was introduced only to the nearest month or quarter. Another approach is to try to record just the phases in the life cycle of detection and when the defect is judged to have first appeared. In practice this is a lot easier than trying to estimate the actual date and can be used to derive a reasonable age measure that I have found to be quite effective.

To compute the measure we first assign numbers to each project phase (for example "requirements" might be given a 1; "design" a 2; "implementation" a 3; and ongoing "support" or "production" a 4). The "age" of a defect is then calculated by subtracting the phase number it was detected in minus the phase number where it was first introduced. Any defect found in the same phase as it was introduced has an age of 0. A defect introduced in design (phase 2) but found one phase later in implementation (phase 3) would have an age of 1. If that same defect was not found until production or during support or maintenance (phase 4), the age would be 2 (4 − 2 = 2).

A Simple Average Age Measure

$$\text{Average Age} = \frac{\Sigma \, (\text{Phase Detected} - \text{Phase Introduced})}{\text{Number of Defects}}$$

The formula above gives a normalized *average age* measure. One alternative I've also seen used on a few occasions uses the square of the phase numbers; that gives even more emphasis to not finding a problem as soon as possible and may be preferred. Another is to present the data in graphical form plotting the number of defects found and introduced at each phase to present a visual picture of what was happening. Note that "average age" will decrease over time if the organization is finding its defects earlier—a nice thing to be able to discern and measure. We want to be able to look at defects introduced and found by phase anyway. Average age highlights defects that get missed and are not found until subsequent phases.

Defect Response Time

In addition to analyzing the time from defect introduction to detection, it is also desirable to track the time from detection to fix, or what is commonly called the *defect response time*. Figure 3.8 illustrates an example of such a response time measurement provided by Ashton-Tate for its DBase product.

The age distribution (number of weeks open) of the Program Trouble Reports (PTR's) is displayed graphically. A clear bi-modal distribution can be observed with the large majority of problems being less than two weeks old and another group that are two to three months old.

Note once again how data like this raises more questions than it answers. Is this response time profile what we want? How should we try to change it? What is the significance of the few items over four months old? Are the problems that are one to three

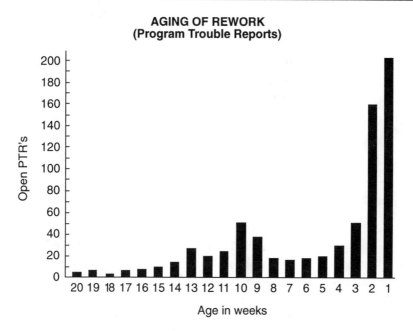

AGING OF REWORK
(Program Trouble Reports)

1990 Applications of Software Measurement Conference.
Steve Wilkerson, Ashton Tate.

Figure 3.8.   Sample defect response time measurement.

months old any different or harder to fix than those that are under two weeks? All of these questions would require further analysis and other measurement data to be answered.

Defect Effort and Cost

Many companies also capture the effort required to fix each defect. This is required to compute and track the *cost of rework* and correction. Those who have tracked such a measure have repeatedly found that a small percentage of defects accounts for a large percentage of the rework.

Figure 3.9 shows an example of the distribution of effort required to correct 1165 reported problems on a large project. The 7 percent most time-consuming defects (those requiring over a week

Effort to Fix	Percentage
< 1 Day	71%
< 2 Days	15%
< 3 Days	7%
< 1 Week	5%
< 2 Weeks	1%
< 1 Month	.08%
< 3 Months	.02%

Figure 3.9. Distribution of rework effort.

to correct) took more effort than the other 93 percent combined! If we can use our measurements to identify this 7 percent and thus focus attention on preventing them in the future, we may be able to greatly reduce the rework.

A number of companies who record and count defects do not measure the effort and cost it takes to fix them because they are reluctant to face the overhead necessary to do so. We can estimate it without having to analyze all the defects if we can find the time to analyze just the small percentage of defects that consume the bulk of the cost and then applying a standard cost to all the rest. A similar approach can be used with failure costs when applicable. The result is a reasonable defect cost measure with a minimum of analysis effort, requiring detailed analysis of less than 10 percent of the total defects that are captured and recorded.

Defect Density

One final defect measure we need to discuss is *defect density*. Quite a few companies who count defects also compute a "density" or ratio measure. The most common form is *defects per KLOC* (defects per thousand lines of code). This is just the ratio of two simple measures we have already discussed—Defect Count and Lines of Code. The intent of the measure is to normalize the count of defects by the "size" or "complexity" of the product. We recognize that larger and more complex products are likely to have more defects, and density is one way of comparing products of different sizes.

Although the measure is rather popular, I personally don't like it much—especially from our practitioner-based point of view. Most organizations are using the measure as a gauge or metric for software quality. Many also try to compare "quality" between projects and companies by comparing the defect density measures. Yet the defects of greatest interest are those still in the product after release, not those already discovered. That means we must wait through several months (or even a year or two) of field experience to get our total defect count and that the measure can't be computed until long after the product is released.

Even when we finally get the density, it is easy to misinterpret it. There is no way to standardize what users choose to report and not report, and with its small numerator the measure is extremely sensitive to any counting inconsistencies. There is some evidence that the measure does not correlate well with customer-perceived quality. Customers are much more sensitive to failures than they are to defects, and satisfaction is also strongly influenced by factors like ease of use, adaptability, and so on.

Like the counting of defects, I believe defect density has been given too much emphasis. What we should concentrate on is problem cost and impact, not problem density. Software quality goals should be concerned with minimizing rework and failures and maximizing customer-measured perceptions. Such an approach eliminates most of the problems with the defect measures and strengthens the overall measurement program. If you can validate that density is a good satisfaction and quality metric in your company, then by all means use it. Otherwise, be extra careful with it, and make sure your manager doesn't view it as a simplistic gauge of goodness or something he can easily compare with his colleagues.

Despite the lack of good definition and collection procedures and the absence of validation, there is a sizeable segment of the industry that uses the density measure. Almost all at least recognize the need to understand defects better in order to make intelligent process improvements. Thus, reporting defects in each work product is certainly something we want to do to make sure we get them corrected and learn from our mistakes. But just how we use such information to evaluate effectiveness and satisfaction remains very much open to debate. We'll see lots of examples in subsequent chapters and try to contrast their strengths and weaknesses to help you decide the best approach for your company.

Defect Measurement Revisited

So where does all this leave us? Regardless of the difficulties in measuring them, we need information about our work product defects (both those we discover and those we miss and get discovered for us). We want to know the causes and when a defect is first introduced; when, by whom, and how it was found. What was its impact or cost? How common is it, and what are the trends? And perhaps most importantly, what could we have done to the process to prevent it or help detect it earlier?

To find out you've got to measure and analyze your defects in all your important work products throughout the development and support life cycle. There are no easy, fully automatable, ways to get such information. Even when we get it, we have problems trying to compare between projects and companies due to the lack of standard definitions and counting rules. However, the need is basic to good engineering, and it is clear to me that we are going to have to improve our defect measurement and analysis significantly. The Problem Tracking building block system is basic to that effort and is a place almost all measurement programs should be concentrating on.

BASELINING WHERE YOU STAND TODAY (CURRENT STATE)

Assessing the existing support systems is part of the important first step to understanding and *baselining* where your company stands on software measurement today. A good baseline requires a systematic inventory of what is currently being measured, how it is used, and what the existing strengths, weaknesses, and needs are. It includes an analysis of the building block systems and any other measurement-related tools and infrastructure and may sometimes include systematic benchmarking and cross-organization comparisons.

Choosing the scope is an important initial decision. The baseline can be focused on just a single project, a unit, a division, or the entire company. If you are unsure of how much to tackle, select the smaller scope to start with. You can always enlarge it later if necessary. Just make sure you avoid making it so narrow that you fail to discover or learn about key strengths that may already be in place in a sister project or peer organization.

It is reasonable to consider the baselining task a measurement activity in itself—in this case a measurement of the current measurement program! As such, the bottom-up IOR model introduced in Chapter 2 is applicable, and the measurements collected need to consider the inputs, outputs, and results of the measurement program (see Figure 3.10).

Let's look at the "outputs" first. All the existing measurements now being *collected* and *presented* should be systematically inventoried and documented, even if poorly defined, not in use, or unvalidated. How the data gets used along with an analysis of measurement activities, resources, and effectiveness can then be assessed as a second step.

A recommended procedure is to interview a selected sample of practitioners and managers to identify any measurement information data or reports that they now receive or use. During these interviews sample copies of any reports received can be tracked down and collected. Each measurement found in the re-

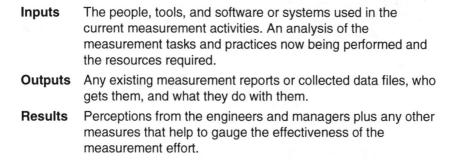

Inputs   The people, tools, and software or systems used in the current measurement activities. An analysis of the measurement tasks and practices now being performed and the resources required.

Outputs Any existing measurement reports or collected data files, who gets them, and what they do with them.

Results Perceptions from the engineers and managers plus any other measures that help to gauge the effectiveness of the measurement effort.

Figure 3.10.   Measuring your measurement program.

ports is inventoried and traced back to its source to establish where it came from and how it gets collected.

The inventory of existing measures, metrics, and meters can be thought of as one of the baseline work products. Figure 3.11 provides a list of some of the key questions to be answered as the inventory is gathered.

As the questions are answered, they should be documented and routed for review and validation by the entire organization being baselined. This process will catch most of the measures and any additional ones can be added as they are discovered or noted. Once the inventory of measures and who uses them is established the resources and activities associated with collecting and reporting along with some selected measures of satisfaction and perceived effectiveness are collected to complete the baseline. Our experience has been that most organizations are surprised to discover how much information they now collect and how little all that is collected is really used for anything productive.

Satisfaction with the existing measures can be assessed by

What are you COLLECTING?
What source collection forms and entry screens are available?
What measures get collected at what frequency?
What files (paper or computer) already exist somewhere?
What measures are captured in the building block systems?

How are you PRESENTING your measurements?
What reports (paper or computer) are produced?
Who gets them and at what frequency?
What analyses and data transformations are performed?
Who performs them?
Do users interact with or analyze data on their own?

What are your measurements USED for?
Who uses the presented information or reports?
What do they do with it?
What metrics and meters exist in the organization now?

Figure 3.11.   The existing measures, metrics and meters inventory.

survey (orally or with a survey instrument completed by the engineer or manager who uses the measure). True effectiveness is harder to assess and validate. For a first-order approximation consider bringing together a hand-picked group of employees and managers to meet and discuss the major strengths and weaknesses of the current system. (In Chapter 8 I'll discuss a more sophisticated effectiveness measurement technique based on objective comparison with industry norms and benchmarks.)

The inventory and baseline information should be packaged and documented in a formal report to the organization. This is an important and visible step that will serve to define where you stand today (your current state). It is important to put it together professionally and carefully. Some organizations like to combine the baseline report with recommendations and an action plan. Given the option, I prefer to treat it as a separate work product. The separation helps focus attention on understanding and gaining problem consensus without the distractions and politics of what ought to be done about it.

COMMUNICATING WHERE YOU WANT TO BE (DESIRED STATE)

The second important step is establishing a high-level vision for what the organization wants its measurement program to be like. The purpose of the vision statement is to help everyone in the organization understand the role of measurement and to outline policies to guide and shape ongoing program improvement.

In theory, a vision statement can be shaped independently from the baseline inventory work. This book is all about building an industry-wide vision for how a software measurement program should or ought to be run. It and other books like it certainly help an organization come to grips with policy setting and objectives. However, in practice it is much more effective if the results of a completed baseline are already on the table. Understanding (and acknowledging) your existing strengths and weaknesses adds realism to the vision statement and helps in focusing and setting priorities. While the intent is to set a direction for the long haul (three to five years or more), you don't want to end up with a vision that is so abstract that it becomes devoid of content and impact at both the practitioner and manager levels. Factoring in the baseline results gives it much more substance.

I recommend that the vision be captured in a formal policy document that is approved and adopted by the entire management team. After approval it should be widely disseminated and shared in open meetings to ensure good understanding and support. The policy should emphasize continuous bottom-up engineering of the measurement effort. That includes ongoing changes and evolution in the vision, so part of the policy should encourage change and define the mechanism for handling it.

IMPLEMENTING AN IMPROVEMENT INITIATIVE

After the two important deliverables of the existing baseline and desired vision have been published, it is easy (well no change is ever easy, but certainly we can say *easier*) to identify individual improvement steps and initiate improvement projects.

The idea is to carve out modest, digestible steps (projects) that have reasonable priority and leveraged payoff. This is shown in Figure 3.12. What we want to do is make progress over time in closing the gap (climbing the steps) between the current state and the desired state. At any one time we may have several such improvement efforts or projects under way. Each project by itself is perhaps only a few weeks or months in duration, but they are tied together by the shared long-term vision and overall policy or architecture for ongoing improvement.

It is important for me to stress that this basic approach to building an effective measurement program is applicable and relevant to large and small companies alike. Don't assume that measurement improvement programs are only for the big guys. Small companies find it much easier to change rapidly and often get the biggest paybacks from even modest improvement efforts.

Measurement plays a fundamental role in every step of the improvement process. We first "measured" our organization to define the current state (baseline) and we may have used measurement (in the form of industry-wide surveys and comparative practice measures) to benchmark and help set our current vision. Next we measure all the ongoing projects and feed back the successes (and failures). That helps refine and adjust our view of the current state as well as our view of where we'd like to be in the

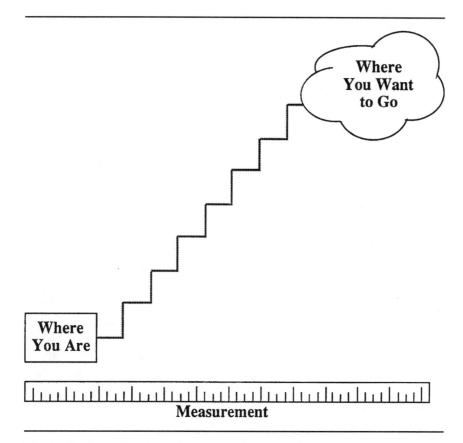

Figure 3.12. Continuous measured improvement.

future (desired state). Periodically, we'll want to come back and remeasure the baseline in order to confirm improvement and reestablish where we are.

It is important to emphasize that both the vision and the current baseline are in motion and continually evolving over time. Thus it might be possible to have actually climbed a few steps (achieved some real program improvements) yet had the gap between the current state and the desired state widen (if, for example, we changed our vision or fell back in other areas). The healthy organization understands the need to manage the evolution of its measurement program and use measured results to both assess needs and evaluate results.

Such an approach not only works as an effective model for

measurement improvement, but can also serve as a "system" for managing all technical process changes. A critical need that many organizations have is learning how to quantitatively select change priorities (based on measured facts) and then evaluate the results (measuring the actual improvement or nonimprovement if that is the reality). At the 1991 measurement conference I participated in a panel session with Howard Rubin, Al Pietrasanta, and Bill Curtis. During the panel I asked the audience to think back over the past year and identify one specific, fairly visible change that happened in their organization. The change could be almost anything—a process change like deciding to add or beef up formal inspections, a technology change like moving to an object-oriented language or installing a new CASE tool, or even management changes like changing the organization, establishing a metrics effort, or setting new quality goals. The only criteria was that the change selected be viewed as fairly important within the organization.

With that specific change in mind, I then asked the delegates if good measurement data had been collected and used as an important element in the decision to make the change. Were hard, measured project results required in order to demonstrate persuasively that any new policy or change was better? Was the change supported by measured results, and was measurement data viewed as a vital and important element in the decision? Just a tiny sprinkling of hands across the room signaled the affirmative.

This demonstrated for me how tall a challenge we really face. I think we all can agree that the reason we measure is to help people make decisions and to improve their understanding and insight. Yet few in the industry really seem to depend on measurement to support important actions and decisions. Getting started with the kind of long-term, ongoing measurement program we've advocated here can help enormously and is an industry objective we all need to be working toward.

SUMMARY

Our goal in this chapter was to lay out what it takes to get a good bottom-up practitioner-based measurement engineering program under way.

We've stressed four basic steps:

1. Clearly understand and *baseline* where you stand today.
2. Focus initially on the three building block systems—Resource, Work Product, and Problem Tracking.
3. Publish a policy vision stating your intent to establish a bottom-up measurement engineering program for the future (your desired state).
4. Identify and prioritize the differences between the desired state and the current state defined by your baseline.
5. Fund and complete projects (small steps) to close the gap.

The baseline serves to define the measurements now being collected and the current meters and metrics in use. It identifies strengths and weaknesses of the existing effort and helps them to be communicated and understood throughout the organization.

The building block systems form the core foundation for all measurement engineering efforts.

1. *Resource Tracking* provides basic I measures of effort and input activity by work product and project phase.
2. *Work Product Tracking* provides basic O measures of size and complexity for the work products produced or modified.
3. *Problem Tracking* provides basic R measures of defect counts, classifications, rates, densities, and so on to help evaluate work product results and quality.

For most organizations, and for any just getting started, the best way to work on developing a strong bottom-up measurement engineering program is to concentrate on the three building block systems.

We've also stressed that there are no quick-hit, simple solutions. Management must make a commitment to invest in and manage their measurement effort over the long haul. Small, steady improvement steps working toward a well-thought-through vision with a measured fact base for where you stand now is what is required to succeed.

CHAPTER 3 EXERCISES AND DISCUSSION POINTS

1. Describe the foundation support systems (Resource Tracking, Work Product Tracking and Problem Tracking) that are available in your current organization. Highlight any key weaknesses or limitations.

2. Why must effort be accumulated by activity or task? How are such measurements used?

3. Explain the differences (if any) between terms like bugs, errors, defects, faults, failures, problems, incidents, etc.

4. List at least five problems with defect density as an R measure for a software work product.

5. Identify at least two apparent inconsistencies in the defect classification data shown in Figure 3.5. What questions would you want answered before you could interpret the data or use it to make decisions?

6. Why do defects cluster within programs or files? What does this imply about the techniques for measuring them?

7. What decisions can be made using a defect rate plot (such as the example in Figure 3.7). Be careful to list any assumptions you are making.

8. Why is measurement of defect age important? How can it be used?

9. Outline the basic steps for starting a bottom-up measurement program.

10. Why is a measurement program always changing? What aspects are the most stable? What aspects are the most variable and likely to change?

11. Discuss what a "requirements document" for a software measurement program might look like in your current organization. How would you organize it? List examples of typical requirements you would include. (*Note*: Team projects could be assigned to provide a complete requirements package.)

12. Describe how you would "measure" the existing "cost" of measurement in a hypothetical company. List or note any key assumptions important to your method or approach.

PART II

Practitioner-Based Measurement

"My vision of the future is not of software metrics in isolation. It is a vision of software engineering where metrics help engineers to measure and help manage software change and complexity."

Robert B. Grady

INTRODUCTION TO PART II

In Part I we introduced the systematic engineering process and outlined how to get started using it in your organization to improve and structure your software measurement program. In Part II we'll be looking at practitioner applications of the process and sharing industry case studies and examples. The intent is to demonstrate practical experiences and help provide ideas for measures, metrics, and meters that you can use successfully.

The material is organized in three chapters, each covering one of the following major practitioner activity areas:

Measuring Software Specifications and Designs
Measuring Software Code and Development
Measuring Software Test and Evaluation

Within each chapter the work products developed are described, and appropriate Input, Output, and Results measures that measure them are presented. Each chapter can be read standalone, but all assume familiarity with the bottom-up, practitioner-based paradigm (Chapter 2) and the three basic building block support systems (Chapter 3).

Part II draws heavily on industry experience and case studies. I am convinced that the best way to spread a good technology is to study how someone else got it to work. So there are lots and lots of examples. Remember, if you like some of the examples, clip them out, and put them in your scrapbook. Better yet, try them out yourself! The overall objective is to share what others are doing and help give you ideas that have been tried or applied in practice and achieved at least limited success.

Since we are working from the bottom up it may not always be clear to the reader just how the measurements described are used in decision making or engineering process improvement. In terms of the structure of the book, much of this connection will be deferred to Part III. However, for the reader who might get a little confused, let me stress again that the book is *not* about theory or measurement research but rather the application of measurement to real-world concerns and problems. Even though we introduce our measures bottom-up as an integrated part of the software process, we must insist on a clear purpose and a *practical* application. That means we should always be able to envision a clear set of decisions (about present or future actions) that our measures should affect and have a model in mind for how they are to be used. If along the way you lose sight of where all this is leading, I suggest skipping ahead to Part III and reading it first. That will help you see where all this is going and remotivate you to climb back into the trenches!

4

Measuring Software Specifications and Designs

"Metrics is a lot like swimming. You can't learn to swim unless you get wet. The wetter you get, the faster you learn to swim."

David Longstreet

INTRODUCTION

Engineers and managers have historically had a hard time measuring the early requirements specification and design phases of a software project. We generally agree on what these phases are supposed to accomplish, a definition for WHAT the software is supposed to do (the requirements) and a blueprint or plan for HOW it will do it (the design). The problems arise in deciding how much detail or abstraction to provide and with the many different alternative forms the WHAT and HOW specifications can take. While virtually all software projects have at least something called "requirements" and something called a "design," there are few standards and little agreement as to the specific form and content these document work products should have.

Projects range from those using "formal" specification languages and very disciplined and structured specifications to those with extremely informal specifications. Some employ CASE tools to describe all or part of the specs; others use prototypes and simulators; and still others may be extremely detailed in certain aspects (for example, interface or user specifications). While leaving other areas loosely defined and subject to implementation decisions by the engineers later in the project during code development. The lack of work product standardization at both the industry and in-company levels has been an obstacle to developing better requirements and design measurements. As we shall see, however, there is much that can usefully be measured, even in organizations with poor and widely disparate requirements and design engineering practices.

The benefits and motivation for good measurement of these front end phases are easily appreciated. Such measurements can help the project anticipate problems that are likely to arise and serve to improve and control the quality of the requirements and design work products. Learning how to measure early helps ensure that we have a solid specification foundation to build upon and provides the basis for meaningful future project estimation.

THE IOR MODEL APPLIED TO REQUIREMENTS AND DESIGN

Our bottom-up IOR paradigm defines the measurement areas that need to be addressed for any work product. For every phase of the software life cycle we must capture information about the inputs, the outputs, and the results.

Input resource measures—Information about the resources (people, effort, time, money, etc.) and activities performed in producing the software requirements and design specification work products. These measure who is doing what; how much effort they expend; and what is required or used to produce any particular specification document.

Output work product measures—Information describing and quantifying each software requirement and design work product (requirements documents, design specifications, interface specifications, etc.).

Results and satisfaction measures—Information quantifying each work product's effectiveness and results of the effort expended (omissions, defects or errors, ability to meet and satisfy internal and external customers, etc.).

Obtaining the input measures does not involve anything fundamentally new or unique to the requirements and design phases. The basic building block *Resource and Activity Tracking System* has the job of capturing the software tasks we perform and how much effort goes into them (see Chapter 3). Whether this is a terrific, fully automated tracking system or just a very crude high-level task reporting (weeks or days of effort on each key task) provided by each project member every week or two is not the critical success factor. What is important is to track and compare effort spent with an accuracy of, say, plus or minus 20 percent. That is accurate enough to develop thumb rules of how long various tasks and product deliverables take and to begin to introduce metrics and gauges as guidelines and comparative measures.

It is also relatively straightforward to collect at least a starter set of very simple work product measures. Many practitioners balk at measuring anything in these early phases because they tend to think measures like the size of a requirements document (crudely measured by, say, a page count) won't have any value.

A key principle underlying the bottom-up measurement engineering model is to start small and keep the primitive measures simple. Yes, we want to get a handle on difficult attributes like the complexity of the design or the comprehensiveness of the requirements. But such measures are not easy to develop and are not what we should begin with. What we can do is make sure we establish what the requirements and design deliverables are and understand who produces them and who uses them. Then we can measure the resources and activities that go into producing each deliverable; some limited product measures (page-count, number of changes, etc.); and a few "satisfaction" measures that help assess perceived "happiness" with the results of the deliverable (like number of defects or a subjective opinion survey at a document review).

This chapter introduces some of these simple measures and

describes how they can and have been used to help improve specifications and produce better designs as well as bring effective visibility and control to the early phases of the software project.

BASIC SPECIFICATION MEASUREMENTS

To compare specification work products we need some basic measures of "size" and "complexity." Deriving effective quantitative measures of underlying software complexity (functions as well as structure and design) has proven to be fairly tough. However, we can easily capture simple measures like the number of lines or pages in a document, and such simple counts often meet our needs nicely. When measured, the volume of documentation can be surprisingly large. On several big projects I have been involved with there has been over a full page (250 words) of documentation produced for every line of source code!

Clearly there is a need to "measure" this work. Fortunately, there are a number of simple measures available to help "size" our specifications and design efforts. Figure 4.1 contains a list of some that various organizations use effectively.

All of these have the virtue of being easy to define, understand, and collect, and most can be gathered automatically from a static analysis or scan of the completed requirement or design deliverable.

Size in words, lines, paragraphs, or pages

Number of requirements or features

Changes or revisions in words, lines, pages, or percent

Number of design objects—inputs, outputs, interfaces, files, calls, or bubbles

Design Lines (DLOC)—if the design is in a PDL-like language

Fan in—number of design objects that call a given object

Fan out—number of design objects called by a given object

Figure 4.1. Some primitive specification size and complexity measures.

What is not clear is how relevant they turn out to be as metrics or meters that give support and insight to the practitioner and manager. Until an organization experiments with the measures and tries them out, it is generally far from intuitive as to which give useful predictive insights and which do not.

As an example, consider the scatterplot shown in Figure 4.2. [Kitchenham and Linkman 90]

This scatterplot between design effort (in hours) and the design specification size (in pages) for a Pascal-like language cross-compiler was used to specify test sequences for burn-in tests of

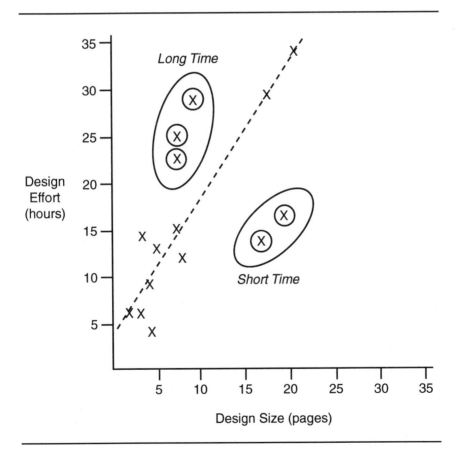

Figure 4.2.   Analyzing design effort vs. size.

semiconductor components. Each point on the plot represents one of the design documents developed in the project. The plot shows a general linear relationship between size and effort, but it also highlights several documents that took relatively longer and shorter times to prepare.

One purpose of such simple measurements is to help the design team better understand and control their process. Documents that took a relatively long time may represent particularly complex parts of the system, may have been carried to greater detail, or may just have been given to an inexperienced team member. Documents that took a relatively short time may represent particularly simple parts of the system, may be similar to already designed components, may be incomplete and need further work, or may just have been performed by a more knowledgeable team member.

Note that the measurement doesn't *answer* which of these (or perhaps other) possibilities is the underlying cause. What it does do is help the project to identify the *unusual* components and support knowledgeable action if appropriate. As has already been stressed, interesting measurement data serves to *raise* new questions, rather than produce simple answers. When organizations start examining data, they will gain more insight and bring up new and more probing questions. The goal is to be able to use the measure as a metric or meter to guide the process and support the design team in producing better or more efficient work products.

Another scatterplot, taken from the same Kitchenham and Linkman article is shown in Figure 4.3. This plot shows fan-out (defined in this case to be the count of the number of calls a program makes plus the count of the external data structures written to) plotted against the number of defects or faults reported against the program.

The relationship is generally linear, but there are four programs (circled in the plot) that have an unusually small number of defects relative to their fan-out value. After analysis by the project team (the data was taken from a real time embedded system controlling an electronic peripheral device), it was determined "that the large fan-out program with the low defect count was a critical program that had been given particularly intensive

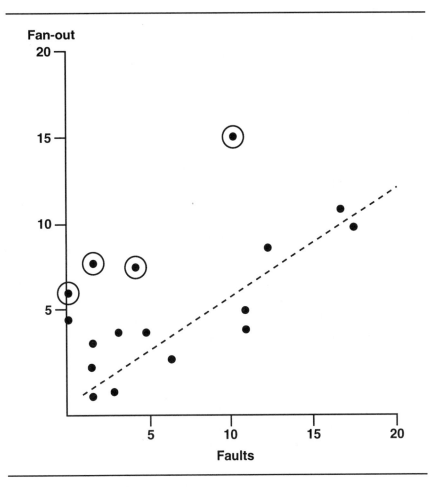

Figure 4.3.   Creating a simple meter.

code and design inspections. It thus had fewer residual defects than other programs during subsequent testing. The other programs were judged to be small and simple in spite of their relatively large fan-out values." The analysis helped the team to appreciate and decide to use the *fan-out measure* as a *potential* indicator of problems. Eventually the designers adopted it as an informal meter triggering additional review whenever a threshold value of 10 was exceeded.

FUNCTION POINTS

The obvious criticism of the simple specification measures (like page count) is that they don't really measure the system functions and features. A measure of the design size and complexity called *function points* has been developed to overcome this problem and deserves special discussion. It is not my intent to teach the reader the fine art of counting function points. However, we do want to explain the measurement and provide enough understanding to allow evaluation and a discussion of the benefits and potential uses. The measure was originated by Allen Albrecht at the Data Processing Services organization of IBM in the late 1970s and is now promoted and standardized by the International Function Point Users Group (IFPUG). For more information and details on the counting procedure, the reader should contact IFPUG (See Appendix B).

The principles behind the function point measurement are straightforward and simple. Function points for an application are counted by itemizing and weighing the "functionality" as seen by the user—namely the inputs, outputs, inquiries, files, and interfaces of a system. Counts of these data components are made using a prescribed set of rules and counting guidelines.[1]

The formulas and rules for counting appear to most practitioners as arbitrary and complicated. Indeed the rules reflect empirically derived, rather arbitrary choices. However, one of the strengths of function points is that one basic procedure is shared

---

[1]Note: In practice there are several variations in use within the industry. The approach described here is the most common one, but the reader needs to be aware that others exist. A variation called Mark II Function Point Analysis enjoys substantial usage in Europe. Readers interested in this variation should obtain Charles Symons' book *Software Sizing and Estimating: Mark II Function Point Analysis* [Symons 1991]. Hallmark Cards helped introduce another variation. They expanded the levels of complexity for each data component (from 3 to 5) and reduced the number of application characteristics (from 14 to 8). Software Productivity Research (SPR) created a version in 1985 that could be directly automated. They use only one level of complexity and apply an adjustment multiplier from .5 to 1.5 based on scoring two questions that characterize the overall application problem complexity and data complexity. SPR also introduced a technique for "backfiring" an *estimated* function point count from source code.

and recognized by a broad community of organizations. The oddities of the counting rules are much less important than the availability of a common approach and the resulting ability to compare data between organizations.

The function point formula is the following:

$$\text{Function Points} = \text{Unadjusted Count} \times (.65 + .01 \times \text{Influence Rating})$$

To use this formula we need to calculate two items: the "unadjusted count" and the "influence rating."

To obtain the unadjusted count there is a fill-in-the-blank counting form to record the various data components in the application. See the sample calculation in Figure 4.4. The function point counter studies the design to identify (count) each of the inputs, outputs, inquiries, files, and interfaces. These are then classified as either *low, average,* or *high* in complexity using guideline tables and rules provided by IFPUG. An excerpt from these guideline tables is shown in Figure 4.5. (*Note:* The tables are not completely reproduced here, but there should be enough for the reader to see how the complexity determination is made.)

As an example, the complexity classification for a customer record master file with two record types (individuals and businesses) and over 50 data elements in each would be "high." The counts of low, average, and high components are entered in the function point counting form and totaled to obtain the overall

Components	Low	Average	High	Total
Logical Internal Files	$1 \times 7 = 7$	$\times 10 =$	$2 \times 15 = 30$	37
External Interface Files	$\times 5 =$	$\times 7 =$	$1 \times 10 = 10$	10
External Inputs	$2 \times 3 = 6$	$3 \times 4 = 12$	$1 \times 6 = 6$	24
External Outputs	$5 \times 4 = 20$	$3 \times 5 = 15$	$\times 7 =$	35
External Inquiries	$6 \times 3 = 18$	$6 \times 4 = 24$	$1 \times 6 = 6$	48
Total Unadjusted Function Count				154

Figure 4.4. Sample unadjusted function point calculation.

External Interface Files and Internally Updated Files

Number of Record Types	Number of Data Element Types		
	1 to 19	20 to 50	Over 50
1	Low	Average	Average
2 to 5	Low	Average	High
Over 5	Average	High	High

Inputs

Number of File Types Referenced	Number of Data Element Types		
	1 to 4	5 to 15	Over 15
0 or 1	Low	Low	Average
2	Low	Average	High
Over 2	Average	High	High

Outputs

Number of File Types Referenced	Number of Data Element Types		
	1 to 4	5 to 15	Over 15
0 or 1	Low	Low	Average
2 to 3	Low	Average	High
Over 3	Average	High	High

Figure 4.5.   Complexity guideline tables.

Unadjusted Count. In the example shown in Figure 4.4 there are three internal files—one with low complexity and two with high that totaled to a count of 37. The total unadjusted count is 154.

To complete the count we need to calculate the "Influence Rating." This is obtained by rating 14 factors on a 0 to 5 scale. The scores denote the degree of influence the factor has on the particular application, with 0 indicating no influence and 5 reflecting a strong influence. Rating guidelines are provided for each factor. For example, the rating guideline for the "transaction rate" factor is the following:

0   No peak transaction period

1   Monthly peak transaction period

2   Weekly peak transaction period

3   Daily peak transaction period

4   High transaction rates required—requires performance analysis

5   Requires performance analysis during development and installation

For an application with a month-end peak transaction rate to consider but no special weekly or daily transaction rates to be concerned with, the rating selected would be a 1. Figure 4.6 shows a sample influence rating calculation with all 14 factors included.

The 5 for transaction rate would signify that consideration for transaction rates and peak loads was at the strongest level. The total influence rating for all 14 factors is 43.

With the unadjusted count and the influence rating we can go back to our formula and calculate the final function point count as follows:

$$
\begin{aligned}
\text{Function Points} &= 154 \times (.65 + .01 \times 43) \\
&= 154 \times (1.08) \\
&= 163
\end{aligned}
$$

Data Communications	4	On-line Update	4
Distributed Functions	3	Complex Processing	2
Performance	5	Reusability	2
Heavily Used System	4	Installation Ease	1
Transaction Rate	5	Operational Ease	4
On-line Data Entry	5	Multiple Sites	0
End-user Efficiency	1	Facilitate Change	3

Total Characteristics Influence   43

Figure 4.6.   Sample characteristics influence rating calculation.

The influence factor in this example increased the unadjusted count by 8 percent to a total of 163.

We have now presented a complete sample function point calculation. You can see for yourself that the counting rules are quite arbitrary. However, one of the reasons why function points have enjoyed success within a small loyal segment of the industry is just that arbitrariness and the standardization efforts of IFPUG. A broad base of industry experience has now been accumulated with thousands of applications having been counted using essentially the same rules and standards. The experience has demonstrated that the function point count correlates fairly well with effort and can serve as a predictive metric for it.

One recent study published in the August 1990 issue of *Systems Development* by Roger Betteridge, David Fisher and Paul Goodman [Betteridge 90] examined data from eight projects—three new development efforts and five major enhancements at Inland Revenue in the United Kingdom. Function points for the projects were counted twice by two different non-DP trained tax officers with no significant differences (suggesting that the count is not unduly influenced by subjective judgments) using the functional requirements documentation as input. Even for the largest project (approximately 1200 effort days for design and coding) the count took only several hours to complete.

The counts were then correlated with actual project effort required for completion. High correlation was reported with a correlation coefficient of .89 for the three new development efforts and .7 for the 5 enhancements. Lines of code (see Chapter 5) were also counted on the new development projects and resulted in a correlation of .94. Since the function point count can take place much earlier (as soon as the design firms up and well before code becomes available), it emerges as a clear winner over lines of code as a metric to help predict project effort.

Several other studies have suggested that the counting rules could be made simpler. For example, the Influence Factor has been shown to add little value—in most instances the Unadjusted Count correlates with effort just as well as the final Adjusted Function Point Count.

In Part III we'll present several case studies showing how function points have been used. Those chapters address measurement for managers and to date most of the success stories with function point counting have been aimed at management needs. Most practitioners remain rather unaware of the measure. The few who do have some experience seem skeptical of its value and potential usefulness. That is a shame and is likely to change over the next decade. There are now several dozen vendors offering tools that facilitate function point counting. (*Warning*: Unfortunately the tools do not all calculate the count the same way, even though they all call it function points!). I anticipate rather broad adoption and extensive industry use over the next few years.

What we know now is that most applications can be counted in a day or less and that the counting procedures are reasonably consistent. We also know that the count can be completed early in the detailed design activity and that it correlates reasonably well with the eventual effort required to build and test the system. On the few occasions when two counts of the same system are far apart, the reason is that the design is being interpreted or understood differently, and that is certainly desirable to get fleshed out early. In fact, one strong argument for continuing to count the application manually is to make sure the designs are understood. Norms and reference guidelines for what to expect from the measure and how it equates with some of our other simple measures are beginning to be shared. For example we are learning that *on average* a software developer implements about five function points a month; that one function point equates to somewhere between 50 to 150 lines of code and requires an average of two pages of documentation and specification. (*Caution:* All of these are average ranges and can vary considerably in individual cases or in special situations, such as a new project with a lot of reuse of existing functionally. All such averages are also very sensitive to project size. Very big projects will have much lower productivity rates and produce much more paper work. Several projects I have measured produced over 5 pages of documentation per function point and one had as many as 10!)

What we don't know much about is when it doesn't work and how sensitive the measure is to specific applications and environments. We also still have a lot to learn about a variation of the counting rules called *Feature Points,* which was introduced in order to apply function point counting to systems software. It was recognized that counts of systems applications such as operating systems and real time software were too low. Feature Points were created by adding a new component of the number of "algorithms" and reducing the weighting applied to the count of the number of logical files. Counting Function Points and Feature Points on classical data processing applications should give about the same result while Feature Point counts will be considerably higher (25 percent or more) for applications with high algorithmic complexity. We need much more experimentation and validation work. Substantial research and pilot program work is under way and we should expect to learn much more about function points over the next few years.

DESIGN COMPLEXITY MEASURES

There are a number of other design "complexity" measures that deserve discussion, including Tom McCabe's extensions of his original cyclomatic complexity ideas to apply to designs and David Card's proposed design complexity metric.

McCabe Design Complexity

In the next chapter we will introduce McCabe's cyclomatic complexity as a measure of structural complexity (paths) in a module and an aid to specifying the tests required to "cover" the coded logic (executing all branches and statements). McCabe has recently extended these ideas to apply to designs and help specify the integration tests needed to cover all the interfaces and calls.

The formulas and procedures for computing McCabe design complexity are rather imposing and put off most practitioners who are at all wary of anything theoretical or mathematical. Fortunately the concepts have been packaged in an automated tool (ACT—Analysis of Complexity Tool) that anyone using the measure in practice will employ. (See Appendix C for further information and a description of this tool.)

The input to the tool is information about which modules and components in the design call each other—or what is sometimes referred to in the literature as a design *call tree*. The output is a complexity number that specifies the minimum number of tests that will ensure coverage of all the call paths and the test cases themselves if desired. The tool can be used to help the designer (by warning when design complexity is getting too high) and the implementer by facilitating in the selection and creation of integration tests. Within the few companies where it enjoys substantial use, it is an excellent example of good bottom-up measurement tightly integrated within the software engineering process. One senior designer who used it didn't even think of what he was doing as measurement; to him, measuring complexity and whether any call paths were not executed at integration was "just part of doing the design job." In fact, he told me rather solemnly that he didn't really believe in measurement! You know you are succeeding when the practitioner doing the work gets so used to the measuring device that he no longer thinks about measuring anymore.

Card Design Complexity

In his book *Measuring Software Design Quality*, David Card [Card 90] also introduces a design complexity measure that he calls C_T. The formula for this measure is the following:

$$C_T = \frac{S_T}{n} + \frac{D_T}{n}$$

S_T is the sum of the *fan out* squared (over each module in the design).

D_T is the sum of the number of module input and output variables divided by *fan out* + 1 (over each module in the design).

n   is the number of modules in the system.

This is an example of a composite calculated measure based on a variety of studies and analyses performed by Card in an effort to develop an overall design metric. An independent validation study performed on data taken from eight projects (some 2000 modules) showed a correlation between C_T and the defect density (errors per thousand lines of code) of .83.

Coupling and Cohesion

Coupling and cohesion were design concepts popularized by Myers and Constantine in the early 1970s. "Coupling" refers to the way different modules connect to each other (ranging from full module independence to extensive use of common variables), and "cohesion" refers to how focused the elements of the module are on a single function (ranging from no cohesiveness to all elements related to one single function).

As part of Card's effort to develop the design complexity metric, he conducted a study evaluating coupling and cohesion as metrics (predictors) for defects and fault rate. A group of several hundred modules for which defect data was available were classified into three groups based on their coupling rating (parameter coupling only, mixed coupling, and extensive common coupling)

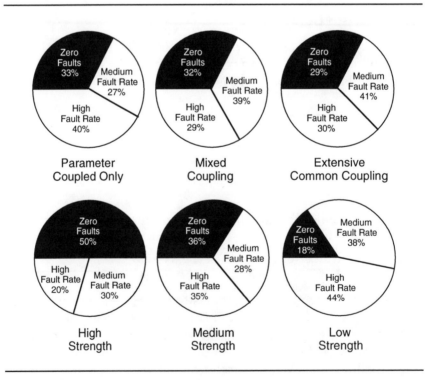

Figure 4.7. Coupling and cohesion vs. fault rate.

and their cohesion strength (only one function, two functions, three or more functions). The defects and fault rates for each of these groupings were then analyzed and are shown in Figure 4.7.

Note there is no relationship shown between coupling and defect rate while the relationship between cohesion (functional strength) and defect rate is significant. The high-strength modules had a much higher percentage of zero faults (50 percent versus 18 percent) and a lower percentage with high faults (20 percent versus 44 percent) than the low-strength modules. This is an example of a somewhat surprising finding that should again trigger more questions in the minds of most readers.

RESULTS AND EFFECTIVENESS MEASURES

Besides the input and output measures we also need measures that help to quantify the effectiveness of our requirements and design work products. Requirements and design specifications are "used" by the project team to build and implement the software. They are also used to help define and describe the product to the end users and customers. Measures of satisfaction in meeting and fulfilling these purposes are necessary—both in terms of the *perceptions* of the internal (development) and external (user) customers and through *quality measures* such as the amount of rework required because of wrong or deficient specifications or the count of defects and problems.

Figure 4.8 lists satisfaction measures in use by companies we

---

Project Team Perceptions—How good are the requirements and design products? Are they meeting expectations and needs?

Customer Perceptions—Are the requirements complete and understandable? Will the system fulfill expectations and provide needed features?

Rework—The effort or time required to correct problems or resolve issues due to defects in the requirements and design products.

Defects—Mistakes or omissions in the work products that must be corrected and fixed listed by major type and category.

Figure 4.8.   Sample satisfaction measures.

have inventoried that I believe can and should be collected on most software projects.

We need to know the amount of rework caused by defective specifications or omitted, forgotten, or changed requirements. This isn't easy to measure precisely, but it can be approximated whenever a baseline document is changed or as part of the work product review or inspection. The review (whether a formal or informal one) offers an excellent opportunity for analyzing the effectiveness of the work product and obtaining basic quality measures like the list of defects and the amount or percent of change and rework required. Such measures can be used as metrics or meters to determine the need for re-review of the work product or other special management actions like a project review or audit.

One example of a meter employed by a number of organizations using inspections is requiring another inspection if the percentage of the work product that has to be changed or corrected exceeds some threshold value of, say, 5 to 10 percent. The number of major defects or the rework impact might also have defined thresholds.

We also need to know how satisfied the practitioners are with the specifications and how our customers feel. Are the early project deliverables understood and felt to be thorough and complete? Does the system contain the features and elements they feel it should or must have? Such perceptions are clearly important to the success of the software effort, and measurements should be

"Good" Product   "Bad" Product   Undecided

Figure 4.9. The smiley face metric.

available to help us answer them objectively if possible. A recommended approach is to employ a simple survey completed by the project members and key external customers at periodic points in the project. The purpose of the survey is to measure gut perceptions and feelings about the quality of the requirements and specifications. This could be collected initially at the requirements and design phase reviews and then again at the end of the project. Simple gauges (even something as simple as a face without a mouth that is "filled in" to show a frown or a smile) will work well (Figure 4.9).

I also like to ask selected questions that can be tabulated and trended over time. Some sample questions that are appropriate are provided in Figure 4.10.

A similar survey approach can be used to sample the perceptions of the end user customers. Completing short surveys like this at the end of various phase reviews or project checkpoints requires only a minute or two of each respondent's time, yet the results over time will help bring visibility to the underlying attitudes and satisfaction trends and in some cases actually reveal major project problems. They are well worth the effort to collect and track.

How would you compare this requirement/design work product?

Real Mess   Below Average   Average

Above Average   One of the Best

Rate the following attributes on a scale of 0 to 5 (0 is awful; 5 is terrific).

Ease of understanding by others

Ease of projected implementation

Your overall confidence

Do you anticipate (or did you have) any major problems with this product?

No   Yes (If yes, please explain.)

Figure 4.10.   Sample Perception Survey.

SUMMARY

As an industry we've done a poor job of measuring software requirements and designs in the past. Most organizations have none of the
three basic IOR measurement areas covered. We don't regularly
track how much effort goes into producing and revising the documents, what the specific work product characteristics (size, complexity, etc.) are, or the quality and satisfaction with the results.

Measurement efforts, even in many of the best projects, fail to
provide the needed visibility for developer and customer perceptions, defect introduction and removal, and the impact of required
changes.

This can and must be changed. We've emphasized very simple
bottom-up measurements that are admittedly crude but that have
been demonstrated to bring visibility to the front-end specification
phases:

I measures (for all specification work performed)

Activities	—Major categories of work (requirements, high-level design, detailed design, rework, review and inspection)
Effort	—Time (days, weeks, or even months of effort) spent in each activity

O measures (for each work product created or modified)

Size	—Pages or counts of lines, paragraphs, and so on
Changes	—Amount and frequency
Complexity	—Dependent on product type—possibly function points, fan out, or the McCabe or Card design measures

R measures (for each work product used)

Rework	—Amount of effort required to fix defects and problems
Defects	—Lists of problems by category and reason
Satisfaction	—Perceptions (developer and user trended over major time checkpoints)

None of these are highly sophisticated. The design complexity measures are the only ones that require tool and training support to implement; the rest just require energy and commitment.

Launching a measurement improvement effort in the requirements and design phases of the life cycle is one of the highest payoff steps available for many organizations. Once the building block systems are reasonably solid, this is clearly the best place to begin. At first analysis it may appear daunting, but persevere and push forward—you'll be rewarded many times over.

CHAPTER 4 EXERCISES AND DISCUSSION POINTS

1. Debate the following proposition: Simplicity is a critical measurement attribute.
2. Why is *Lines of Code* so much more used in practice than *Lines of Documentation*? How do the measures compare in terms of strengths and weaknesses?
3. List at least three problems with using function points as a system size (output) measure.
4. Why are function points preferred to lines of code?
5. Function points for existing systems are sometimes calculated by "backfiring" the count based on lines of code. (See for example, Jones 91) What assumptions are implied by such a technique? What potential problems can you identify?
6. Describe or list some aspects of design complexity that are *not* measured in Card's measure.
7. Why do you think fan-out is more correlated with observed defect density than fan-in? Can you outline a validation experiment that might be conducted to support your hypothesis?
8. Given the experimental results showing the correlation between cohesion and fault rate, why isn't cohesion a highly recommended measure for any software organization?
9. Contrast the advantages and disadvantages of rework vs. defect count as an R measure for specification work products.

5

Measuring Software Code and Implementation

"The number one factor common to companies scoring high in quality was that they were quantitative and had instituted measurement programs."

Dr. Curtis Reimann, Chairman of the Board of Overseers
Malcolm Baldridge National Quality Award

THE IOR MODEL APPLIED TO CODE WORK PRODUCTS

In the previous chapter we examined bottom-up measures for the front-end requirements and design phases. Now we'll look at integrating measurement into the coding and implementation activities.

The work "products" produced during implementation are new or modified modules and system components that are made available to integration and system configuration libraries for further testing and operational use. In some instances documentation work products (including updates to the requirements and design specifications produced in the front-end phases) and special analyses to help in understanding the software implementation may also be supplied.[1]

The framework for what we want to "know" and measure about these work products is provided by the hopefully now familiar IOR inputs, outputs, results) bottom-up model. First, we want information about the effort that went into producing each of the work products. The breakdown of activities should include categories like coding modules, making changes to modules and components, documenting design details, reworking code to fix problems, and so on. We assume that the input measures (effort by major activity) are being collected by a resource tracking system that is tracking effort for all phases, not just implementation.

Most of the time, the key input to be concerned with is "people time." As long as we know where most of it goes, we can put together a fairly good measurement picture of the input side. Coding also depends on the quality of the work products that precede it (requirements and design specifications), so the input measurements for coding include the output and results measures for specifications. An additional resource that we are sometimes concerned with in implementation is computer time and workstation or specialized tool usage.

For the output and results side, we want to know what the work products are, how they change and evolve, and how effective they are. Results and effectiveness measures include defect and rework tracking as well as developer perception—just as with the front-end phases. Inspections and testing play critical roles in providing insight about implementation quality and effectiveness. The measurements applicable to these evaluation activities are covered in the next chapter.

Code with its machine-readable syntax and structure is by its nature the most measurable software work product we have.

---

[1]*NOTE*: All the evaluation and test-related work products, including inspection reports, special analysis reports for evaluation purposes, test plans and specifications, and testing reports, are covered separately in the next chapter. Some readers may find this separation a little confusing. We do recognize that test and evaluation work is an integral and parallel part of any software effort. The reason for the separation is purely pedagogical convenience. We can't cover everything at once, and it was easier to help understand the applicable measurements by separating them and covering them in two chapters.

There are a large number of tools that "read" code in and spew out a sometimes bewildering array of measures. The confusing part is deciphering what it all means and figuring out how to turn the measures into useful metrics and meters. The earliest tools were the language compilers themselves. Although not designed for measurement purposes, most compilers provide a good deal of quantified information about the programs they process:

Compilers As Primitive Measurement Devices

- Object size—Bytes of compiled object code
- Symbols and variables—Symbol table with a listing of internal and external variables
- Cross-references—Cross-reference listing to all labels
- Statement count—Listing with numbered statements

Most compilers have options that can be invoked to produce symbol table and cross-reference listing outputs, as well as a number of other specialized code analysis features. Taken together, the information provides at least a high-level measure for code "size" and "complexity."

Additional information about code should be captured from the Work Product Tracking building block system. (Most companies refer to this system as their source library or configuration management system. See Chapter 3.) This system can be used to measure the following:

Source Library Systems As Measurement Devices

- Code inventory—Number and index listing of all code modules in the library
- Versions—Number of versions (changes) to each module
- Change dates—History of change dates and the date of the latest change
- Module size—Number of statements, lines, characters, or bytes in each module
- Related documents—Listing, size, and changes for related documents that support the code

---

Source library or configuration management systems were initially established to control code changes and maintain the source code and object code versions. They have evolved over time to become quite sophisticated. Most companies require any code module that is developed or changed to pass "through" configuration management as a control point for all code moving from development into formal test or production libraries. This makes it an ideal time to automatically capture and collect measurements of the code. It is usually quite easy to extend the configuration management system to provide baseline tracking measurements on each code work product—for example, the current version, the date last changed, the number of lines or statements in the module, number of lines changed, number of changes, percentage changed, and so forth.

Configuration management is also increasingly being used to control document work products (such as design specifications, test plans and specifications) as well as the code work products. This is an important and encouraging step toward a comprehensive bottom-up measurement process since it allows the capture of basic size measures on all the software work products with one consistent and automated collection procedure.

An effective Work Product Tracking building block is a critical factor in all leading edge measurement engineering programs. As measurement tools (such as those that we'll be discussing here) are introduced, they should be embedded within the building block system so that the measurements are produced automatically whenever a work product is added to the library or changed.

LINES OF CODE SIZE MEASURE

Specialized code measurement tools began appearing more than a decade ago. One of the most basic and widely used is the "line counter." Many organizations have various counters (one for each language or coding environment) built into their configuration management systems. These counters can collect a Lines of Code (LOC) size measurement on all the modules and systems within the source library easily.

Despite rather widespread use and experience, the measurement remains fairly controversial. Most practitioners have tended to resist the use of LOC. One problem is a lack of clear definition and standardization for just *what* the measure is counting. Some counters count only executable lines; others count the data definitions and declaration lines; still others may include comment or even blank lines. Some of the counters also try to distinguish between lines and executable statements so that one statement spread out over several lines for readability or convenience would not add to the count. Still other issues that the counters must resolve are how to handle job control statements and any included or invoked code such as macro statements (should the macro be counted as one line or expanded and counted as the full length of the included code?). The result is that each person's line count algorithm is a little different. Even within organizations, there are sometimes significant variations and many different automatic counters in use.

A second (and rather more legitimate) concern that practitioners voice is over how the LOC measure is going to be used. They worry that management will use it unfairly to gauge performance— by computing lines delivered over a period of time and interpreting the result as a measure of personal productivity. Overcoming this kind of fear is one of the motivations that inspired me to write this book. Yes, it is true that many managers mismeasure and misinterpret the productivity of their staff (and a lot of other things as well). But pragmatically our choices boil down to choosing (1) no measurement (and thus all judgments are made subjectively); (2) some measurement (typically those pushed hardest for by a few of the managers); or (3) systematic engineering measurement (such that all important aspects of the engineering work become visible, and questions that arise can be answered).

Given such a choice, there is no doubt in my mind that the professional practitioner of the '90s will choose number 3. He or she would much rather work for an organization that systematically collects all kinds of relevant measures (of which LOC just happens to be one) and then equally systematically analyze and present this information to help raise questions and make improvements.

The definition problem is also not as important as it might seem, and it is not an argument for not collecting it in your own organization. A general consensus is emerging in the industry: most now define a line of code as "any line of source text that is not a comment or blank line, regardless of the number of statements or fragments of statements on the line." The big advantage of any automatic counting tool is uniformity. We may quibble with the particular counting algorithm, but once we standardize on a tool, we can depend on it to count the same way every time. That provides the *relative* consistency we need for using it as a measure.

So for me there is no controversy. I accept that Lines of Code is simple and has no truly standard industry definition, BUT it (along with many other basic measures we'll be introducing) is also easy and cheap to collect in a uniform way in any given organization. As we shall see this has proven to be helpful as a basic code product-sizing measure. Like the height or weight of a person it doesn't have much utility by itself, but it is a measure we should gather to help in describing and comparing that person to others.

OTHER CODE SIZE AND COMPLEXITY MEASURES

In 1977 Maurice Halstead published a book called *Elements of Software Science*. The book proposed a number of code-based measures that Halstead hypothesized could be used to establish a "scientific measured basis" for program development. While such a lofty goal proved to be unobtainable, the measures have had a significant impact on the field of software measurement and need to be understood by the working practitioner.

The most important Halstead measure is a basic size measure called *Length:*

Halstead Length Measurement

$N = N_1 + N_2$ where N_1 = total occurrences of **operators**

N_2 = total occurrences of **operands**

Operators were defined by Halstead as the symbols or key words within the program that specified or performed action. This includes the various arithmetic operations $(+, -, /, \times)$ and logical operations $(=, >, <, (), \neq)$ as well as most punctuation and command names and verbs (READ, CALL, IF, DO). The *operands* were the data or items operated on, such as the program variables, constants, and labels. To compute Length, one adds up all the occurrences in the program of the operands and operators. Like Lines of Code, Length is a primitive measure of code size and complexity.

Halstead also defined a number of other code measures that are frequently obtained as outputs from commercially available code measurement tools. While not especially important in terms of practical use, a list of the more common ones and their formulas is provided in Figure 5.1 for reference.

Halstead Length, Vocabulary, Volume, and Effort are used in the same way we use Lines of Code. They give us a crude output measure of the size and complexity of the code or module work products. They correlate with Lines of Code and to a large degree are measuring similar output attributes. They have been shown to correlate with effort and defects in several studies and to have weak correlation in others. One such study examined five fairly large products developed in IBM's Santa Teresa Lab. [Conte 1986] This study found strong intercorrelations between all of the size and length measures (Halsteads and LOC), but it also reported that the "best" predictor for the total number of defects and the number of modules with no defects was n_2 or the number of unique operands (variables, constants, and label names). As expected, larger modules have more defects, and all of the size-related measures showed reasonable correlations to the count of

---

VOCABULARY $n = n_1 + n_2$ where n_1 = number of unique operators

n_2 = number of unique operands

PREDICTED LENGTH $N = (n_1 \times \log_2 n_1) + (n_2 \times \log_2 n_2)$

PROGRAM VOLUME $V = N \times \log_2 n$

EFFORT $E = \dfrac{(n_1 \, N_2 \, N \log_2 n)}{2 \, n_2}$

TIME $T = \dfrac{E}{B}$ (B a productivity factor varying between 5 and 20)

PREDICTED BUGS $B = \dfrac{V}{3000}$

Figure 5.1. Some of the other Halstead code measurements.

defects found both after the completion of coding and the completion of formal test.

For the practitioner the significance of the Halstead measures is due to the fact that most common code measurement tools compute and display them. For example, Figure 5.2 shows a sample output from one of the readily available, low-cost PC-

Procedure	n1	n2	N1	N2	N	N^	P/R	V	E	VG1	VG2	LOC	<;>	Sp
pushproc	7	7	19	12	31	39	1.3	118	708	1	1	9	6	1
popproc	10	10	29	18	47	66	1.4	203	1827	2	2	15	9	2
topproc	8	8	20	12	32	48	1.5	128	768	2	2	11	6	1
loadccp	7	7	24	14	38	39	1.0	145	1015	1	1	10	7	2
addccp	13	7	43	27	70	68	1.0	303	7597	3	4	16	11	4
removeccp	13	7	37	22	59	68	1.2	255	5209	3	4	14	9	2
createnod	11	14	37	22	59	91	1.5	274	2368	2	2	14	10	0
addtotree	18	16	83	56	139	139	1.0	707	22271	7	8	26	14	5
inorder	23	26	121	78	199	226	1.1	1117	38536	9	10	38	17	10
gettoken	31	51	364	264	628	443	0.7	3993	320380	44	53	130	73	31

```
                Summary Complexity Report for: SAMPLE.RPT
                -------------------------------------------

                Unique Operators (n1):        17
                Unique Operands (n2):         37
                Total Operators (N1):         67
                Total Operands (N2):          72

                Software Science Length (N):                  139
                Estimated Software Science Length (N^):       262
                Purity Ratio (P/R):                          1.89

                Software Science Volume (V):          800
                Software Science Effort (E):        13231

                Estimated Errors using Software Science (B^):      0
                Estimated Time to Develop, in hours (T^):          0


                Cyclomatic Complexity (VG1):               4
                Extended Cyclomatic Complexity (VG2):      4
                Average Cyclomatic Complexity:             4
                Average Extended Cyclomatic Complexity:    4

                Lines of Code (LOC):                       1
                Number of Comment Lines:                   0
                Number of Blank Lines:                     0
                Number of Executable Semi-colons (<;>):   14
                Number of Procedures/Functions:            1
```

Figure 5.2.   Sample code measurement output report—PC-Metric.

based tools—in this case a tool called *PC-Metric*. The practitioner needs to be able to understand the output from these tools and know how to use and interpret the measurements provided.

The PC-Metric information is presented in a spreadsheet format with each row providing data on one source module. (This type of presentation format was illustrated in Chapter 2 when we first introduced the systematic measurement process.) The first nine columns of PC-Metric output are all Halstead-defined measures.

Two additional examples of source code measurement tools, Logiscope and PATHVU, are displayed in Figures 5.3 and 5.4 .

These tools are typical of the fairly broad range available in the marketplace, and all display Lines of Code and the primitive Halstead measures we've already discussed. Some are specialized to certain language environments (for example, many of the columns in Figure 5.4 are COBOL-specific, such as the number of verbs, fall thru's, and so on). Other than that the tools are fairly similar, and it really doesn't matter which one you select for your organization. They all produce similar numbers and measures. The question is what we should be doing with the information and how we use it to help the practitioner and manager in performing day-to-day software work.

Which specific measures and which source code measurement tool we pick isn't very important. In a bottom-up systematic measurement process our goal is to track the measures over time and develop averages and typical ranges. We want to better understand the "normal" so that unusual values will stand out and can be examined more closely. Not only are we preparing to answer the next unanswered question, but we want to generate questions and help force issues to the table.

Some tools do a better job than others when it comes to obtaining averages or spotting special cases. An example is Logiscope with its ability to specify upper- and lower-range bands for the measures it collects and then graphically present the observed values in the form of a Kiviat diagram. The bounds are shown as inner and outer circles (see Figure 5.3) and can be thought of as guidelines set by the practitioners to trigger additional review. Points outside the outer circle or inside the inner circle deserve special attention.

Axis	Lower	Upper	Mean
NB_STMT	2	31	21.99
P_LENGTH	11	185	139.20
V_SIZE	9	60	38.20
P_SIZE	0.00	5354.00	175.21
INT_CONT	11	48	19.06
NB_ERROR	0.00	0.30	0.47
P_LEVEL	0.03	0.31	0.06
EFFORT	143.00	96400.00	2.15E+05
P_TIME	8.00	5356.00	11995.91
P_NODES	0	1	0.80
VG	1	8	6.63
C_D	0.16	0.30	0.19
NB_LEV	1	4	3.34
NB_DEG	1	5	3.28
COM_RAT	0.18	3.39	0.37
ETA_2	4	35	13.93
N_2	5	79	42.53
ETA_1	4	23	24.27
N_1	6	104	96.66

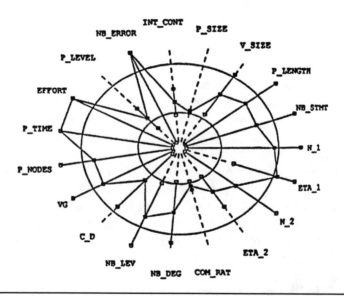

Figure 5.3.   Sample code measurement output report—Logiscope.

	PROGRAM	SYS	SEC SID	ARC SCR	CMP SCR	DPST LVL	LEVEL COEFF	PCT CTL	NUM IF	NUM LPS	LOCC PRGM	LOCC PROC	NUM VRBS	NUM PARA	NUM GOTO	NUM FALL THRU	GOTO THRU	FALL THRU	PERF THRU	PERF PARA	PERF SECT	TERM VERB	DIAG IND
1	APQ00029	XXX	4 TA	264	415	14	3.01	56	516	20	6213	2800	2054	236	207	45	443	84	67	2	0	-	44
2	CPWR0004	XXX	3 PA	124	52	4	0.87	20	102	28	3018	962	694	46	52	20	34	20	0	2	0	-	5
3	CPWR0009	XXX	3 TA	213	203	13	3.79	20	113	13	2874	739	559	75	84	27	105	37	11	2	0	-	0
4	CPWR0033	XXX	3 TA	126	153	8	1.69	45	302	18	4833	1991	1376	87	63	16	148	31	29	19	0	-	0
5	CPWR0058	XXX	3 TA	76	85	7	1.78	34	147	11	3459	1193	875	59	5	8	57	27	19	17	0	-	2
6	CPWR0073	XXX	3 TA	177	106	11	2.34	34	124	19	3268	972	789	105	57	33	78	48	29	3	0	6	2
7	CPWR0117	XXX	1 TA	4	59	6	1.18	23	61	0	1065	911	531	68	0	1	14	34	33	0	2	-	-
8	EAEHE014	XXX	4 PA	528	664	40	7.63	47	291	86	3542	2100	1690	263	286	141	308	141	21	30	2	-	46
9	EHRLAH02	XXX	4 TA	518	548	23	4.65	41	930	92	9541	5474	4095	411	403	175	562	192	49	14	2	1	60
10	EHRLAH14	XXX	4 TA	425	404	23	4.13	43	503	85	5448	2998	2150	229	264	124	333	125	22	13	2	-	21
11	EHRLM945	XXX	4 TA	343	643	58	15.08	50	257	53	5405	1759	1282	200	184	56	244	59	31	12	14	-	8
12	GCTL0008	XXX	3 PA	402	160	14	3.10	41	147	41	1804	991	935	146	90	91	103	91	26	34	0	3	8
13	GCTL0013	XXX	3 PA	281	117	12	2.43	42	40	26	836	301	258	47	41	20	52	20	4	5	0	-	5
14	GEYS0036	XXX	3 TA	189	85	10	2.06	36	64	9	1189	447	344	49	15	16	24	27	14	8	0	-	0
15	GRUM0032	XXX	4 TA	383	296	15	3.27	43	455	101	5056	2781	2153	255	282	83	386	86	33	4	0	58	58
16	GRUM0058	XXX	4 PA	532	695	28	5.95	44	701	110	6611	3956	3175	335	411	136	528	136	18	31	0	-	57
17	GRUM0085	XXX	3 TA	427	66	7	1.32	37	23	2	325	160	190	42	20	27	19	29	9	2	0	1	6
18	GRUM0407	XXX	4 TA	1215	795	44	8.49	43	1449	211	14011	8562	7231	801	1069	358	1134	387	68	42	21	-	59
19	GRUH0416	XXX	4 TA	319	547	32	8.41	45	229	15	2818	1347	1150	147	247	38	267	42	7	5	2	6	17
20	GRUH0605	XXX	4 TA	978	612	20	2.49	60	1227	106	6582	4432	4299	338	867	118	1020	125	20	77	2	-	51
21	GUIGE013	XXX	3 PA	164	144	13	2.84	32	157	31	2374	1345	1111	104	97	20	118	20	10	33	0	-	20
22	GUIGE163	XXX	3 PA	175	176	12	3.31	46	169	28	1499	733	606	66	43	17	56	17	15	29	0	-	19
23	IEOCH079	XXX	4 TA	320	404	21	4.62	46	377	70	3629	2130	1854	228	218	64	397	68	12	12	0	-	80
24	IEOCH099	XXX	4 PA	364	775	92	15.57	36	520	41	19000	8718	7692	456	306	149	332	149	31	210	2	1	8
25	KTPEL063	XXX	3 TA	186	174	15	3.14	45	149	49	1583	854	686	61	74	28	112	31	12	12	2	-	-
26	KTPEL149	XXX	3 TA	220	150	8	1.54	45	205	55	3525	1616	1364	131	111	32	166	46	26	28	0	-	3

SYSTEM XXX   TOTAL PROGRAMS   26: TOTAL STATEMENTS   121,508.

CLIENT ABC   TOTAL PROGRAMS   26: TOTAL STATEMENTS   121,508.

GRAND TOTALS   TOTAL PROGRAMS   26: TOTAL STATEMENTS   121,508.

Figure 5.4. Sample code measurement output report—PATHVU.

STRUCTURAL ANALYSIS AND DECISION COMPLEXITY

The code-based measures we've discussed so far are often criticized by practitioners as not measuring "real" program logical structure. One measure directly dependent on the decision logic within the code that has gained some acceptance is called *McCabe Complexity*. It originates from work Tom McCabe performed in converting programs to flowgraph form and applying concepts from mathematical graph theory to develop a testing technique to exercise all the decisions and branches in the code (Figure 5.5).

McCabe Complexity is also called *Cyclomatic Complexity* (its graph theory name), and is another measure provided by almost all commercial code measurement tools. The measure can usually be calculated by simply adding 1 to the number of decisions or branch points in the program (this won't work for decision

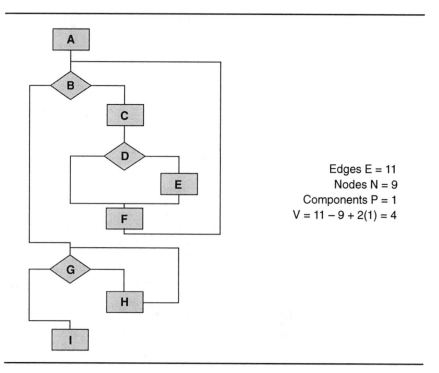

Edges E = 11
Nodes N = 9
Components P = 1
V = 11 − 9 + 2(1) = 4

Figure 5.5.   Sample flowgraph and McCabe Complexity calculation.

points that have more than 2 branches, such as the CASE statement)[2] and it is fine for the practitioner to view the measure as just a *decision count* and not be daunted by its fancy name.

When program code is represented as a flowgraph (see Figure 5.5), McCabe Complexity can be calculated by counting up the number of *edges* (lines in the graph), subtracting the number of *nodes* (the lettered boxes and diamonds), and adding two to the result or even more simply by just counting the regions (bounded areas within the graph), and adding 1.

In Figure 5.5 there are 11 edges and 9 nodes giving a complexity value of 4 (11 − 9 + 2). The same number can be found by adding up the regions (there are three—one to the right of nodes B, C, D, E, and F; one to the left of nodes D and E; and one to the right of nodes G and H) or the decision points (also three—the diamond nodes B, D, and G) and adding 1.

What the McCabe measure *counts* is the amount of structural logic (decisions) in the code. The logical complexity can also be displayed pictorially. Several commercial measurement tools are available that will analyze the code structure and produce graphical representations and models of it. Two examples (Logiscope and ACT) are shown in Figures 5.6 and 5.7.

The two tools use different output representations but perform similar functions and help the practitioner to "see" the underlying logical structure of the code. The McCabe measure and the graphical outputs have been used successfully in a number of companies to control or meter logical complexity. As new modules are produced, they are measured and graphed. Values above selected preset levels (typically 10 to 20) act to trigger review or design simplification so as to bring the complexity down.

An example of one of a number of successful experiences reported in the literature is provided by a medical products division of Hewlett Packard. In an article published in the *Hewlett Packard Journal* by William Ward [Ward 89], cyclomatic complexity is shown to be strongly correlated with defect density, at least for new modules where there was not a lot of reused code.

---

[2]The actual mathematics are a bit heavy and beyond what the casual reader would want or need to tackle. For a more theoretical treatment, consult any of McCabe's papers on the subject.

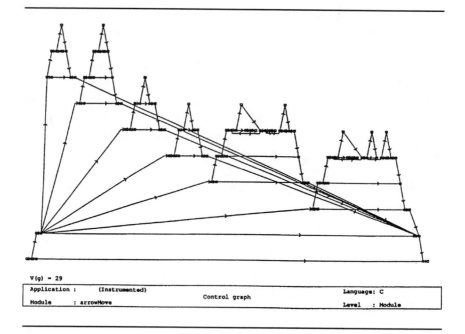

V(g) = 29

Application :	(Instrumented)		Language: C	
		Control graph		
Module	: arrowMove		Level	: Module

Figure 5.6.   Sample code structure graph—Logiscope.

(The Conte study referred to earlier also correlated cyclomatic complexity and found it to be a close second to Halstead's little n_2 as the best predictor for number of defects.) Once this relationship was validated, practitioners readily adopted the measure as a working meter. Ward also comments that "the flowgraphs were a better motivator than mere numbers. An ugly picture of the code had much more impact than a high complexity number." We'll see more examples later where the form of presentation makes a considerable difference. In metrics (as in perhaps all things) form may be as important as substance!

A measure related to McCabe Complexity that the reader should also be aware of is *Essential Complexity*. Essential Complexity is defined as the McCabe Complexity of the flowgraph that remains after all possible attempts to simplify it through simple structural abstraction (i.e., treating a group of nodes with a single entry and exit point as a single node) have been made. This sounds complicated, but what it boils down to is a measure

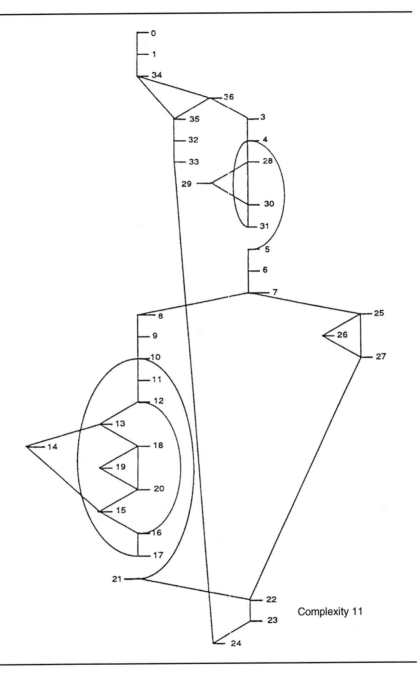

Figure 5.7.   Sample code structure graph—ACT.

of structured programming. Any fully structured program (no GOTOs) will have Essential Complexity equal to 1 (the lowest possible complexity value).

McCabe & Associates market a tool called Battlemap that uses Cyclomatic Complexity and Essential Complexity to classify the existing modules in a source library in terms of those they believe are most likely to require rewriting or maintenance attention. A sample output from Battlemap is shown in Figure 5.8.

The two complexity measures are computed for the modules in the system (see Figure 5.8) and used to flag or identify those likely to be unreliable (lots of decisions and high Cyclomatic Complexity) or unmaintainable (poor structure and high Essential Complexity). Notice that although Battlemap is actually *measuring* just two very simple structural properties (McCabe Complexity and Essential Complexity), it reports its results in terms of very complex multidimensional properties (Reliability and Maintainability). While this might help tool sales, it certainly is not good measurement practice. Potential purchasers should make sure they know what the tool *actually* measures and not be misled by the label or the name applied to the output into thinking something more is going on under the covers!

CHANGE ANALYSIS AND VOLATILITY MEASURES

An important part of code measurement is tracking changes and maintenance effort. Making changes is a significant part of all implementation and system support efforts. In some (perhaps quite a few) environments changes are the primary coding activity with little major new development under way or planned. Systematic measurement can be used to support this activity very effectively.

We've already seen examples of how basic code measures can be used to target programs or modules for improvement. A tool designed specifically for use in a maintenance environment is a product called Inspector. The tool analyzes input programs and calculates a *Maintainability Rating* ranging from 0 to 100 based on a set of measurements very similar to those already presented in this chapter. Maintenance organizations commonly employ the tool to score their maintenance effort and help make sure

Module Index

Module Number	Module Name	v(G)	ev(G)	Chart Location (col,row)
1	main	2	1	1,5
2	optimize_sys	22	14	2,3
3	optimize_terr	47	21	2,6
4	optimize_acct	7	3	2,8
5	shutdown	1	1	2,9
6	load_data	2	1	3,3
7	close_files	3	1	3,9
8	diag_eval	13	3	4,1
9	load_index	5	2	4,2
10	isolate_accts	9	1	4,3
11	regroup	6	4	4,4
12	compact_index	2	1	4,9
13	recomp_hash	17	6	5,2
14	examine_rels	20	3	5,4
15	optimize_rels	18	11	6,4
16	combine_verts	16	3	7,4
17	combine_edges	14	3	7,5

Battlemap Structure Chart

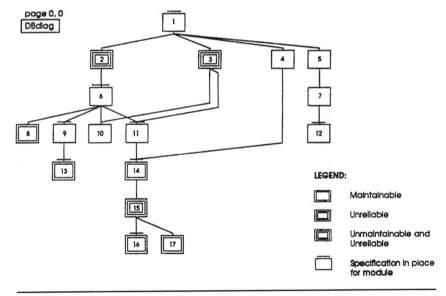

Figure 5.8.   Identifying "maintainable" modules with Battlemap.

that their programs get better (have higher scores) over time. Figure 5.9 displays some data on the use of Inspector at the Ford Maintenance Center.

Figure 5.9 shows the distribution of maintainability rating scores in 1988 and again two years later in 1990. Over that time a substantial number of programs moved up the ladder (the percentage scoring "excellent" went from 2 percent to 25 percent), and the results in terms of staffing and headcount validate the measure's success. As the scores went up, the number of programs being supported per programmer nearly doubled (from 25 to 40), and total headcount decreased from 162 to 123 despite the fact that the total number of programs being supported increased significantly (4006 to 4894).

Another similar maintenance success story on a much smaller and more limited budget environment was reported in the May 1990 issue of *Software Quality World* by Nathan Lowell at the Bath Iron Works. Lowell didn't have the money to go out and buy tools, so he made a simple one on his own—in this case, by just adding a counter to the source library management system (COBOL production environment) that could count decision points and thus calculate Cyclomatic Complexity. The maintenance staff was then challenged to make fixes in such a way that the complexity number

Maintainability		1988		1990	
Rating	Index	Programs	%	Programs	%
Excellent	90–100	70	2%	1,249	25%
Good	70–90	2,425	60%	2,346	48%
Acceptable	60–70	675	17%	586	12%
Difficult	50–60	446	11%	370	8%
Complex	0–50	390	10%	343	7%
Total		4,006	100%	4,894	100%
Headcount		162		123	
Programs/Programmer		25		40	

Figure 5.9.   Maintainability rating with inspector.

always got smaller. They found that fixing programs became easier, and the number of production abends fell as the complexity got lower. The practice was so successful that it migrated from maintenance to new development and led Nathan to observe, "It's been a turning point in my career. It's really helped me to advance."

Certainly there may be other causes and factors involved in the success of these examples, but they do offer strong evidence of the value of using simple code measures to help motivate and assess maintenance work. The principle at work is fundamental. Establish a measurement before and after all code modifications that "scores" the effect of the change. The score is tangible and visible in the organization, and practitioners will be motivated to raise the bar and improve their scores. Scores will rise over time, and if the scoring measure is valid, you achieve real process and product improvement. Many of the code measurement tools facilitate this type of before-and-after measurement. We illustrated PATHVU earlier in the chapter. Figure 5.10 displays the optional before-and-after output that may be obtained from this tool.

Jerome Landsbaum describes Monsanto Chemical's success using PATHVU in a nice little book titled *Measuring and Motivating Maintenance Programmers* [Landsbaum 1992]. As with the Ford and Bath Iron Works success stories, the tool was a significant aid to motivate the maintenance staff. Recall that PATHVU computes a complexity score and an architecture score based on the set of measurements it gathers from the code. Monsanto added a simple measurement that they called a "maintainability score." This was the "distance" from the 0 point on a plot of the complexity and architecture scores (mathematically the square root of the sum of the squares of the complexity and architecture scores that PATHVU provided). Monsanto's senior technical staff felt comfortable that a reduction in this maintainability score signified meaningful improvement. Figure 5.11 shows the results achieved after the first year of using the tool.

As with the other case studies, the perceptions of the maintenance staff were very positive. The overall 8 percent improvement was modest but real. New programs that were added during the year averaged just under 100 on the maintainability scale, and the project teams were able to convince their clients that their efforts to improve were paying off. They could argue persuasively that the

PATHVU USER
METRIC ANALYSIS

BEFORE AND AFTER REVISION

PAGE NO 1
DATE 07/28/87
TIME 10.21.01

PROGRAM COMPLEXITY AND ARCHITECTURE

	PROGRAM	SYS	SEC STD	ARC SCR	CMP SCR	-NESTING- DPST LVL	LEVEL COEFF	PCT CTL	NUM IF	NUM LPS	---LOCC---- PRGM	PROC	NUM VRBS	NUM PARA	-NON-STD- NUM GOTO	FALL THRU	NUM GOTO	FALL THRU	PERF THRU	PERF PARA	PERF SECT	TERM VERB	DIAG IND
1	PDKL0032	XXX	4 TA	383	296	15	3.27	43	455	101	5056	2781	2153	255	282	83	386	86	33	4	0	1	58
		XXX	2 PA	0	331	15	3.46	43	464	94	6608	3669	2380	227	0	0	94	0	0	223	0	1	0
2	VOIDT010	XXX	3 PA	164	144	13	2.84	32	157	33	2374	1345	1111	104	97	20	118	20	10	33	0	1	20
		XXX	1 PA	0	111	8	1.45	36	163	37	2916	1622	1212	110	0	0	37	0	0	106	0	1	0

SYSTEM XXX	ORIGINAL	TOTAL PROGRAMS	2;	TOTAL STATEMENTS	7,430.
SYSTEM XXX	REVISED	TOTAL PROGRAMS	2;	TOTAL STATEMENTS	9,524.
CLIENT ABC	ORIGINAL	TOTAL PROGRAMS	2;	TOTAL STATEMENTS	7,430.
CLIENT ABC	REVISED	TOTAL PROGRAMS	2;	TOTAL STATEMENTS	9,524.
GRAND TOTALS	ORIGINAL	TOTAL PROGRAMS	2;	TOTAL STATEMENTS	7,430.
GRAND TOTALS	REVISED	TOTAL PROGRAMS	2;	TOTAL STATEMENTS	9,524.

Figure 5.10. Measuring code changes with PATHVU.

	Number Programs	Average Scores		
		Complexity	Architecture	Maintainability
Start	3521	104	93	157
1 Year Later	4482	96	92	145
Percent Change	+27%	−8%	0%	−8%

Figure 5.11.   Maintainability improvement at Monsanto.

new programs they were writing were markedly better than the old ones, and the programmers now had direct feedback from the job itself to steadily improve further (a meter was in place!).

RESULTS AND EFFECTIVENESS

In addition to the basic input and output measures described so far, our IOR model tells us we need measures that quantify the "effectiveness" of the coding and implementation work products. How can we really determine that the coding work was done well? It is nice to have scores like maintainability ratings that show improvement, but we also need to make sure those scores are valid and that we really are improving on the things that count (long-term results and perceptions, for example).

Much of the answer is provided by evaluation activities like reviews and testing. If we find a lot of defects in the evaluation activities, we know the coding work was not very effective. If we don't find defects, it may be because the work was defect-free, or it may be because our evaluation effort was ineffective. To find out we have to collect other measures or be patient and wait to see if defects get reported during customer use of the software after its release to production. We described many of the defect measures in Chapter 3 and will expand on them further in the next chapter when we discuss measurement of the test and evaluation activities.

Ultimately we are interested in using measures taken during coding to predict the reliability and defects that are found later in testing or by customers. Many studies have been performed trying to understand these relationships. David Card conducted one typical study examining the relationship between module size and defect rate. [Card 1990] Several hundred modules were grouped into "small," "medium," and "large" size categories based on the number of lines of code in the completed module. The modules were selected so that the mean "complexity" (as measured by Cyclomatic Complexity or the number of decisions in the code) was the same for each of the three size categories. Fault data (number of defects found in formal testing and customer use) was available for each of the modules and was also grouped into three categories—"zero" defects, a "medium" or average number of defects, and a "high" number of defects. The relationship between size and defects was then examined in a contingency table as shown in Figure 5.12.

Note the surprising result that module size, per se, does not affect the fault rate. The small modules tended to be either perfect or rather bad with very few (just 6%) having an average or medium number of defects. The medium-sized modules had approximately equal percentages of zero, medium, and high numbers of defects, while a disproportionate share of the large modules (52%) had a medium number of faults.

What explains this observed data? What questions would you want to ask before you could make a stab at why the data looks the way it does? (Remember that each size group was selected with the same average complexity in terms of the number of program decisions.) The likely explanation lies in how the modules were tested. Small modules may not have been tested at all (in the mistaken belief that they did not need it!), while the larger modules probably underwent more thorough review and testing. Unfortunately we can't be sure because data on test effort and practice was not col-

	Fault Rate		
Size	Zero	Medium	High
Small	58%	6%	36%
Medium	34%	37%	29%
Large	21%	52%	27%

Figure 5.12.   Module size vs. defects.

lected, but notice again how good measurement raises new questions and spurs the desire for more measurement. That is what our bottom-up measurement engineering paradigm tells us to expect. As we learn more, we learn we know less! This results in more intelligent questions and leads to a new round of more focused measures as we travel around the MQG spiral.

To validate relationships like this, we must have meaningful results and effectiveness measures. Measuring the "perceptions" of those who use the coding work products (users, maintainers, testers, etc.) provides one perspective on the results. Objective questions like those provided for requirements and design (see Chapter 4) also work well with code. Questions that ask the practitioner to compare his or her program to others, rate its attributes, and predict operational reliability will give a view of the perceived quality. This qualitative view can then be correlated with objective measured defect data and field experience.[3]

Perceptions also play a useful role in measurement experiments and research. A good example is a study performed by Kitchenham and Linkman to determine if simple code size and complexity measures could "predict" which programs caused the biggest headaches and most problems. Four measures that we have already introduced were collected on several hundred operational programs—fan-in and fan-out (see Chapter 4) plus the number of branches or decisions and the number of noncomment lines. Actual experience with the programs in operation and maintenance was used to "rate" each program. Programs in the upper quartile of number of known faults, number of planned changes, or perceived as complex and difficult to work with by their maintainer were classified as "problem" programs. The top quartile of each of the measures was then examined to determine the percentage of these problem programs within it. Figure 5.13 shows the results.

As we can see, using the top quartile of fan-out, branches, and lines would have predicted about 80 percent of the problem pro-

---

[3]*NOTE:* Measuring perceptions can also be misleading. In his book *Software Metrics: A Rigorous Approach,* Norm Fenton reports on a study that showed that programmers are very bad at subjectively rating the maintainability of programs about to go into production (especially their own!). The study compared the subjective ratings with actual repair time data and showed no correlation.

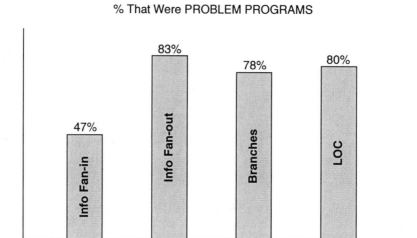

% That Were PROBLEM PROGRAMS

Figure 5.13. Size and complexity measures as problem program predictors.

grams. Remember that fan-in and fan-out may be measured from detail design specifications, while branches and lines require coding to be completed. This gives a little further evidence of the importance of fan-out and why it is a key primitive in Card's design metric.

The study approach used above can be generalized as a technique for constructing preliminary metrics and meters. First, collect a set of measurements for several attributes of interest and obtain a distribution of actual values within a project or organization. Classify values in the top quartile (the upper fourth) as "high," values in the bottom quartile as "low," and any values in between as "normal." Next obtain one or more results or effectiveness measures by surveying the perceptions of the practitioners and customers. Classify the perceptions as high (above average), normal, and low (below average). Now you can produce scatterplots relating the high and low measured attributes to the high and low perceptions. If you find good correlation, you have a metric that the staff will support!

We mentioned Monsanto earlier when describing their use of

the PATHVU tool. Monsanto also collected many other measures and statistics that they trended over time to provide an indication of the amount of activity and work being performed by the maintenance staff. These included the number of compiles per year, compiles per program, batch and online jobs, transactions, abends, emergency repairs, enhancements, and changes. Tracking such activity and relating this to their staffing effort and cost enabled them to demonstrate significant long-term productivity improvement. Their case experience demonstrates how much can be achieved with well-thought-out bottom-up measurement engineering.

SUMMARY

Code is the *most measurable* software work product.

All practitioners employ some measurement of their code (even if they do not realize it) whenever they use a compiler or source library configuration management tool.

Extending the Work Product Tracking building block to provide systematic, automated measurement of the code when it is placed in the configuration library and whenever it is changed is a key and critical step in successful measurement engineering.

The code measures we need to collect are simple, almost primitive. Automated tools collect them for us without effort. The big job is to organize the data and interpret it meaningfully. O measures that should be collected include counts of the number of lines, decisions, inputs and outputs, fan out and simple Halstead measures like operators, operands and length.

Results and effectiveness (the R measures) are the hardest part of code measurement. As with requirements and design, we need to track rework and defects along with the perceptions of developers and users and look for ways to validate the primitive measures and be able to use them as working meters and metrics.

Maintenance changes are particularly measurable because we can measure the code before and after a change and provide direct feedback (metering) to the maintainer. This enhances motivation and has led to significant productivity and quality improvements in a variety of case studies.

CHAPTER 5 EXERCISES AND DISCUSSION POINTS

1. Describe why version control over code and documents is so important in the bottom-up measurement engineering approach.
2. What can (should) the various static measures of code provided by common static analyzer tools be used for?
3. Explain the difference between a call graph and a control graph. How is each typically used?
4. Compare McCabe Complexity and Lines of Code. What are the advantages and disadvantages of each of these measures?
5. Why do simple static measures work better measuring changes vs. new development?
6. Outline an experiment to compare two hypothetical static code measures. Explain any key assumptions. What can and can't be validated in such experiments?

6

Measuring Software
Test and Evaluation

"If you measure speed without also measuring quality, you can end up with a lot of junk in a hurry."

Bill Smith

"The difficulty in managing the testing effort is another result of poor or nonexistent measurement."

Tom DeMarco

INTRODUCTION

The purpose of software test and evaluation is to examine the other software work products (specifications, designs and code, etc.) that we've been learning how to measure in the previous two chapters. The goal is to help assess software effectiveness (by providing information such as defects found, inspection or test results, etc.), and hence the test and evaluation activities are themselves measurement activities! This chapter is about how to measure them. So what we have to deal with is making measurements of measurements. If you've been thinking all this measurement stuff is hard, measuring a measurement activity (meta-measurement) is harder! Fortunately, there is a lot that is very similar to what we've already covered, but there are also some key differences and problems to contend with, too.

Taken together, the evaluation activities consume a significant percentage of total practitioner effort (ranging from 25 to 75 percent and more depending on the application and its criticality) and require special measurement attention. Chapter 1 presented some survey data that indicated the general lack of good software measurement practices. This is especially true for measurements of testing and evaluation. Software Quality Engineering has conducted an annual survey of testing practices and trends for the past six years. Two questions included every year are whether the organization measures testing effort or cost (what is going in) and tracks its effectiveness (what comes out). Figure 6.1 shows the results.

	Percentage of companies reporting common use in system testing practice					
	1987	1988	1989	1990	1991	1992
Testing effort or cost measured	24	21	25	28	31	29
Test efficiency and effectiveness measured	15	18	14	16	15	23

Figure 6.1. Annual survey of test measurement practice.

The survey has consistently shown the rather gloomy result that less than one organization in four claims to be measuring testing efficiency and effectiveness.[1] Even more discouraging is the fact that we have seen little change over the years. There is a small group of companies that track and provide management visibility for their testing effort, but it doesn't seem to be getting any larger.

---

[1]*NOTE:* Industry reality is even worse than these figures suggest. This survey is given at the major annual international testing conference. Attendees at the conference come from companies at least progressive enough to send their employees and who typically have better than average testing practices. It should also be noted that "claiming" to measure testing cost and effectiveness is not the same as actually doing it. In a number of cases I have visited organizations making such claims only to discover that the actual data they had was limited or unusable due to accuracy and collection problems.

Consider the following multiple choice question that we often use as a discussion starter in seminars and management briefings.

Choose One

What we spend on testing each year is:

    a.   just about right.

    b.   too little and needs to be significantly increased.

    c.   too much and needs to be significantly decreased.

    d.   a mystery to me.

Managers, especially senior managers, tend to select "c" (costs are too high and need to come down). Practitioners, essentially those doing the bulk of the testing, tend to select "b" (costs are too low and need to go up). This occurs within the same organization and often sparks lively discussion and debate. The sad truth (confirmed by Figure 6.1) is that neither group really knows what is actually being spent or how effective the results are.

So it is clear there is much to be done. Doing a good job in test and evaluation is a critical element of bottom-up systematic measurement since it provides us with important result and satisfaction measures for how good our other software work products are. To define the measurements required, we once again will use our bottom-up paradigm as the framework. As with specifications and code (and for that matter in order to measure anything at all) we need information on each of the three fundamental IOR (input, output, results) elements. The I measures quantify the activities and the resources that are expended on the input side; the O and R measures provide information about the work products produced and their effectiveness on the output side.

Organizations need to be able to measure the percentage of total effort that goes into test and evaluation and how this is spread between analysis, review, test development, test support and test execution. Without such information we (practitioners and managers) are not able to see what the evaluation effort really costs, and we can't make meaningful conclusions about its effectiveness. We also need measures that describe and quantify each of the test and evaluation work products that are produced and enable us to assess their effectiveness and how good they are. This is nothing more than our basic IOR measurement set. The next three sections of the chapter discuss each in turn.

INPUT MEASURES

To measure test and evaluation effort and activity we first have to have a clear understanding of what the evaluation activities are and the work products that result. Figure 6.2 is a list of high-level activities and the resulting major test and evaluation work products that Software Quality Engineering teaches as a part of its STEP (Systematic Test & Evaluation Process) methodology.[2]

Analysis includes specialized studies performed to evaluate some aspect of a system as well as time spent by individual practitioners in examining their own work or the work of others. There are many forms of specialized analysis (for example, deadlock analysis, ripple analysis, data flow analysis). Some of the specialized forms imply automated tool support; others are purely mental exercises and judgments. The output work product from an analysis effort is an opinion or evaluation of the work item analyzed and is often represented as a formal analysis or study report. When the analysis is performed as part of an inspection, the output work product is typically a list of defects found along with issues and questions to be raised in discussion.

Review activities include any effort associated with formal or informal group peer reviews of selected software work products. The key word that distinguishes a review activity from analysis is *group*. The review includes some planning and preparation to organize and prepare a work package for analysis; group meetings to provide an overview of the work package and to discuss or locate defects in it; time spent by reviewers and inspectors to evaluate and look for defects; and appropriate post-review follow-up time. Work products that result from formal reviews are some sort of inspection report or summary along with a list of the defects and issues uncovered.

Testing activities include any effort expended in planning for, specifying, developing, executing, reporting, or analyzing tests.

---

[2]STEP is a proprietary methodology developed by SQE and presented in its Systematic Software Testing and High Impact Inspection seminars.

Activities	Resulting Work Products
ANALYSIS	
Special Evaluation Studies	Study Reports
Desk Checking and Personal Review	Defects or Issues Found
REVIEW or INSPECTION	
Review Planning and Preparation	Review Plans
Pre-Review Analysis	Defects and Issues Found
Review Meetings and Discussions	Inspection Reports
Post-Review Meeting Follow-Up	
TESTING	
Test Planning and Preparation	Test Plans
Testware Acquisition	Test Specifications and Test
Testware Support	Procedures
Test Execution	Test Environments
	Test Reports

Figure 6.2. Test and evaluation activities and products.

Work products produced include test plans and specifications, test procedures, test execution environments (testware), and test reports to describe what has been tested and any defects or problems discovered.

Note that debugging effort (time spent fixing defects) is not one of the evaluation activities. In the previous two chapters on measuring specifications and code we recommended that there be a *rework* activity. Effort spent on corrective fixes should be tracked as rework on the work product that is corrected and should not be lumped in with test or review effort. Changes required on test and evaluation work products (such as having to rewrite test code or fix a test procedure) are legitimate test effort and should be tracked.

The bottom line is that you have to define your test and evaluation activities carefully and make sure you capture the effort for each activity and output work product that results. Activities as least as detailed as those in Figure 6.2 should be defined, and staff resource effort (usually in days) should be collected for each.[3] The total evaluation effort should include any special analysis for evaluation purposes, all forms of informal and formal reviews and inspections, and all testing (test planning as well as test execution at all levels—unit, component, system, acceptance, etc.).

The reader should also understand that evaluation activities overlap and complement each other in many ways. Test cases can be used in a review or in analysis to walk through a work product or simulate its execution. Analysis is used to prepare for a review or inspection and is also employed during group discussion, test planning, and test evaluation. Reviews can be performed on any analysis or testing work product and can even be a review of a review! What is clear is that all three activities are a core part of modern evaluation practice and must be carefully blended together in a balanced, complementary fashion for optimal effectiveness.

Besides measuring the time spent on evaluation, we also need to assess and track any other inputs or work products used in the process, including the item that is being evaluated or tested. If the item we are evaluating is complete and understandable, we should expect all or nearly all of the defects in it to be uncovered during evaluation. On the other hand, we cannot expect evaluation of an incomprehensible design or undocumented code to be very effective. This is a property observed in all engineering work: the quality of an output work product depends directly on the quality of any supporting work products that are put into it. From the measurement engineering point of view this means we must measure the effectiveness of input work products and gauge the likely effectiveness of output work products accordingly.

SQE's High Impact™ inspection methodology is an example applied in practice. The "input" to the inspection is a "work package" that includes the item to be inspected (such as a piece of code or a specification) along with supporting materials and documen-

---

[3]In most cases it is also desirable to further break down the effort by testing level (unit, integration, system, acceptance, etc.). I also like to separate the effort spent on the test environment and test tooling from any effort on test development and execution.

tation that will help the inspector to understand the work item and the approach the author used to create it. Inspectors are "briefed" on the overall package and asked to "examine" it with several hours of individual analysis aimed at unearthing any major defects. An "analysis log" is completed to record the effort spent and any defects found or issues to be raised. This same log is also used to record the inspector's overall assessment of "comprehensibility" of the work package that was examined. Each inspector grades the work package from "very easy" to "very difficult" in terms of how hard they found it to comprehend. This is scored from 1 to 5 and allows for a measure of average comprehensibility of the inspected package to be computed and collected. Figure 6.3 is a sample extract from the section of the analysis log where the comprehensibility measurement is recorded.

At the completion of the inspection each inspector must verify that "some," "most," or "nearly all" of the major detectable defects in the work product have been identified and addressed. "Nearly all" is applicable to comprehensible packages that are well understood by the inspectors (average score of 4 or above), while "some" applies for very difficult packages (average scores below

---

PACKAGE COMPREHENSIBILITY

☐ Very Easy　☐ Easy　☐ Moderate　☐ Difficult　☐ Very Difficult

If Moderate or harder, identify up to 2 major causes:

☐ Inadequate background knowledge

☐ Inadequate information in package

☐ Poor work product description

☐ Poor work product design

☐ Poor work product organization

☐ Significant work product compexity

Figure 6.3.　High Impact™ inspection comprehensibility measurement.

2). In this way the predicted or expected inspection effectiveness is directly tied to measured input comprehensibility.

OUTPUT MEASURES

The output measures quantify the work products produced during testing and evaluation activities. The objective is to make the output visible. The most direct measure is probably just a count of the number of tests. Figure 6.4 is an example of a typical test status report showing the counts of tests grouped by major category. The first three categories show the number of tests defined but not yet executed as well as the number of tests "passing" or "failing" (whether the test met its exit criteria the last time it was executed). Two additional categories show any tests "holding" (awaiting some decision as to status or classification) or tests that are "invalid" (awaiting a fix or correction).

Tools that execute or play back tests should have built-in measurements to log test execution and present the test results in a format similar to Figure 6.4 whenever possible. Other measurement data such as the date and time of each test run, run time (elapsed and CPU), and any aborts or abends are also typically recorded and logged during test execution.

Category	Counts
NOT TESTED	264
PASSING	1464
FAILING	191
CRITICAL	6
MAJOR	9
MINOR	176
HOLDING	37
INVALID	7
TOTAL	1963

Figure 6.4.   Sample daily test status report.

The count information should be plotted over time to show trends. Several examples of such plots are shown in Figure 6.5.

The top plot displays the number of tests specified, implemented (coded and ready to execute), and executed over time versus the total number planned. This can be converted to a percentage of tests so that various system components or subsystems can be plotted together (as shown in the bottom plot).

The third example plot in Figure 6.5 shows test execution results by "build number" or version of the software under test. In a number of organizations a new build will be created every day or two during the latter phases of development and testing. The vertical axis indicates the number of tests executed and executed successfully (shown darkly shaded) on that build. As the release nears completion more and more tests can be executed and a larger percentage execute successfully. To be practical, such plots require automated test recording and logging.

Test counts are not very meaningful when some of the tests are complex and others are trivial. General guidelines for how "big" a single test case should be will evolve over time and tend to vary by organization and application. Some organizations also separate the counting of test objectives (functions and features to be covered) from the count of tests (executable test programs or cases). Others find it useful to relate or normalize the count to the size of the system being tested. An example from one organization where this is done is shown in Figure 6.6.

Each point in the plot represents a separate project and the fitted line in this case shows a linear relationship between the number of tests and the system size in lines of code. (*Note:* Organizations that do track the number of tests versus the size of the system under test usually discover a fairly linear relationship. The author, however, is aware of several rather extreme exceptions. You'll have to track it for yourself and find out what your own organization's experience is.) Keeping such a plot helps in estimating how many tests may be required on a new system and to size or scope the test effort.

Besides counts, there are a number of other O (output) measures that have direct analogues to those we've already introduced and discussed for specification and code. Test plans, test specifications, and test or analysis reports are all "documents," and the simple measures of document size—like the number of lines or pages that we found useful for specifications apply here as well. Similarly, the code size and complexity measures (such as lines or decision counts)—may be applied to test procedures and test support code (testware) just as they were to software. All that is required is a simple line counter to count the document pages or lines and the lines of test code and test data by work

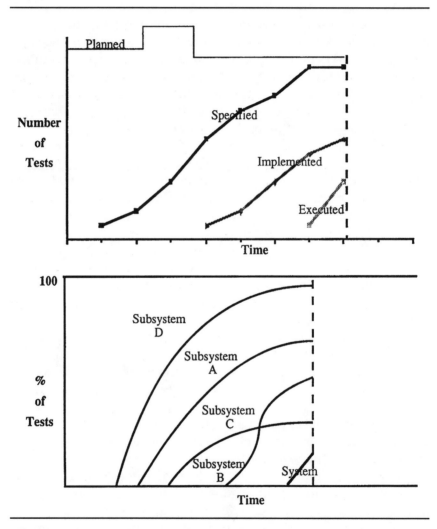

Figure 6.5. Examples of test status plots.

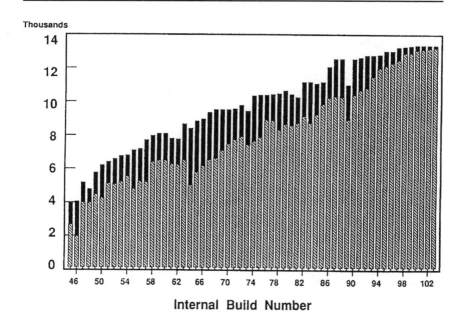

Figure 6.5.   *Continued*

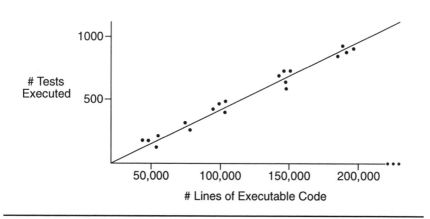

Figure 6.6.   Tests vs. system size.

product. With a little effort this counter can also pick up the lines changed or modified in a particular change. Such measures allow describing the "size" of a test set as so many KLOC (thousands of lines of code), thousands of bytes, and so on.

As with specifications and code, the best time to collect the output measures is whenever the testing work product is finished or modified. The same Work Product Tracking building block system used for code and the software documents should be used for tracking the test code and the test documents. If formal reviews of any of the testing work products (test plans, test designs, etc.) are performed, there will be additional measures collected as a part of the review process. For example, Figure 6.7 shows a test plan review rating form used in one organization.

The form allows each reviewer to grade 10 topics on a 1 to 5 rating scale. It is given to each person attending the test plan review and provides a quantified overall score that reflects the perceptions of the individual reviewers as to effective coverage of the listed topics. Many other organizations that inspect the test specifications or test code also produce inspection summary reports. Typically the summary report records when the inspection was held and who participated, lists the number of defects found in the inspection (often broken down by category), and records the effort spent by activity (preparing for the inspection, holding the review meeting, and reworking to correct or resolve any problems found). Such reports serve as a signal that a work product has been completed (in many organizations the review or inspection is a required gating step that must be conducted before the work can be considered complete) and provide a measure of the quality of the work performed. If used regularly they also offer a good place to summarize the I and O measures that are collected.

RESULTS AND EFFECTIVENESS MEASURES

To complete the IOR model we must obtain the R measures. The count of the number of defects found during testing is a poor gauge for test and evaluation work comprehensiveness and effectiveness. Finding few or no defects could mean that the software is terrific, but it could also mean that the evaluation effort was poorly done. When most students in a class ace an exam, it may

Topic	Coverage	Comments
1. Test Objectives/Summary		
• Reliability	0 1 2 3 4 5	
• Performance	0 1 2 3 4 5	
• Availability	0 1 2 3 4 5	
• Usability	0 1 2 3 4 5	
• Error Recovery	0 1 2 3 4 5	
2. Testable Items List/Matrix	0 1 2 3 4 5	
3. Test Schedule	0 1 2 3 4 5	
4. Resource Requirements	0 1 2 3 4 5	
5. Test Descriptions	0 1 2 3 4 5	
6. Retesting Approach	0 1 2 3 4 5	
7. Error tracking/ Reporting forms	0 1 2 3 4 5	
8. Causal Analysis/ Corrective Action plan	0 1 2 3 4 5	
9. Test Emphasis/ Test Coverage	0 1 2 3 4 5	
10. Test Limitations	0 1 2 3 4 5	

Overall Rating (1–5): ☐

General comments (use back if required): _____

Rating Legend: 0—Not Applicable
1—Needs work
2
3—Average
4
5—Excellent

Figure 6.7.   Sample test plan review rating form.

mean the teacher has done a great job and they all know the subject material; it may also mean the exam wasn't well prepared or was too easy. What we need in addition to defects found are true measures of test and evaluation effectiveness—like the defects not found—that help us evaluate how we've done.

As noted in the chapter introduction, industry does a poor job of measuring test and evaluation effectiveness. We are just beginning to learn how to do this better. Figure 6.8 lists five categories of measures in use that have proven to be beneficial in helping assess the "goodness" and "completeness" of test and evaluation work products. Each of these are further described and illustrated in subsequent sections.

Evaluation Detection Efficiency—Percentage of defects found that were present at the time the evaluation activity was performed. Highlights the defects that are missed.

Test Coverage—Percentage of items (requirements, features, test objective inventories, programs, branches) covered in test. Highlights the thoroughness of test coverage.

Product Reliability—Measured failure rate during the test period and after release. Highlights failures as opposed to defects.

Product and Evaluation Perceptions—Direct measures of perceived effectiveness and satisfaction from practitioners and customers.

Test Analysis—Analysis and study of the tests to measure effectiveness. Includes sampling, seeding, and mutation analysis.

Figure 6.8.   Test and evaluation R measures.

Defects Missed and Detection Efficiency

To measure testing we must not only measure what we detect but also what we don't. One measure that has been successfully used is called Detection Efficiency. It is computed with the following formula:

$$\text{Detection Efficiency} = \frac{\text{Defects Detected} \times 100\%}{\text{Defects Available to Detect}}$$

The measure is expressed as a percentage and measures the percent of the defects present that were discovered during a given test or evaluation activity. Figure 6.9 shows a sample calculation.

The data provided in the table shows defects reported throughout the development of a hypothetical project. With this data Detection Efficiencies can be calculated for each of the inspection or test activities. In the example shown, code inspections detected a total of 98 defects (66 of these were in the code and 32 in the design). They did not detect the 101 other defects that were discovered subsequently in unit testing, system testing, and a representative period of production (6 months in this example). That computes to a Detection Efficiency of 49%. (Note: To test your understanding of the measure, try calculating Detection Efficiency for system testing. You should get 70%.)

The biggest problem in using Detection Efficiency is that we can't fully calculate it until after we've found all the defects that are left, and we can never know if or when that point is reached. This is the same problem we have with defect density. Even after six months or more of operation we can't be sure we've found *all* the defects. (Recently I learned about a critical defect that stayed hidden for 19 years in a system in use at over 700 user sites!) The

Step	High Level Design	Low Level Design	Code	Total
Design walkthrough	40			40
Design Inspections	9	82		91
Code Inspections	1	31	66	98
Unit Tests	0	20	48	68
System Tests	5	7	11	23
6 Mos Operation	2	5	3	10
	57	145	128	330

$$\frac{\text{DRE}}{\text{(Code Inspections)}} = \frac{98}{98 + 68 + 23 + 10} = \frac{98}{199} \times 100\% = 49\%$$

Figure 6.9.   Defect Detection Efficiency calculation.

only way around the problem is to try to estimate the additional defects likely to be discovered based on similar project histories.

Another problem is the need to track when a defect is introduced and becomes available to detect. To obtain a more accurate Detection Efficiency, you must measure defect age (see Chapter 3) and subtract any defects that are introduced after the evaluation activity took place. (*Note:* In the simple code inspection Detection Efficiency example, we ignored this and assumed that all the defects found in subsequent testing and operation were present at the time of the inspection. Since this is not likely to be true, the Detection Efficiency we calculated is somewhat understated. However, we also assumed that there were no more defects to be found after the 6 months of operation, and if that is not true, the calculated percentage is overstated. Perhaps if we are lucky these two inaccuracies cancel each other out!)

A results measure like Detection Efficiency is very important, but I should also warn you that it is quite conducive to misinterpretation. The first tendency is to assume that some particular evaluation activity is *better* than another because it found more defects or had a higher Detection Efficiency. It has been reported in several studies that the Detection Efficiency of good inspections is as high as 90 percent, while the detection efficiency of good unit testing seldom exceeds 70 percent. *Even if accurately measured and validated, such a result does not mean that inspections are "better" than unit testing as an evaluation technique!*

You must remember that the defects found and missed in each case are different and that unit testing comes *after* inspections.[4] Perhaps if we reversed the order and put unit testing first the detection efficiencies would turn out very differently. I call this the Easter Egg Fallacy after a rather painful experience with an Easter egg hunt I was put in charge of at my church. Our hunt was organized in three age divisions—Toddlers, Little Kiddies, and Big Kiddies. We hid 200 eggs early in the morning, and each age group got to hunt for them in the same field in turn. The Toddlers and Little Kiddies each had a great time and hauled in lots and

---

[4]Despite these rather obvious points, I must note rather sadly that almost all the published studies comparing testing and evaluation methods rely on the number of defects found as the only criteria for assessing or comparing effectiveness.

lots of eggs. The problem came on the third hunt. By this time very few eggs were left in the field and those still around were well hidden and difficult to spot. When the final hunt was over, only two of the Big Kiddies had found any eggs, and a large group of parents (and in this case grandparents and other visiting Easter relatives as well) were glowering at me for messing up the big day. The Big Kiddies' combined Detection Efficiency ended up at a paltry 40 percent (finding just 2 of 5 remaining eggs). Even the Toddlers' percentage exceeded 50 percent. They found more than half of the original 200 eggs we hid, but I am sure no one would want to claim it was because they were "better" hunters!

Defect Analysis

In Chapter 3 we emphasized the importance of analyzing defects to determine why they occurred and how to prevent them or detect them earlier. One organization I have worked with analyzes defects missed in testing and decides what phase they should have been detected in. They use that information to compute a Detection Efficiency for those found that should have been found as well as the overall Detection Efficiency percentage for the phase.

Figure 6.10 displays an example of the form used by that organization to gather the data needed for the calculation. This form is filled out for any defects not found in system testing that are subsequently discovered and reported in acceptance testing and operation. The tester analyzes the problem that was reported and classifies it into one of several categories (blocks 1 and 2). A judgment is then made as to where the tester believes the problem should have been first found and why it was not found by the system test group (blocks 3 and 4).

The forms are collected and reviewed once a month in a *joint* meeting between testing and development. A consensus is reached in the meeting, and if needed, the initial tester response is modified. Once every quarter overall results and trends are analyzed and the "true" Detection Efficiency for system test is presented and reviewed.

Other variations on the basic Detection Efficiency measure may also be desirable. One possibility is to classify subsequently discovered defects by type and impact and then compute the de-

PROBLEM CLASSIFICATION

1	

(a) NEW PROBLEM   (b) DEFERRED   (c) NO PROBLEM FOUND

(d) DUPLICATE   (e) PROPAGATION   (f) ENHANCEMENT

(g) DEV. MAINTENANCE   (h) INSUFFICIENT INFO   (i) NONTESTED AREA

(j) OTHER

Continue only if you answered "a" to question 1.

PROBLEM CATEGORY

2	

(a) SOFTWARE   (b) DOCUMENTATION   (c) JCL

(d) DATABASE   (e) SUPPORT SOFTWARE   (f) OTHER

PROBLEM SHOULD HAVE BEEN FOUND FIRST BY

3	

(a) REQUIREMENTS   (b) UNIT TEST   (c) INTEGRATION TEST

(d) SYSTEM TEST   (e) OTC TEST   (f) PRODUCTION

PROBLEM WASN'T FOUND BY SYSTEM TEST BECAUSE

4	

(a) NEED FOR TEST CASE NOT RECOGNIZED   (e) DEPENDENT ON LOCAL/USAGE DATA

(f) SECURITY/NETWORK DEPENDENT

(b) INADEQUATE TEST CASE   (g) DEPENDENT ON VOLUME

(c) MISSED DURING ANALYSIS   (h) OTHER

(d) RECOGNIZED BUT DEEMED A NONESSENTIAL TEST CASE

FORMAL TEST CASE PLANNED: (Y or N)

5	

Figure 6.10. Analyzing when a defect "should" have been found.

tection percentages for each type or category. This gives visibility as to detection results by problem severity and may show which types and kinds of problems are found by different evaluation or testing activities.

Test Coverage

A second category of result-oriented measurements helps to quantify the degree of testing thoroughness or "coverage" actually achieved. For coverage to have meaning we must first have an agreed-upon list of test objectives (for example, a detailed list of product functions and features) and then analyze the percentage of this list that have been covered by at least one test case or test procedure. Objectives of interest include both functional or requirements-based coverage as well as structural design and code-based coverage.

Coverage measurements identify specific objectives not tested and indicate the percentage of objectives actually covered and executed in a given testing phase or activity. Figure 6.11 displays some plots tracking the functional and structural objectives and coverage over time.

The top plots show the number of features (requirements and

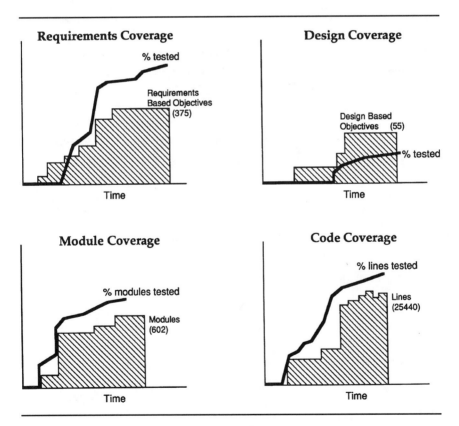

Figure 6.11.   Sample test coverage plots.

design based) and the percentage of those features executed in test. The bottom plots show the number of modules and statements integrated in the test library and their coverage percentage achieved. The list of features is assumed to be an output from the software specification activity, and the count should be one of the O measures we get out of the specification phase. If it isn't, a separate list can be compiled by the tester during the test design and specification activities. The count of the number of modules and statements is assumed to be provided by the Work Product Tracking system and is updated whenever software is delivered into the build. Both counts (functional and structural) will increase (or decrease) over time as the project configuration changes.

A "test coverage matrix" (see Figure 6.12) is normally used to record the relationship between test cases and features. Requirements and design-based coverage can be directly measured from the information maintained in the matrix. The matrix lists test objectives (in this case features of a hypothetical airline reservation system) and denotes with check marks any test cases that cover them. It is completed by the tester as the tests are designed and can be verified in a review or as the test cases are executed.

For this example, five of the six main features and one of the two subfeatures are "covered" or exercised by at least one test

Test Objectives or Functional Features	Test Case or Procedure Number			
	1	2	3	4 ...
1. Enter city and date request	✓	✓	✓	✓
2. Display flight alternatives	✓	✓		
2.1 All airlines	✓			
2.2 Selected airlines				
3. Display seats available			✓	
4. Display reservation				
5. Enter new reservation		✓		✓
6. Cancel reservation			✓	
...				

Figure 6.12. Sample test coverage matrix.

case. (Features 4 and 2.2 are not yet checked off against any of the test cases.) The measured functional coverage percentage is 83 percent of the high-level features; 71 percent of all features; and 50 percent of feature 2.

Maintaining and updating the coverage matrix is generally impractical without effective tooling and automation support. A relational database is needed to track the many-to-many relationship between tests and features and an easy to use outliner is important to list features and objectives and make it easy to update and change them over time.

Besides requirements and design feature coverage we are also interested in measurements of the number of modules, paragraphs, code segments, calls, decisions, statements, and so forth that have been tested and not tested. In the literature this is referred to as "structural coverage," as opposed to "functional or feature coverage." A variety of tools are available to provide such measurements. Typically these tools take a source program as input and "instrument" it so that it can track and record what parts are executed during a test. Most of the tools allow for a cumulative analysis to be made over a number of different test runs and to identify any parts of the program not tested. The measurements are used as a meter to determine that the tests that have been run are minimally sufficient and to identify and suggest further cases so as to cover omitted parts of the program. Functional tests created from the test coverage matrix can be executed and measured to determine the extent of structural coverage. At unit testing, statement and decision coverage tends to be most appropriate, while at higher levels of testing (integration, system, and acceptance), we are more concerned with module, paragraph, and call coverage.

Structural Coverage Analyzer Tools

As an illustration of how the structural analyzer tools work this section contains sample outputs from two of the common analyzer tools now available. The first example in Figure 6.13 is output from a tool called TCAT™ from Software Research, Inc. The tool provides an annotated source listing that identifies each segment (defined as a part of a program which has the property that if any

```
                char menu[13][79] = {
                  "SOFTWARE RESEARCH'S RESTAURANT GUIDE \n",
                  "      What type of food would you like?\n",
                  "\n",
                  "      1        American 50s    \n",
                  "      2        Chinese     - Hunan Style \n",
                  "      3        Chinese     - Seafood Oriented \n",
                  "      4        Chinese     - Conventional Style \n",
                  "      5        Danish             \n",
                  "      6        French             \n",
                  "      7        Italian            \n",
                  "     .8        Japanese           \n",
                  "\n\n"
                };
                int char_index;
                main(argc,argv)
                int  argc;
                char  *argv[];
                {
                  int  i, choice, c;
                  char str[79], answer;
                  int ask, repeat;

C1 = 74.07      /** Module main **/
                  int proc_input();
2               /** Segment 1 <> **/
                  c = 3;
                  repeat = 1;
                  while(repeat) {
5               /** Segment 2 <start while> **/
                    printf("\n\n\n");
                    for(i = 0; i < 13; i++)
65              /** Segment 3 <start for> **/
                      printf("%s", menu[i]);
5               /** Segment 4 <end for> **/
                    gets(str);
                    printf("\n");
                    while(choice = proc_input(str)) {
5               /** Segment 5 <start while> **/
                      switch(choice) {
                      case 1:
1               /** Segment 6 <case alt> **/
                        printf("\tFog City Diner              1300 Battery   982-2000 \n");
                        break;
                      case 2:
*****           /** Segment 7 <case alt> **/
                        printf("\tHunan Village Restaurant  839 Kearney    956-7868 \n");
                        break;
                      case 3:
```

Figure 6.13. Structural test coverage—TCAT.

part of it is executed, then all parts of it are excuted). It also displays the number of times that segment was executed in the left-hand margin. The last segment (segment 7) contains asterisks in the margin indicating that it was not executed at all. The tester can then analyze the code and determine if additional tests are needed and what would be required to execute this segment.

TCAT™ also provides a "cumulative coverage" report as well as a "not hit" report (see Figure 6.14). The coverage report high-

Cumulative Coverage Report

```
Options read:   1
TCAT: Coverage Analyzer.  [Release 7]
(c) Copyright 1990 by Software Research, Inc.  ALL RIGHTS RESERVED.
```

Module Name:	Number Of Segments:	Current Test			Cumulative Summary		
		No. Of Invokes	No. Of Segments Hit	C1% Cover	No. Of Invokes	No. Of Segments Hit	C1% Cover
main	27	1	19	70.37	1	19	70.37
proc_input	24	8	15	62.50	8	15	62.50
chk_char	3	8	2	66.67	8	2	66.67
Totals	54	17	36	66.67	17	36	66.67

```
Current test message(s) (saved in archive):
Runtime vers 4.9, last updated 12/4/89
```

Not Hit Report

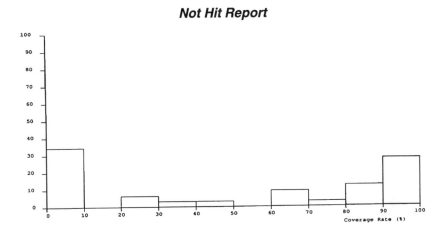

Figure 6.14.   TCAT "coverage" and "not hit" reports.

lights the number and percentage of code segments hit in the most recent or current test as well as cumulatively overall testing since being reinitialized. In the example only one test was run, so the current and cumulative results are the same. The report tells us that the modules exercised contained a total of 54 segments of which 36, or 67 percent, have been invoked or executed at least once. The "not hit" report lists all the segment numbers that have not been executed. This is used to refer back to the annotated source listing and quickly reference each part of the code that still remains to be tested.

Software Research also markets a companion tool with similar outputs that provides an integration or system test-oriented coverage measure of the possible "call-pairs" that a test or a group of tests exercises. It can be used to measure test coverage during integration and high-level system or acceptance testing and determine if all interfaces and intermodule calls have been exercised.

A second example of a coverage analyzer tool is LOGISCOPE from Verilog. LOGISCOPE is both a static and dynamic analysis tool. Statically the tool will analyze a source program and graphically depict its call structure and global architecture as well as the control graph and logical structure for each of its modules. Along with the graphs the tool calculates and displays many of the measurements we have been discussing in this book. For the call graph the number of call paths in the call graph as well as its structural complexity and testability are shown. For the control graphs the number of basis paths (McCabe Complexity), arcs, nodes and control density is provided. These measurements help to estimate the unit and integration test effort and the minimum number of test cases that will be required. Additional information provided by the tool highlights the unit and integration test conditions and paths and provides assistance in defining and specifying the tests required.

Logiscope also tracks the parts of the call and control graphs that are executed during testing and displays the coverage graphically. Figure 6.15 is an example. The leftmost plot in Figure 6.15 shows a call graph of an overall design and how the modules within it are interrelated. The plot to the right shows a control graph for one of the modules within the design. In both plots paths that have been tested are represented by a solid line while those that have not been tested are indicated with dashed lines. Looking at the plots we can see that eight call paths have not been invoked and four logical paths within the one module remain untested.

Logiscope also provides a dynamic analysis report that shows the number of times each decision point in the module is executed by each test case. This can be used to identify branch points or paths not hit and to evaluate test case independence

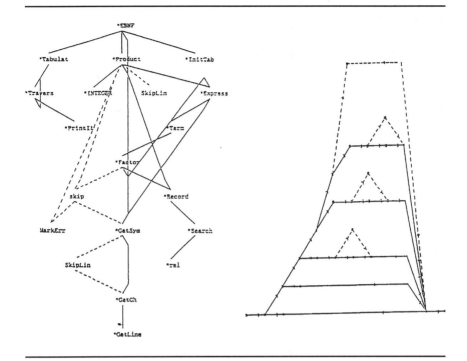

Figure 6.15.   Logiscope test coverage.

and redundancy. The tool will also display a histogram of the module coverage for all modules being tested and help provide an overall evaluation of the thoroughness of structural test coverage. (Samples of these supplementary outputs are provided in Figure 6.16.) These two examples are typical of the better and more powerful tools that are now available to support testing and structural coverage measurement. They have been selected only for pedagogical reasons. The reader should know that there are many equally good competitive offerings available and certainly not try to make a selection based on the limited information sketched here.

Reliability

Software Reliability Engineering (SRE) is a new testing-related discipline that has emerged to predict, measure, and manage the reliability of software-based systems. Reliability is defined as the

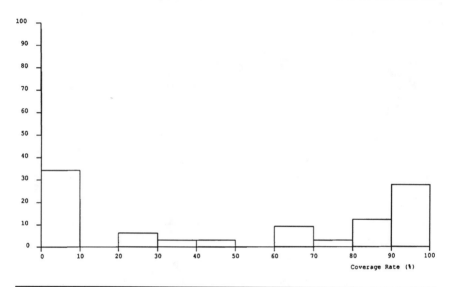

DDP Tests	1	2	3	4	5	6
TEST1	641	0	641	0	641	1
TEST2	376	0	376	0	376	1
TEST3	91	0	91	0	91	2
Total	1108	0	1108	0	1108	4

16	17	Rate of Coverage
1	640	76%
2	372	82%
1	89	76%
4	1101	82%

Figure 6.16.   Example of Logiscope's dynamic analysis report.

probability of failure-free operation for a specified period and gives us a direct measure of a software system's stability and operational success. We can (at least theoretically) obtain high reliability without doing good test and evaluation, but low reliability certainly means a dissatisfied customer and ineffective testing. We don't intend to cover the specific techniques of SRE in any detail. Our intent is to consider the measurement aspects and provide enough information to help the reader decide if the measure should be considered further within their organization.

For any reliability measurement the critical aspect to define is the notion of a failure. A failure occurs when a program does something that is a departure from the user requirements or customer needs. Note the distinction between defects and failures. A simple defect can cause repeated failures, often with many different symptoms. Conversely, a majority of defects never produce failures, or it may take a combination of many defects to lead to a single failure. The point is that failures are implicitly defined in terms of how the software is intended to be used. Failures can occur in production use or be induced through the running and execution of a test.

To measure reliability we must first understand how the software will be used and build up a set of tests that simulate that operation. (This is referred to in the literature as creating an operational profile.) Once we have tests that mimic operational use, we can run those tests over time and count the failures we observe.

Various models have been developed to "predict" the growth in reliability (decrease in failure rate or number of failures per unit of test execution time). Through these models it is possible to measure reliability during the latter stages of testing. The measure is used to help assess how much additional testing and time might be

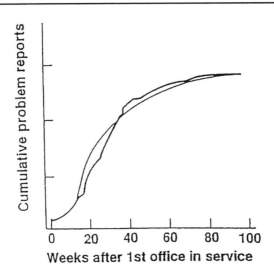

1990 Application of Software Metrics Conference. John Muse Presentation

Figure 6.17.   Predicting reliability.

required to reach a desired failure intensity level and predict the likely number of field failures that will be experienced upon release. Figure 6.17 shows a plot of the predicted versus actual failures for a release of AT&T's #5 ESS switchboard.

The close observed fit to actual experience indicates that SRE technology can be used successfully to measure and predict software reliability. Successful predictions like that shown in the example have been reported in a number of applications. Reliability measurement based on statistical testing is one of the technologies embedded within the cleanroom methodology. Reliability measures are also being used to help predict and control the end of system testing. The technology is still very young, but there is sure to be significantly expanding use during the coming decade.

Perceptions

As we have emphasized already it is important to capture people's "perceptions" and feelings as an integral part of the measurement engineering program. How testers, developers, and customers think and feel gives important insight for the overall quality of both the development and evaluation efforts.

Measurements and surveys of satisfaction are becoming more and more common. We can use them to help validate many of our other bottom-up measures. For example, does perceived satisfaction go up when failure intensity and/or defect density goes down? Do practitioner feelings about quality and confidence in their work products correlate to measured defect counts and densities? Earlier in the chapter we gave an example of the comprehensibility perception measure SQE uses in its High Impact™ inspections. Recall that this measure is collected from each inspector after they have completed their review of the work product being inspected. We expect that the inspection detection efficiency will drop when comprehensibility does. This allows us to measure it and find out. We also collect a result or "value" measurement from each inspector at the completion of a High Impact™ inspection. Participating inspectors are asked to assess value on a scale of 1 to 5 with 5 being "extremely worthwhile" and 1 representing "worthless." This information is included as a part of the inspection summary report and is correlated with actual detection efficiencies as well as other direct work product quality measures to help track the inspection program effectiveness.

Perceptions are usually sampled through some sort of survey or interview technique. Process assessments and audits may use one or both of these techniques and provide a good opportunity to sample practitioner and customer perceptions. Many companies conduct "post-mortem" reviews of their projects a few months after they are completed. I like to sample perceptions right after the project is completed and then use the post-mortem to "measure" their accuracy. Were the initial perceptions about the product quality and reliability realized? Were the perceptions about key process issues (strengths and weaknesses) confirmed?

Test Analysis

A final category of R measures comes from direct analysis and study of the test and evaluation products. As with specifications and code we can (and should) measure any defects found in our testing and evaluation work products. We may use testing to find defects in other work products (in fact, the count of those found is one measure of output from the test process), but we also indirectly discover defects in our test work that have to be fixed. These can be tracked as a work product density (number of defects per number of tests or lines of test code or pages of test specification) or as a percentage of the nontest-related defects found. Typically we'd expect a small percentage of all the defects found to be ones that require fixes or corrections to the testing work products. When that is not true it suggests insufficient care in planning and specifying the testing or a lack of appropriate quality input work products to work with. Tracking test product defects allows us to understand what causes them and then change the process to eliminate them— just as we do with defect analysis on the software side. One company that performed such an analysis found that most of their defects were caused by erroneous or missing information from development. (A common example is when a change is made to a routine, but the design is not updated, and testing is unaware of an impact on the test case.) They were able to use this information to help educate developers as to what was needed for test specification and bring about a significant improvement.

One special form of test analysis that is worth commenting on involves "testing" established tests by measuring their ability to detect known or intentionally inserted defects. In literature the technique is referred to as "seeding" or "mutation analysis." The basic idea is to insert some defects in the software system under test and then measure how effective the tests are at picking them up. In mutation analysis, multiple defective versions of the system are created, each with a single defect. Typically the "mutant" versions are created under program control by deleting a random statement or arbitrarily changing a constant (for example, a 1 to a 0). The tests are rerun against the seeded or mutant versions, and we measure the number of known defects that are discovered. The technique helps to gauge the effectiveness of a test set and can be used to estimate the number of unknown defects yet to be found. While the technique is seldom used in industry, it does show some promise, and interested readers should consider experimenting with it. In general a test set that performs poorly in detecting the seeded or mutant defects can be expected to do poorly in detecting real-world conditions. The converse is much less likely, but some experimental research has shown the technique to be quite robust and that good mutant detection is a reliable indicator of high overall detection efficiency.

SUMMARY

In this chapter we have reviewed the broad range of measurements required to measure test and evaluation work. A few readers may feel bewildered by the many different measures we have discussed. Don't despair. The fundamentals of measurement engineering apply to measuring evaluation just as they do to measuring anything else. What ties everything together is our by now familiar IOR model. We must measure the Inputs, Outputs and Results from each evaluation or testing work effort.

I measures—the evaluation inputs

Resources (effort)

Activities (tasks performed)

Work products used and their comprehensibility

Size and complexity of the software evaluated

O measures—the evaluation outputs

Work products produced or created

Testing status (tests specified and executed)

Size and complexity of the testware created

Software defects found

R measures—the evaluation results

Detection efficiency (defects missed)

Test coverage (features and structure)

Software reliability

Testware defects found (rework)

Perceptions (testers, developers, and customers)

This is a lot to measure, but it is all necessary if we want to make the evaluation effort visible and complete an effective measurement engineering program.

Our three bottom-up building block systems are particularly important to support test and evaluation. Resource Tracking, Work Product Tracking, and Problem Tracking may be strong on the software side but also have to be strong on the testware side. Historically they have not been, and that must change.

Automation and tooling is also important. As with the coding area we have useful and valuable tools to support test and evaluation measurement. Automated test status logging, test coverage analysis and measurement (both functional and structural), and reliability measurement must become the norm. Extensive investment in automation is required to achieve effective results.

CHAPTER 6 EXERCISES AND DISCUSSION POINTS

1. Why is measuring the reviewed work product comprehensibility considered important in a High Impact™ Inspection?
2. True or False—A test that uncovers lots of defects is a good test. Explain and defend your position.
3. True or False—A test that detects all or nearly all the defects that are present is a good test. Explain and defend your position.
4. True or False—A test that fails to detect some important defects is a bad test. Explain and defend your position.

5. Calculate the Defect Detection Efficiency for all of the evaluation activities (steps 1 through 5 combined) listed in Figure 6.9.

6. Explain why a higher defect Detection Efficiency does not necessarily imply a more effective test or review process.

7. Outline an experiment to compare two hypothetical testing techniques. Explain any key assumptions and what results you would need to be able to conclude that one technique is "better" than the other.

8. Explain what problems you would have with a testing approach based on random sampling from a list of test objectives or program components.

9. Explain how "seeding" is used to provide a test effectiveness measurement. What assumptions does such a measurement depend upon?

10. Suppose a high correlation were discovered between the number of defects found in testing in the small (inspections and unit tests) and testing in the large (system and acceptance tests). How would you interpret such a result? What questions would you have about such a result?

PART III

Measurement for Managers

"As our industry becomes more and more quality conscious, it's beginning to dawn on all of us that we'll never achieve much quality without gaining quantitative mastery of our projects. As long as we set budgets and schedules politically, then all the talk about quality is just talk. Until we learn to derive expectation from the empirical patterns of the past, then our problem is not so much how to assure quality as how to make it possible at all."

Tom DeMarco

INTRODUCTION TO PART III

In the first two parts of this book we have introduced a systematic measurement process and shown how to build bottom-up from the three basic measurement building block systems (Resource Tracking, Work Product Tracking, and Problem Tracking) to a proven software measurement engineering program that serves the needs of practitioners effectively.

For the project leaders and managers (along with any would-be managers) who have come this far with the book, you may be wondering when we are going to get around to discussing how the measurements help and support managers. Well, that time is here. This part of the book is for managers. We will show how bottom-up measurement engineering also serves top-down management needs and requirements and does so without introducing any new requirements!

The material is organized into three chapters:

Chapter 7 Measuring Projects

Chapter 8 Measuring Processes

Chapter 9 Measuring Best Processes

Chapter 7 describes how the basic IOR (inputs, outputs, results) measures are used to support project management needs of estimation, planning, tracking, and reporting. Chapter 8 reviews the important and evolving technology for measuring software processes (surveys, studies, and assessments) and shows how these relate to our fundamental IOR measures as keys to any successful process analysis or comparison. Chapter 9 examines the special issue of trying to understand and measure the "best" processes and provides industry-wide benchmarks.

Measuring Projects

The investment of a modest amount of skilled effort in a Plans
and Control function is very rewarding. It makes far more
difference in project accomplishment than if these people
worked directly on building the product programs. For the
Plans and Control group is the watchdog who renders the
imperceptible delays visible and who points up the critical
elements. It is the early warning system against losing a year,
one day at a time.

Fred Brooks

WHAT MANAGEMENT NEEDS

Most managers are pro-measurement and at least desirous of, if
not clamoring for, more quantified information. What does a software project manager need to know to manage a project effectively? What should a manager expect (require?) from the software
measurement program? Just what is it that they want, and why
has it been so difficult to satisfy? How useful is the measurement
information, and what should managers be doing with it? How do
we engineer our measurement programs to properly support managers as key measurement customers?

No two managers' needs are identical. Managers have different styles and different measurement requirements. However, all managers need some basic information across the broad spectrum of project issues, and most will agree that what they currently have available falls far short of what they would like to have.

There have been many attempts to provide a top-down answer for what should be measured. The Basili GQM paradigm (see Chapter 1) says start with goals and compile questions and metrics that will help you determine if your goals are being realized. In a book called *Making Software Development Visible*, David Youll [Youll 1990] offers what he calls the 5 Ps (see Figure 7.1) as his answer for what management should measure. Another answer comes from an Air Force Systems Command study that sought to identify key management indicators all software managers should have available (see Figure 7.2).

These top-down approaches give us useful insight into what most managers should be measuring, but there are still many managers who don't even know what their goals are, let alone how to measure them. It is rare to find a manager who has really thought out measurement needs and information requirements carefully. It is rarer still to find those who have invested the energy and effort to define and specify workable measurement systems. Those that do, find it tough to get implemented and even more difficult to sustain. Practitioners must understand and support the effort if the data they are being asked to supply is to be trusted. A whole lot of other managers may know very clearly what they need but end up resisting the measurement program because they are afraid it may expose what is really going on and make them look bad. Reorganizations and realignments are at least annual events in most organizations, and when a new man-

PLANS	Activities coming up—forward visibility
PROGRESS	What has been achieved—backward visibility
PRODUCT	Status and quality of what has been produced
PROCESS	Methods and tools used and their effectiveness
PERIPHERALS	Status of supporting activities

Figure 7.1. Youll's five Ps—making software development visible.

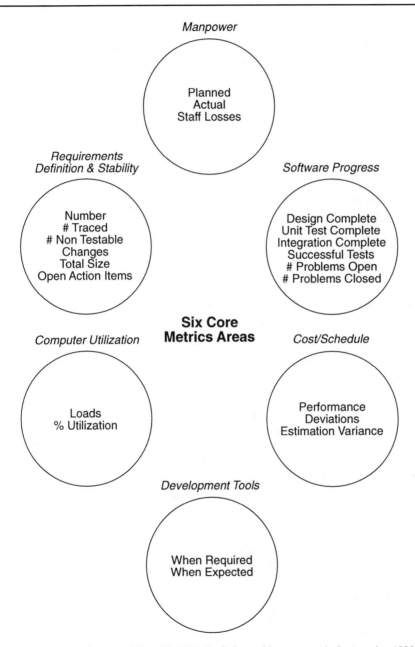

Air Force Systems Command Pamphlet 800-43, *Software Management Indicators*, Jan 1986

Figure 7.2. Air Force core metric management indicators.

ager comes into the fray, she brings with her a different set of visions and needs that can be extremely disruptive.

Even without these problems management wants are ultimately constrained by the engineering realities of what is practical and reasonable to provide. Every manager needs to track activities and process steps that are taking place; what resources have and will be expended; what the products are that are being produced and their status; and how good those products are or are likely to be. *This is nothing more than our by now familiar bottom-up Inputs—Outputs—Results measurement model.*

Today's manager needs accurate and timely information to *estimate* and *plan* more effectively; to *assess* projects and products; to *anticipate* better and be able to *predict* potential problems; and to specify changes and *take action* when required. We'll demonstrate in this chapter that measurements that support those needs are not any different from those we have already presented and recommended. Whether you drive top-down or bottom-up, you end up at pretty much the same place. Engineering the measurement program bottom-up is the *quickest and most practical* (only?) way to supply management with the information it needs. The bottom-up approach is as much in the best interest of management as a customer as it is the practitioner!

MEASUREMENT ENGINEERING FOR THE PROJECT MANAGER

In this book we've introduced the bottom-up inputs-outputs-results (IOR) model as the foundation for systematic measurement engineering. Figure 7.3 shows an expanded version of the model emphasizing the retention of the IOR measurements in a project history database and their use to support the project manager in planning and controlling the project.

Measurements from prior projects are assumed to have been gathered and stored in the history database as a company "experience" repository. That experience is then used to help plan each new project. The output work products or *deliverables* to be developed during the project are specified by extracting what was produced on a similar project and adjusting it as needed. Measurable *goals and objectives* are specified for each of the deliverables using

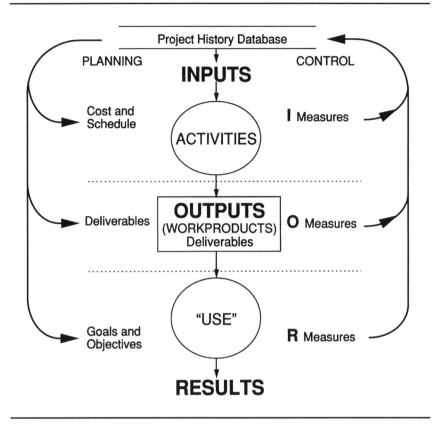

Figure 7.3.   Extending the IOR model for project management.

actual experience of what the O and R measures were on prior projects. With the deliverable output and performance criteria results understood, we then *schedule* the project resources and activities required. The measured history is drawn on once again, and the actual activities and resources used on similar projects and deliverables (our I measures) are adjusted as necessary to produce the final plan.

As the project proceeds, we collect new IOR measurements on each of the project activities and work products. These are fed back to the database for comparison and tracking to assess where the project stands against schedule, deliverables progress, and its goals and objectives. Using measurement to provide ongoing control and feedback alerts the manager to problems early and provides the basis for replanning as necessary.

Systematic use of bottom-up measurement engineering provides the database needed to quantitatively address most project management issues and questions that arise. Youll's backward and forward visibility (*p*lans and *p*rogress) is obtained by comparing the I and O measures of actual achievement against the target schedule and deliverables. The O and R measures describe the *p*roducts (outputs) produced, who uses them and how good they are. The I measures record the *p*rocess (by activity) that was used to produce them. Most of the common management questions have straightforward quantitative answers. Questions like where do I stand today? What is supposed to happen next? What is the status of the project?

We can even provide fair answers to the typically murky questions like how *well* are we doing? Are we meeting *objectives*? How does our *productivity* compare with the last project we delivered? For example, we can judge how well we're doing by comparing the planned outputs and objectives to the measured O and R actuals, and we can at least broadly assess productivity by comparing the O/I ratio for similar work products that achieved similar results and effectiveness.

Productivity is a hot topic for many managers and practitioners and deserves a few extra words. More than a few measurement programs have failed because productivity was misunderstood or misapplied. The common definition for productivity is some ratio of output to input. We get a measure of productivity whenever we pair up one of our O measures (like size or complexity) with the I measure of the effort it took to "produce" it. For example, we might look at a particular design work product and calculate the ratio of output measured in function points) over input (measured in effort hours). We might then be tempted to report productivity for the design phase as something like X hours per function point or, even more dangerously, compare it with what it was on the last major design effort. Note, however, that *before* the statement can be used to gauge real productivity, we must "use" the design and obtain some R measures as to its value and effectiveness. If we later learn through such use that this time our design product was not nearly so "effective," we must take that into account and adjust the productivity score accordingly.

The problem is that "true" productivity is really a ratio of results to input, not output to input. We may have produced more stuff, but the question is did we really get more results—more bang for the buck? With software (as with a lot of things) we often don't understand the results until after the product has been delivered. We can capture O measures as we build the work products and even use those as *preliminary* gauges of our productivity but we must always remember to come back and apply the R measures to see what we really achieved.

Another Example

We hope we've already convinced most of our readers that bottom-up measurement engineering not only supports the working practitioner, but also the line manager. For the few who remain skeptical and unconvinced I'd like to offer one more example to support the validity of our IOR model.

Near the end of my toil in drafting this tome I came across a set of guidelines developed by the Department of the Army Operational Evaluation Command that contained a recommended minimum set of 12 metrics. The intent of this metric set was to specify what project measurements should be collected to control and manage critical and operational software issues from an overall life cycle test and evaluation point of view.

The metrics are grouped into three broad categories (see Figure 7.4). The *management* group deals with contracting and overall management issues that may impact test and evaluation. The *requirements* area focuses on the specification, translation, and volatility of the system and software definition, and the *quality* area deals with the technical work product characteristics and testing.

The most interesting point to bring out is that the set of recommended measures that emerged from this largely top-down initiative is *not very different* from the set of measures that resulted bottom-up from our measurement engineering approach. It includes almost all the I, O, and R measures we've introduced as candidates, and more, and this is a *minimum* set![1]

---

[1]Note each of the metrics really consists of multiple measures, and in total there are more than 100 different data items. For example, there are 9 in the Software Complexity metric: statements; decisions; Halstead Length and vocabulary; knots; changed lines (added, deleted, and modified); and percent comment lines.

Management

1. **Cost**—Budget and actual dollars by major activity for each configuration item and for the overall project.
2. **Schedule**—Planned and actual start and end dates for each project milestone.
3. **Computer Resource Utilization**—CPU, channel, memory, and mass storage projected and actual utilizations for each target resource.
4. **Software Engineering Environment**—SEI maturity level.

Requirements

5. **Traceability**—Count and percentage of the software requirements traced through the functional design, software design, code, and test cases.
6. **Stability**—Number of open and closed requirements issues as well as the number of user and development engineering changes and the impact they had on requirements measured by the number of requirements added, deleted, or changed and the source lines impacted.

Quality

7. **Design Stability**—Count and percentage of software modules (units) added, deleted, and changed per delivery or release.
8. **Software Complexity**—For each software module added or changed, the number of source lines; the percentage of comment statements; cyclomatic complexity; Halstead Length and vocabulary; and the number of crossing control paths.
9. **Testing Breadth**—Number and percentage of requirements and features tested by priority level.
10. **Testing Depth**—For each software unit the count and percent tested of the number of total paths, source statements, and decisions. Also the number of inputs tested with at least one legal and one illegal value.
11. **Fault profiles**—Open and closed faults (defects) by priority level and by source (requirements, design, code, document, or other). Also the average days open by priority.
12. **Reliability**—For each system level test the measured failure rate (In failures per month), an applicable reliability model data to project MTBF.

Department of the Army Operational Evaluation Command Guidelines for Software Test and Evaluation.

Figure 7.4. Department of the Army recommended minimum metric set.

I don't believe this is accidental. The measures emerge not because management wants them but because we have the practical engineering technology to provide them. They are part of what good engineering is all about, and they enable practitioners to engineer and managers to manage based on visible, quantitative information.

The point is we don't need *more* data or measures to support management. What we do need is to make sure that the measurement information that arises out of our engineering efforts is valid and that managers understand how to use it properly. What we want is *better* data that our managers can and will use for better decision making.

The rest of this chapter gives examples of how managers are using the bottom-up measures to plan and control their projects effectively. Before we leave this example, I should emphasize that I seldom encounter any project with all or even most of the measures this metric set calls for as a *minimum*. Indeed, I can't support the recommendation to require all these measures and am extremely skeptical about the *practicality* of even trying in many organizations. It is not that the recommended measures are wrong—indeed, we see them as offering the *right kind of vision* for where any measurement program should be going. But to get there you must embark on a rather long and arduous journey and engineer the measures in gradually from the bottom by strengthening the building block systems. Imposing them from the top requires some magic dust that is in awfully short supply.

PROJECT PLANNING AND ESTIMATION

One of the basic purposes of any measurement program is to support project planning. All managers will acknowledge that having some good data on old projects helps in planning and estimating new ones. Before the advent of any organized project data histories or estimating tools, managers had to develop project time and cost estimates from their personal experience base—by comparing the job at hand to previous experiences and applying intuition and expert judgment. A few managers were good at this, but most were not, and by the late 1970s overruns and schedule slips had become almost synonymous with large software efforts.

Software projects grew rapidly in numbers, size, and complexity, and the estimation problem gained national and international attention. This spawned a variety of methodology-based improvements in the estimation process as well as significant research efforts in trying to collect project history data and model the underlying patterns. Even with the methodology improvements and the estimation tools, the estimation problem remains serious. A 1984 study by the U.K. Department of Trade and Industry covering 60 companies and over 200 projects found over half the systems had significant cost overruns and two-thirds had significant schedule slips. Another more recent study in 1989 of 344 projects performed by Chris Woodward at Butler Cox PLC found the effort and schedule overruns to average at over a third of the project.

Estimating and scheduling large projects has been a big problem for many managers for a long time. Although the data in Figure 7.5 is old [Boehm 81], the fantasy factor phenomenon is not.

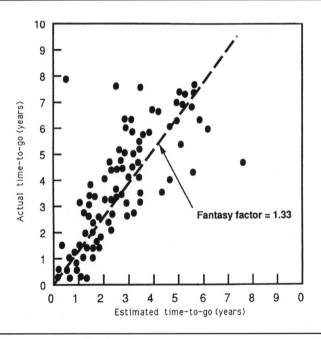

Figure 7.5. Fantasy factor.

Boehm cites three reasons for why people so consistently underestimate. Two of those reasons tie in directly to not having good historical data—people are *not familiar* or experienced enough with the entire software job and omit some of the tasks required. Also, people *don't remember* their previous experience and *forget* some tasks. The third reason is political and derives from people's basically optimistic nature and desire to please. Use of measurement to support estimation helps counterbalance all three.

To overcome the fantasy factor and improve the estimates, project managers began "breaking down" their projects into small, reasonably sized "tasks." They then estimated each of the tasks individually—preferably with the involvement and buy-in of the individuals who would be expected to work on them. This made for more realistic plans, but it proved cumbersome and time consuming in practice. Even when it was done carefully, there was a high likelihood that important tasks would be left out or the plans would change. Capturing and measuring actual tasks performed (our basic I measures) helped to improve the work breakdowns and the individual task estimates but still did not enable the estimator to respond quickly or answer various "what if" or tradeoff questions.

To meet that need researchers worked on analyzing project history data and providing empirical models that managers could employ to help them develop estimates. One important source of early data was collected for a diverse set of nearly 500 DoD projects throughout the 1970s by the Rome Air Development Center (RADC). Data on each project was sparse but included our primitive O and I measures—output source lines and input effort months and duration. The projects ranged from very small (one month of effort) to very large (thousands of months of effort and over a million lines of code). At the time most project managers viewed effort and duration as interchangeable. If they wanted to reduce by half the time to complete a project, they assigned twice as many people! The hard knocks of experience coupled with measured project data like the RADC database soon showed that the underlying relationships between effort and duration were fairly complex nonlinear functions. A variety of empirical studies based on measured project data demonstrated that manpower in large projects builds up in a characteristic pattern and that productivity was a rather complex power function of system size and duration. This set the stage for the empirical estimation models that were introduced in the 1970s—the best known of which was called the COCOMO or COnstructive COst MOdel.

Such models began appearing in the literature of the 1960s and have continued to the present. (See Figure 7.6 for an illustration of the typical inputs and outputs and data flow for these models.)

By the 1980s the models had matured enough to find their way into various commercial tool offerings, and today we have a

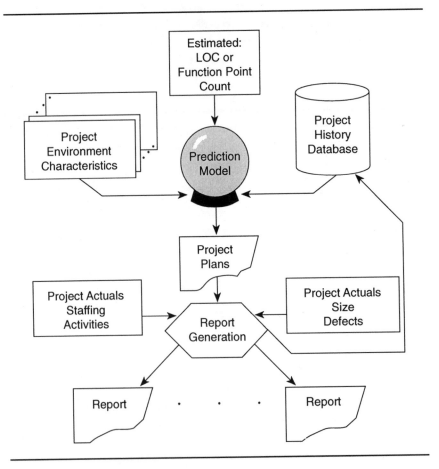

Figure 7.6.   Project estimation model inputs and outputs.

wide range of project management packages to choose and select from (see next section). Use of these packages and estimation tools remains low, but it is gradually growing and should become the norm in the 1990s.

ESTIMATION TOOLS

As noted above, one of the earliest estimation tools (software to help produce an estimate) relied on the COCOMO model. While Boehm's book describing COCOMO is lengthy and rather ponderous to digest, the basic nature of the model is rather simple (see Figure 7.7).

The major input required by the model is an estimate of the size (source lines) of the system to be built. The output is the predicted effort and duration (months) to build the system.

Secondary inputs describe the type of project and the environment and are used to adjust the value of the constants and calibrate or "tune" the model. The COCOMO model spawned many variations and led to a number of the commercial estimating tools that became available. Currently there are more than 20 such estimating products operating in environments ranging from the PC to high-end work stations and mainframes. Some of the more popular ones include ESTIMACS (Computer Associates), CHECK-POINT (SPR), and SLIM (QSM). (See Appendix C.)

All these estimating tools require an estimate for the size of the system to be built as a starting point. To use them you must be able to provide the initial input size estimate. The garbage in, garbage out law certainly applies. If your input estimate for size

---

EFFORT = C $\times$ KDSI^M

DURATION = 2.5 $\times$ EFFORT^N

> **C, M,** and **N** are constants dependent on project type and characteristics. (Typical values for the constants are $C = 3$; $M = 1.1$; and $N = .35$.)

> **KDSI** is the size estimate in thousands of delivered lines.

Figure 7.7.   Simplified COCOMO model.

is off, the estimate for effort or duration that the tool gives you is going to be off accordingly. *There is no magic in the tools!*

I am often surprised by how naive some managers can be about this. As Barry Boehm has observed, "There is no substitute for a thorough understanding of the software job to be done; a thorough understanding of our basic tendencies to underestimate; and a thoughtful realistic application of this understanding to the sizing activity." To be able to provide the input estimates you must have been measuring for a while and have an accumulated history of actual size measures on similar projects. You also have to make sure any other input characteristics are properly described and that your tool is properly calibrated for your own environment.

Any estimating tool projection will be wrong if:

1. The input size estimate (source lines or function points) is wrong.
2. The inputs describing the project and environmental characteristics are wrong.
3. This project is unlike any others in the past.

More recent versions of many of the popular estimating tools accept a Function Point count as the input size estimate. Since this can be an *actual* measure of the high level design taken fairly early in the project it is much preferred over lines of code.

Even with careful inputs the tools are not going to give any miraculous answers. One study published in *Information and Software Technology* by Kusters, van Genuchten and Heenstra [Kusters 90] tried to objectively measure how good the estimation tools and their underlying models were. The study concluded that "estimates obtained with tools were no better (and no worse) than *good* manual estimates" and "that the most positive result of using the tools was to draw attention to issues which would otherwise be overlooked." These findings should not be surprising to the thoughtful measurement engineer. The value of measurement as a "prediction" tool has been rather oversold. What measurement can and does do very nicely is capture actual history and make sure we *remember* it when we consider the next project.

The study also emphasized that calibration for the *specific project environment* was a must to even equal the results of good manual estimates. What that means is that managers can't expect to pick up some shrink-wrapped estimating tool and get much value from it in terms of useful estimates for their environment until they have built up their own history data base. What the tool provides is a vehicle for gathering the history data and putting it to effective use once it is available.

PROJECT TRACKING AND CONTROL

Once a project begins, our bottom-up measurement program will provide a fairly heavy flow of ongoing information: I measures describing the activities and effort; O measures describing the work products and deliverables; and R measures describing their use and effectiveness.

All of this information must be analyzed, summarized, and presented in a manner that helps the project manager to visualize trends and spot issues or generate questions. *Graphs and plots are the keys to success.* Many effective ways to present and track our project measures have been developed. This section offers examples that demonstrate how other managers are using the measures to provide project status and control their projects more effectively.

Input Measurements

Effort needs to be summarized at least monthly and plotted to show trend information throughout the duration of the project. Figures 7.8 and 7.9 are examples of the type of charts managers find useful to track staffing and effort.

Figure 7.8 shows an actual plot for the first 12 months of a large development effort. Staffing on the project started at 20 and has grown to over 60 (the dashed line at the top). The chart shows the planned versus actual count of experienced staff as well as total staff, and it graphically highlights unplanned losses such as resignations or transfers that the manager did not expect or plan (the dashed line at the bottom).

The manager should also be tracking effort as well as head-

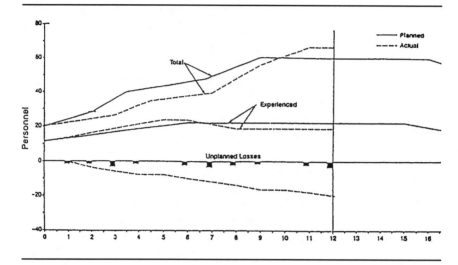

Figure 7.8.   Project staffing sample plot.

count. (This is critical if the project is using a number of people on a part-time or matrix-management basis.) Figure 7.9 shows a graph of planned versus actual versus "earned" effort months. "Earned effort" is defined as planned effort for all completed activities. If activities are taking much longer to complete than planned, then the gap between earned and actual will grow. If activities are completed in less time than planned, the earned effort will exceed actual effort.

Also shown in Figure 7.9 is a simple example of how the manager might track planned versus actual project effort each month by major activity category (our fundamental measurement engineering I measures). The first column under each month indicates planned effort (months), and the second shows the actual effort. Such a table will highlight issues like the fact that two person months were planned on high-level design in February and March, but only one was achieved.

Tracking activities and tasks is a key part of any project control effort. One of the most popular graphical charts used is the *Gantt chart*. There are many variations to the basic Gantt display, but all list activities versus time (usually in weeks or months) and

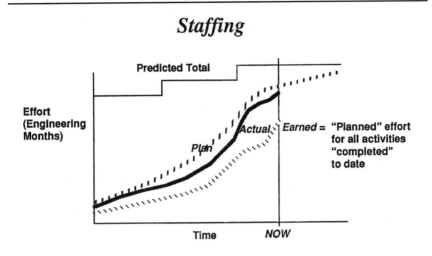

Activity	J		F		M		A	• • •
Requirements	1	1	1	1	1	1		
Test plan			.5	1	.5	0		
High level design			2	1	2	1	3	
Totals	1	1	3.5	3	3.5	2	3	

Figure 7.9.   Project effort tracking samples.

display the planned or scheduled duration for each activity (see Figure 7.10).

Each activity in the Gantt chart is shown as a line with a small box on either end signifying the planned start and finish date. (In the example, the requirements activity is planned to start at the beginning of January and finish at the end of March.) The boxes

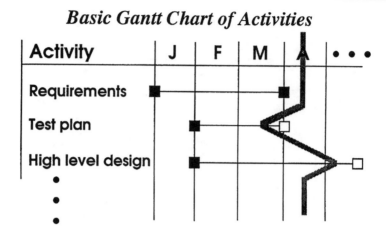

Basic Gantt Chart of Activities

- Boxes signify start and end dates of the activity
- Shaded if activity has started or completed
- Step Lines used to highlight status as of a given date and indicate activities ahead or behind schedule

Figure 7.10.   Activity tracking using a Gantt chart.

are colored in to signify that the activity has actually been started or completed. (The example indicates that the requirements activity is completed and the test plan has been started.) The thick vertical line is called a *step line*. It highlights the project status for the current month (April). For a task behind schedule (like the test plan that was supposed to have been completed in March), the step line jogs to the left. For an activity ahead of schedule (like the high-level design task), it jogs to the right.

Output Measurements

Basic output measurements should also be summarized and tracked as the project proceeds. Two of the common charts used by many managers are shown in Figures 7.11 and 7.12. The deliverables plots (Figure 7.11) track the *number* of work products produced. One plot shows the actual versus planned number of deliverables to be completed by week. The second shows actual

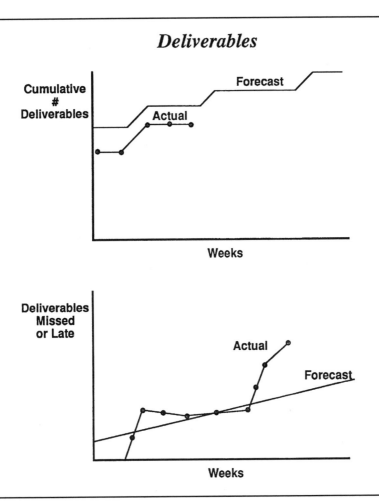

Figure 7.11.   Deliverables.

versus planned for the number of deliverables that are late (missed). Some readers might find it surprising to see a planned forecast for the number of missed deliverables, but this reflects real maturity and is a sign of a highly effective measurement program. What the measurement does is acknowledge reality and make it visible so that the project manager can respond more rapidly and effectively.

Figure 7.12 tracks another aspect of output progress—planned

Size

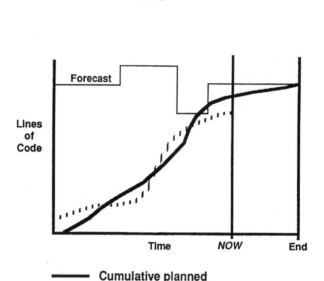

Figure 7.12.   Source lines sample plot.

versus actual source lines. The top line in the plot shows the forecast for total delivered lines at project completion. (For the example shown the forecast has been changed three times during the project.) The dashed line shows the total number of lines delivered to date (completed unit development and released to the integration test library) versus the current plan.

If an estimation tool that relies on projected source lines has been used, it is especially important to track the actual lines being developed and determine as early as possible if the estimate that the schedule is based on is solid. If it looks like you are ending up building a much bigger (or smaller) system, the manager will need to react and replan the project accordingly.

Any of the other output measures that were introduced in Part II may also be candidates for summarization and graphical presentation for project-management purposes. This is particularly helpful when summarizing code and document measures for an entire suite of programs—for a subsystem or overall product perspective.

As an example, Figure 7.13 is reprinted from a baseline inventory of existing software being supported at Purdue University's administrative data center. The inventory was taken to help managers and customers appreciate the size (in number of programs and lines of code) of the applications currently being supported and tested.

Results Measures

So far we have highlighted the use of I and O measures in support of project planning and tracking. Our third group of measures that track results and effectiveness (the R measures) are also critical to project management. What the manager should care about most is results—both good and bad—and trying to make them visible is a major measurement challenge.

Many of the R measures relate to defect tracking and analysis and have already been illustrated in earlier chapters. Readers should refer back to the discussion of the Problem Tracking building block system in Chapter 3. That chapter described the problems in defining and counting defects and illustrated common defect measures including defect classifications, rates, age, response time, cost, and density. Any of the defect plots in Chapter 3, as well as those presented in Part II when the particular work products (specifications, code and testing) were discussed, are useful for management to help highlight problem areas and trends. Understanding defects and their impact on the project is important for all managers and is a key element in both project and process management.

In a number of organizations defect analysis and tracking has become quite sophisticated and is a key project management concern. Figure 7.14 illustrates what is referred to as a "bug budget" in one organization that I visited. The "budget" includes the total number and number by month of defects or faults that are "expected" for each major detection activity. Each month is represented as a column showing the predicted as well as the actual counts of defects found that month. For the example, a total of 25 defects were expected in January, while only 14 were reported (all in requirements review).

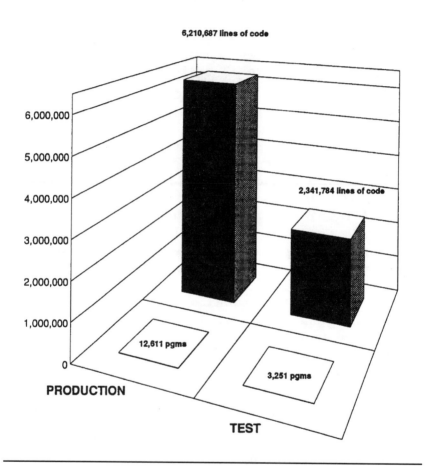

Figure 7.13.   Project baseline graphical example.

DETECTION ACTIVITY	Total # Predict.	Predicted vs. Actual			
		Jan	Feb	Mar	Apr
Requirements Review	20	20 / 14			
Design Reviews	35	5 / 0	15 /	15 /	
Test Design	65		25 /	30 /	10 /
Code Inspections	120				60 /
Unit Test	80				
System Test	40				
Regression Test	10				
Acceptance Test	5				
6 Months Operation	15				
	390	25 14	40	45	70

Figure 7.14. An example of a project "bug budget."

As with almost all measurement examples, this data does not give answers but instead raises lots of questions. Why was the defect count below expectation? Does it signify above average-requirements and design work? Might the cause be poor or rushed reviews? Perhaps there is some other significant explanation such as an inappropriate original prediction, or the work and the reviews were not carried out as planned. As we have repeated many times, measurement's purpose is to raise such questions, not answer them. Budgets don't tell us we've done well or poorly when we do or don't meet them, but they are useful indicators for management to track against and help the manager to better understand his or her project.

The project manager needs to track many other R measures besides defects to get a good handle on overall effectiveness. As we've seen in earlier chapters, the industry is only beginning to emphasize R measures more heavily and learn how to present and use them. Good questions to put before any experienced project manager are "What interests you most? What would you like to have to help evaluate project success?" Figures 7.15 and 7.16 are examples of measures other managers have used and found helpful. These may be copied and tried out—or use your creativity and invent your own built around the basic IOR primitives.

The top plot in Figure 7.15 displays a curve representing the amount of rework (in months of effort or equivalent dollar cost) each month by project phase. The plot is one of several examples in this chapter taken from Youll's book [Youll 90]. Note that all the requirements rework was contained within the first few months of the project. A new "bubble" of requirements rework appearing late in the project would denote a significant problem that required alteration of some of the requirements deliverables.

The bottom plot shows the achievement percent (defined as the effort planned over the actual effort × 100 percent) by month. Achievement is calculated for all activities and deliverables that are completed in a given month. Open or in-process activities are not counted. Such a plot gives the manager a fairly good picture of project progress as long as the plan is valid and isn't changing.

The reality is that changes are common and must themselves be measured and tracked. Figure 7.16 illustrates two plots I have seen used effectively for tracking changes. One shows the effort or equivalent cost of changes (broken down into four categories—required additions, required changes, preferred changes, and non-defect related). The other shows added and dropped activities each week and highlights how the plans are changing. The dotted line plot shows the cumulative change and reflects a characteristic shape seen in many projects. At the start of the project many tasks in the original plan are found to be unneeded and get dropped. Once the project reaches integration, many tasks are "discovered" that must be added to complete the project. Know-

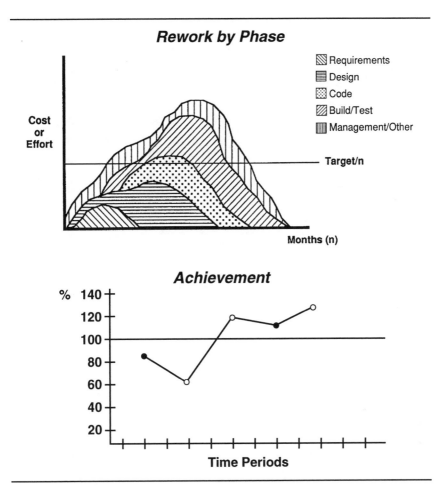

Figure 7.15.   Rework and achievement plots.

ing or anticipating this trend ahead of time can protect the inexperienced manager from surprises near the end of the project.

MEASUREMENTS FOR SENIOR MANAGEMENT

Most of the graphs and plots illustrated in this chapter are targeted to first-line managers and project leaders. Senior managers also need some visibility and are primarily interested in big picture status.

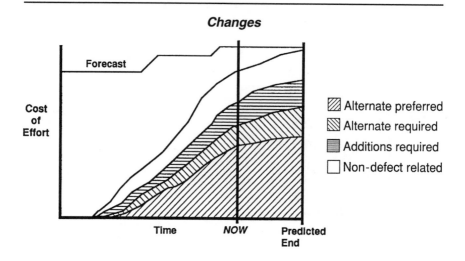

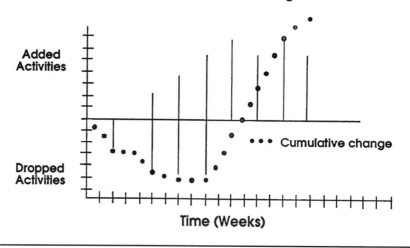

Figure 7.16.   Project changes.

Figure 7.17 combines the visual image of two very familiar gauges, a stoplight and a thermometer, into one high-level management meter. The thermometer is shaded in to show completion of the major project stages—in this case the project has completed Project Definition. The red, yellow, and green lights signify the overall health of the project, with red requiring senior

- **General Market Availability**
- **Trial Readiness**
- **Product Realization**
- **Project Definition**
- **Concept Closure**

Figure 7.17. A high-level management meter.

management review and action, and yellow denoting the usual "proceed with caution." High-level managers want this kind of summarized information, *but* it must be backed up with full supporting detail of all the individual IOR measurements that we have already seen. The presenter should make sure that clear procedures are used to summarize any data and be prepared to explain in detail how the overall status was determined.

SUMMARY

The software project manager's needs vary widely, but all managers need and should have available the basic IOR measures that bottom-up engineering provides.

A fundamental requirement for improved and more measurement-based project management is to save and maintain past project measurements in a project repository or history database.

The project history database is used to support better estimation and planning of all new projects. Retrieval and analysis of data from similar projects in the past helps the manager to baseline the new project goals, deliverables, schedules, activities, and tasks. Modern measurement-based project management means learning from the past and building up a measured corporate history to accelerate learning in the future.

After the project plan is produced, measurement engineering controls and tracks against it. Actual progress versus the planned goals, deliverables, activities, and tasks is captured, analyzed, and communicated. This ensures that management stays abreast of the project and can take early corrective actions if required.

As the project is carried out management-oriented measurement tracking and reporting provides visibility for the IOR measures being collected bottom-up. Many forms of presentation are useful and effective. The key is to make the measures visible and ensure management *uses* them for analysis and decision making.

The software project manager's measurement needs are not fundamentally different from those of the software practitioner. Both need to know and understand engineering reality: Where does the project stand? How good are the work products? When can we expect to be finished? The answers depend on effective bottom-up measurement engineering, not top-down management-driven exhortation!

CHAPTER 7 EXERCISES AND DISCUSSION POINTS

1. How does estimating project effort and schedule for software projects compare with the problem of estimating for other types of engineering or development projects? What is similar? What is different (if anything)?
2. Explain the significance of the finding that project size and effort are non-linearly related.
3. Describe the difference between the actual and earned effort plots in Figure 7.9. What does an earned effort that exceeds actual effort imply?
4. Develop a list that identifies what a software project manager should expect to obtain from an effective measurement program. Rank your list in terms of perceived value and importance.

5. Explain how a project that is completing all of its tasks on or ahead of schedule can still be in trouble. What measurements would detect the possible problem areas?

6. Suppose your manager said he or she wanted to track just five "key" measurements. What would you choose? How would you respond?

7. Propose a set of hypothetical criteria for the high level meter shown in Figure 7.17. What measures (and values) would you suggest using to trigger a yellow or red project light?

8. Construct a list of the top problems or frustrations encountered on a recent actual project. What measures would have been appropriate to collect that might have avoided or reduced the significance of these problems? What problems would measurement have helped? Are there any that would not have been helped (even in hindsight)?

Measuring Processes

"If you don't have a measurement system for a process, there is no point in changing anything. You have no way of knowing if it improves anything or not. In fact, if you are not smart enough to measure your working processes already, then I doubt whether you are smart enough to improve them! To prove this wrong you'll have to measure."

Tom Gilb

The immature state of project measurement limits what has been done with cross-project and cross-industry comparison, but promising steps are being made. In this chapter we survey those steps and show how to use our bottom-up measures for successful process (technique or method) measurement.

COMPARISON TECHNOLOGY

A fundamental part of any engineering discipline are the process measurements that describe that discipline and enable learning from its mistakes. When bridges fall down or roadways don't hold up, we change the process and build or maintain them differently. The ongoing learning derived from systematic measurement enables continuous improvement of engineering technique based on hard experience and measured results. That is what we want and need software engineering to be like.

If we have several alternative processes for performing a certain activity, the general question of interest is which one (if any) is better than the others? Is there a "best" practice among the alternatives that should be standardized across the organization or the industry? If so, under what conditions is it best, and what are the key or critical aspects of that process that make it superior? If there is no single "best" approach, which *parts* of each alternative are most helpful in which conditions?

These are tough questions. If we thought getting a good set of measurements for a single project was tough, we can easily understand how challenging it is to measure multiple projects. We may collect some measurements across a group of projects and observe "differences" between the projects. Are the differences "significant"? Are the differences because of the *processes and practices used* or do they arise from other causes—natural differences in people and their skills, the nature of the project, or any of a myriad number of other uncontrolled factors and influences?

You might expect that the technology for sorting such issues out—for measuring and isolating true process differences and determining which practices really work—would be of paramount importance to our industry. Unfortunately, that is not the case; the reality is that our technology is very immature and is just now emerging. Most comparisons that are made have little real "measured" evidence to support them. Many others are poorly described and invalid. To measure whether some process is "better" than another, we need criteria that define the processes and rank the results of using them.

To compare processes efficiently, we must have (1) clear criteria that "define" the processes to be compared, and (2) clear criteria for evaluating or ranking the "results" of using those processes. Both of these criteria are harder to establish than it might seem. For example, consider a commonly accepted "good" practice like code inspections. For many this is a well-defined practice that has clear criteria for application and a specific set of steps and activities that are performed (Fagan inspections with an overview meeting, defined inspector roles, etc.). Others may regard an inspection much less formally and omit key steps or roles entirely. Both will claim to be using inspections, but the underlying process differences may be very significant.

There are also many seemingly small differences in inspection practices that can have a big impact on results. For example, some organizations hold the inspection before any code is executed; others allow a little bit of debugging to get a clean compile and some simple cases through; and still others allow (or don't prevent) significant unit testing. Are all these organizations "using" inspections? The problem is obviously that the criteria defining what is and is not an inspection are not very rigid. With many variations in the practice, our ability to measure comparative results becomes extremely difficult, if not impossible. It would be nice if we had an index of relevant practices along with clear definitions and specifications for each. Lacking this we often end up thinking we are looking at a group of projects that all employed a certain practice only to find out that each is really doing something different!

Even after we solve the problem of defining the practices we are comparing, we still have the often bigger problem of what criteria to use to rank the "results." What we want to know is if a certain practice is better than another. What we mean by a "good" or "better" practice is one that (at least most of the time) gives better results, and that implies having criteria for ranking the results. For inspections, one ranking criteria might be detection efficiency (finding a larger percentage of the defects present is better). Another might give more emphasis to finding just the high-impact defects (finding the larger percentage of "important" or risky defects is better). When we actually compare two different inspection approaches, the conclusion may well be different depending on which criteria are applied.

The issues involved can be very tricky and subtle. Consider the following simple true-false test.

A Short True-False Test

T   F   Brushing your teeth every day is a *good* practice.

T   F   Brushing your teeth after every meal is a *better* practice.

T   F   Brushing your teeth after every bite is an *even better* practice.

Most readers have no trouble accepting the first statement as true. We've all been raised to brush our teeth every day and generally view it as a good practice (for preventing cavities and general oral cleanliness). As a kid my mother would also press me to brush after every meal. While I don't do this anymore (and struggled then), I really don't doubt that it is a "better" practice in terms of reducing or preventing cavities, and I would expect most readers to also judge statement 2 to be true. But what about statement 3? I doubt anyone views this to be true. What happened? Why isn't brushing your teeth after every bite even better?

Well, it probably is better for preventing cavities. (*Note:* Even this presumption is something that we'd have to measure—perhaps we might learn that brushing so often might wear off the enamel and lead to cavities rather than preventing them.) But it is also obvious that some other criteria have entered the picture. Practicality has stepped in and forced us to apply "different" criteria by which to rank or evaluate the practice. It would be hard to be socially graceful and even finish a meal while insisting on brushing after every bite! The lesson is that *more* is not always better.

These sort of complex interactions arise all the time when you try to measure and compare engineering processes. "Results" are heavily influenced by lots of things—the abilities, skills, and even attitudes of the people using the processes; the environment and supporting tools; interactions with other practices, etc.

The immature state of our disciplines and the wide variations in practice limit what can be done, but it is important, and promising approaches are being developed. These approaches may be broadly grouped under the following areas:

1. Surveys
2. Studies and experiments
3. Assessments

In this chapter we'll review each of the approaches and present some of the more successful case studies to show how to use our bottom-up measures for successful process measurement.

SURVEYS AS SOFTWARE PROCESS MEASUREMENT INSTRUMENTS

Surveys are the most common and easiest to use approach for measuring and helping to analyze or compare process issues and practices. Their flexibility has led to an enormous range of examples and applications. We've presented a number of these applications in earlier chapters of this book. In Chapter 1 we described the results from several surveys of measurement practices in industry. Surveys have also been highlighted in other chapters as good vehicles for capturing the perceptions and feelings of people involved in a project or who are users of its work products.

Surveys are common in virtually every scientific and engineering discipline, and there is much we can learn about how to do good survey work by considering how surveys are used in other fields. One critical issue with any survey is to decide on the population of people you want responses from and how to draw a meaningful sample from that group. With many software surveys it is possible and practical to give the survey to the entire population of interest (for example, all participants on a project, or all customers using a new software system). In other situations we may survey a population group of opportunity (like all attendees at a conference, or all subscribers to a certain magazine or journal) recognizing that there will be some bias introduced. We can still draw meaningful conclusions by adjusting for the bias and understanding how it is likely to affect our data (i.e., recognizing that conference attendees typify above-average industry practices).

Once the population and survey objectives are determined, a set of questions of interest are developed or designed. Survey design is a well-established field built on a backbone of empirical experience. It is very easy to design a lousy survey, and any software researchers who are faced with having to do so should get some help.

Speaking from personal experience, I have been amazed at how easy it is to create questions that are misleading, biased, or confusing. The designer must also try to neutralize and out-maneuver respondents who for whatever reasons may be unwilling to answer correctly or honestly. Besides the design issues we also have to make sure we correctly analyze any data that we do collect. Many surveys lack discipline and rigor and are conducted by people or organizations with a vested interest. The result has been a lot of poor surveys that have little or no validity. However, there are also many examples of good survey-based process measurement and insight.

As an illustration of a well-done survey, consider the following case study comparing test practices in various projects at Hewlett Packard that was reported by Cathleen Meyer at the 7th Inernational Test Conference. The objective was to help spread improved testing technology across the corporation. To accomplish this, a survey was designed to measure testing practice and compare different projects. Questions were designed covering testing practices in six broad areas: planning, preparation, execution, organizational aspects, process management and control, and process improvement. An extract of questions from one area of the survey (test execution) is shown in Figure 8.1. (Each of the other five areas of the survey were similarly designed.) Note that each question is answered with a response from 0 to 4 reflecting a measured degree of use of the specified practice within the responding project. A 0 reflects no use of the practice; a 4 reflects standardized use.

The results were tabulated and presented in the form of Kiviatt diagrams that are shown in Figure 8.2. An average score for each of the six areas (groups of questions) was computed and plotted on one axis of the Kiviatt diagram. Lines were drawn to connect the scores, and the area inside those lines was shaded to create a dark shape or blot. A large blot denotes "more" of the surveyed testing practices in use. Regular shaped blots signify even use of the practices within each area; distorted or irregular shapes indicate relative strengths and weaknesses in one or more of the individual areas.

The "model" projects that use the testing techniques most are shown with their names next to them (top half of Figure 8.2). The others are identified by a letter code that is known to the individual project but not to other projects in the survey (bottom half of Figure 8.2). In this way the projects with more of the desired testing practices are recognized so that others may contact them and learn from them. Recognizing and encouraging the better projects served as a positive force to help spread improved testing practices more rapidly.

EXECUTION	0	1	2	3	4	N/D
1. Written test scripts with expected results are used by testers.	O	O	O	O	O	O
2. Regression testing is performed whenever software changes.	O	O	O	O	O	O
3. Standard, reusable test data is used for testing most functions.	O	O	O	O	O	O
4. Test scripts are automated with tools (e.g., Compare from Aldon, Match utility from AutoTester).	O	O	O	O	O	O
5. Test verification is automated with tools (e.g., Compare form Aldon, Match utility from AutoTester).	O	O	O	O	O	O

COMMENTS _____

_____

_____

LEGEND:

0 — Practice not in use
1 — Limited usage or experimental
2 — Common but optional practice
3 — Well-established practice
4 — Standard practice for all projects
N/D — Practice not considered desirable

Figure 8.1. Hewlett Packard testing practices survey (sample questions).

PROCESS MEASUREMENT STUDIES

A second common technology for measuring and analyzing processes falls under the broad umbrella of "process studies." What we mean by a process study is just a focused analysis conducted to help understand or address a software process issue or practice. Process studies come in all sizes, shapes, and flavors. Almost all are based on some collection of empirical data that is then ana-

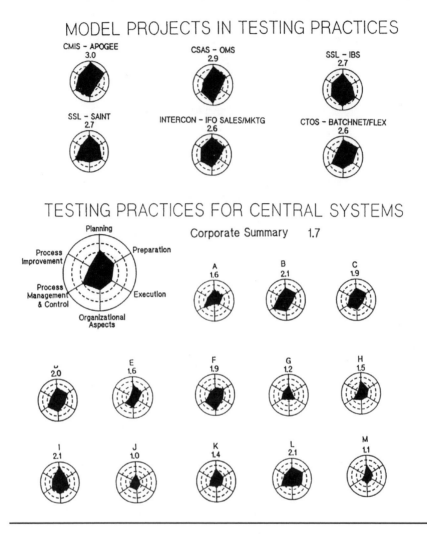

Figure 8.2. Hewlett Packard testing practices survey (results).

lyzed to support various observations and conclusions. There are many examples published in software literature, and like surveys (which some might view as a special class of study), there are plenty of examples of good and bad study work to examine.

Studies have been conducted on virtually every aspect of the software process. Even if we just restricted ourselves to published studies in respectable journals, there are still a rather large number to consider and review. Examples range from simple profiling of coding practices (distributions of code size and complexity measures) to trend analysis of selected measures over time (such as long-term productivity studies) to broad modelling studies that seek to discover underlying process relationships (such as the study work that led to the development of the COCOMO model for project estimation and the various reliability models).

As one illustration of the use of measurement-based studies to compare processes and analyze productivity across organizations, consider the work within IBM that led to the development of function points. (See Chapter 4 for a discussion of what function points are and how the measurement is counted.) Figure 8.3 shows a plot of the number of function points delivered per work month over a five-year period from 1984 to 1988 at three different IBM data centers. The points on the graphs were generated by totaling the function points for all systems developed during the year and dividing by the months worked during the year. The individual organization plots are denoted by letters A, B, and C.

At first glance, data centers A and B appear to be far more "productive" (as measured by function points delivered per month) than data center C. However, we have emphasized throughout this book the problems and dangers of "interpreting" measurement data—especially data that is expressed as a productivity measure (the ratio of an O to an I measure). The reality was that in 1988 the applications built by A and B were able to take advantage of a lot of reuse, while at C they were saddled with having to work on the technology upgrades and database conversions that did not result in new customer functionality or added function points. Thus the study "results" do not imply that C performed "poorly," but they did focus attention on productivity issues and helped IBM management to gain better insight and understanding of what was accomplished.

Collection of the function point data for completed projects led to the introduction of estimation guidelines for new projects, as shown in Figure 8.4. The plot shows actual project experience (function points vs. work months) and a best-fit probability curve. For a new project of 900 function points, the "estimated" effort range is somewhere between 150 months to a little over 500 (see the dotted lines

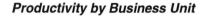

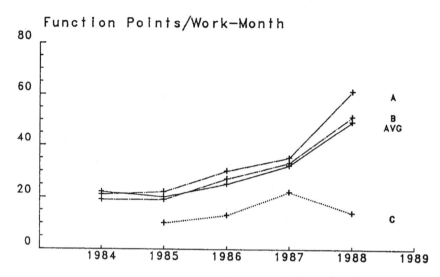

1990 Applications of Software Measurement Conference. Alan Albrecht presentation.

Figure 8.3. Function point productivity comparison.

in Figure 8.4). While this is an extremely broad range, it still served as an effective initial guideline for estimation and project scoping purposes and continues in use today.

Like surveys, the process studies that have been conducted are extremely diverse, and we don't have room to cover more than a few examples in this chapter. Another example of a simple study that arises quite naturally in bottom-up measurement engineering is shown in Figure 8.5.

The study in this case consisted of just presenting the basic I measures (effort by major activity) in a form that highlighted long-term changes and trends in the percentage of effort applied to each phase. The graph shows the organization devoting a larger and larger proportion of total effort to requirements definition while reducing the percentage on management and other overhead activities.

The examples indicate the power of even very simple analysis and graphic presentation to help understand long-term process

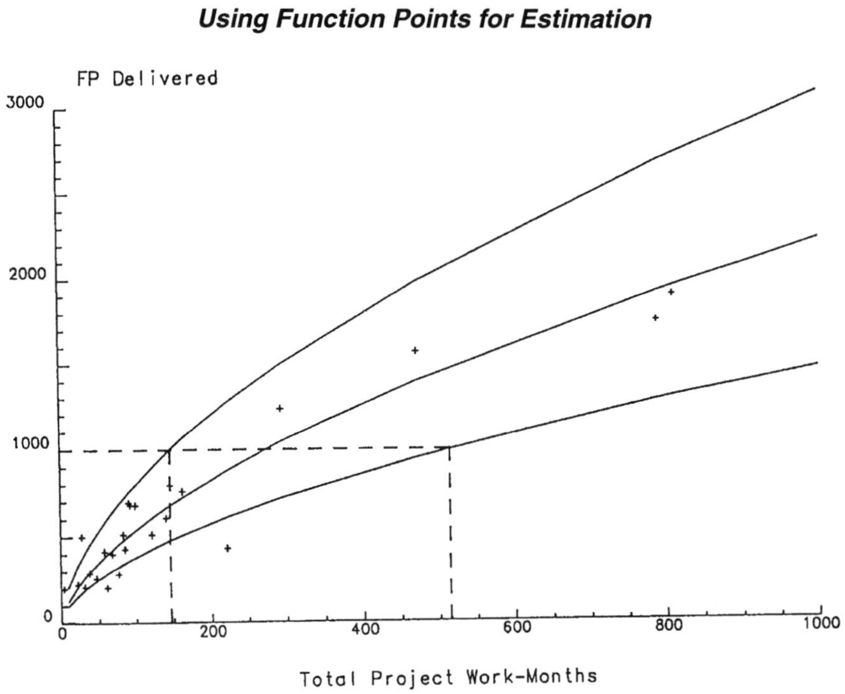
Using Function Points for Estimation
FP Delivered
3000
2000
1000
0
0
200
400
600
800
1000
Total Project Work-Months

Figure 8.4. Function points as a predictor for project time.

changes and their implications. They also typify what can be done when one or more measurements have been collected across a variety of projects and over a substantial period of time. Trends can be plotted and examined, and this invariably leads to more insight and questions about the underlying process differences that explain the observed variations.

PROCESS COMPARISON EXPERIMENTS

One rather special type of study that deserves further mention is the notion of an *experiment*. A central element of the scientific method is the application of careful experimentation to explore and test the validity of various hypotheses. We can compare software practices by experimenting with them under controlled

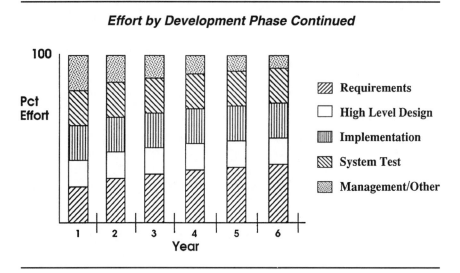

Figure 8.5. Analysis of effort by development phase.

conditions. The aim is to experiment with various alternative methods or techniques under study in a controlled environment that allows differences between the methods (if present) to be isolated and measured.

The first step in any of the experiments is the formulation of a hypothesis believed to be true. In software terms a typical hypothesis might be that some practice A is believed to be better than practice B. Typically A and B are alternative ways to do something (such as different testing techniques), and the objective is to determine (measure) whether there is any statistically significant difference between the two methods.

With the hypothesis established, the next step is to design an experiment in which alternative techniques can be examined in a controlled environment, and any discrepancies between them (if present) can be isolated and measured. Various experimental design approaches have been developed (and in fact fill up complete books in their own right) that permit probability conclusions as to the likelihood of the stated hypothesis being true given the observed experimental results. With such techniques, we are able to make statements such as "the probability is less than 1 in a 1000 that method A is not better than B" (provided we have performed the experiment carefully and not made any mistakes in using the appropriate statistical analysis tools).

A number of such experiments have been conducted and published in the software literature. Some of the earliest were conducted by Sackman [Sackman 1970] who tried to measure differences in effectiveness between batch and online or time-sharing programming environments. In these pioneering studies Sackman assigned a series of small coding problems to various groups of programmers. Each group got to code the same programs using the batch and online environments in different orders and on different programs. The time required to code the programs, the computing resources (number of runs and elapsed online minutes), and various satisfaction measures such as defects made and programmer perceptions were recorded. The design was constructed to cancel out variations due to different programs, programmers, and order.

Many other experiments have been conducted exploring process issues and variables. We have described a number of them in Part II as measures for use in each phase of development were introduced and described. Although a few of these software process experiments have produced important results, their overall legacy and influence on software practice has been limited. One primary difficulty is inherent with the experimental approach. No one is willing to fund repeated development of complex systems just so method and individual differences can be systematically controlled and analyzed. Consequently most experimental results have been obtained on very small problems in artificial environments. Practitioners and managers are quite rightfully skeptical that the results will scale up and apply to real-world work.

A second fundamental problem has to do with the criteria used to evaluate and measure method differences. As we have stressed throughout, the software industry does not have well-developed criteria or even a consensus for concluding that one method is better than another. We can choose various measures (like the number of defects introduced or discovered) and then measure observed differences between methods on those selected measures. However, that does not address the basic issue of what criteria or measures ought to be used to evaluate effectiveness. Even when we select our criteria properly there are many subtle influences that can confound or alter the results. One rather famous experiment conducted by Gerry Weinberg [Weinberg 79] reminds us of how careful we must be. In the experiment Weinberg got 5 different teams to develop the same program. Each team was given a different "success" criteria (e.g., one was to minimize the run time; another was to maximize the understandability of the program, etc.). The result was that every team ranked at the top with respect to its *own criteria*. This may not be an especially surprising result to many readers. Its implication, however, is that software teams act to maximize the criteria they *believe* are important. We have to be sure that what we perceive as method or technique differences aren't just differences caused by different success goals and criteria. This is very difficult to determine in most real-world empirical settings.

Despite the problems, the experimental approach remains an important process measurement tool and one that I anticipate will be employed more frequently in the decade to come. Researchers need more encouragement and support—both from traditional funding sources and from industry. Companies with strong installed measurement programs should be seeking out opportunities to design and conduct their own experiments on an ongoing basis. It is critically important to our industry to perform more quantitative analysis and experimentation on new supposedly more advanced technologies like formal methods, object-oriented design, cleanroom testing approaches and so forth. Such analysis must involve impartial qualified observers rather than relying on the claims of people with obvious or evident self-interest. Even if you are just beginning, researchers are always on the lookout for companies willing to participate in shared studies. While getting involved may be time consuming (and even a little frustrating), I believe the participating company has much to gain and that the long-term benefits will exceed the costs many times over.

COMPARING PROJECTS—EVOLUTION OF PROJECT DATABASES

Many of the most successful process studies performed have benefited from the collection of data over a significant repeated time period or a large number of projects. As discussed in the last chapter, project managers want to be able to look at measures and data collected on previous projects in order to better estimate and plan new ones. This is gradually leading to the evolution of project history databases that incorporate measures across a broad spectrum of projects.

The typical organization has many projects with significant variations in the practices used and employed. Questions of high interest are which (if any) of the process variations work more effectively than the others? Which ones don't seem to matter, and which ones are critical to success? How variable are the processes in use, and how do they compare with other typical or best company practices? Such questions are relevant to every software organization, and one approach toward beginning to be able to answer them is to establish a standard or minimum set of measures that are collected on all projects and maintained in a corporate-wide database. Typically, an organization starts by selecting a small subset of the recommended bottom-up project measures to be collected from every project to enable at least high-level cross-project evaluation and analysis. That set is then refined and expanded over time and gradually a corporate-wide history emerges.

A simple example from one of the earliest such databases is shown in Figure 8.6. The figure shows data collected on a large number of IBM projects over more than a 10-year period. Two measures (Project Effort months and Lines of Delivered Code) have been required as standard data from every major software project completed since the middle 1960s. The ratio (Lines Delivered per Effort Month) was computed as a productivity measure, and the table reflects *average* productivity as a function of project size.

Project Effort (Man Years)	Productivity (Lines Source per Month)
1	439
10	220
100	110
1000	55

Figure 8.6.   IBM large project database.

The averages show an *order of magnitude* drop in productivity as project sizes get bigger. Such data helped lead the industry away from the mammoth projects of the '60s and '70s toward more frequent and smaller-scope projects that had less risk of failure. The database also served IBM in project estimation and helped focus attention on especially high or low productivity rates. The data won't answer why a given project is higher or lower than average, but it does highlight projects we are interested in exploring and analyzing in more detail.

Another more recent description of a company project database is in Bob Grady's book *Software Metrics: Establishing a Company-Wide Program*. Hewlett Packard's standard measures include the Duration and Effort by project phase; size in Lines of New or Reused (Unchanged, Added, Deleted, Modified) Code; Bytes of Object Code; Lines of Documentation; and the Number of Defects Introduced, Found, and Corrected by phase. All of those measures are basic to our IOR measurement engineering approach and have already been discussed in earlier chapters. However, the effort and energy HP had to expend to standardize and establish uniform cross-company collection was enormous and continues unfinished today. HP's story is a reminder of how arduous a job we face in installing systematic engineering-oriented measurement. The benefits of the database for HP are now clear, but it certainly wasn't easy to achieve, and the program is still being continuously adjusted and expanded.

There are also various project databases that cross company boundaries and provide industry-wide comparative data. One of the largest and best known grew out of initial work at the Rome Air Development Center (RADC). This work was subsequently extended and turned into a proprietary database by Larry Putnam at QSM.

The QSM database now contains data on over 2500 projects representing over 200 million lines of code and continues to grow steadily. The data on each project is sparse, and like the IBM and HP metrics includes just duration, effort, size, and some limited defect count data. Figure 8.7 shows several sample plots produced from this database.

The first plot shows project duration versus project size in thousands of delivered source statements. The second shows project effort (months) versus size (again in thousands of source statements).

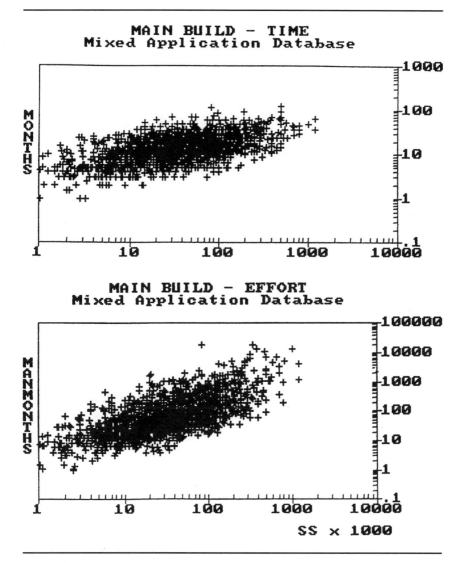

Figure 8.7. QSM project database—sample plots.

Note the immense spread in the data. Projects that took 100 months of effort produced as little as just a few thousand lines to many hundreds of thousands of lines—a range of at least several orders of magnitude! As we have learned before from other real-world measurement samples, variations in our basic measures across projects and organizations are very wide. The QSM database offers yet another example of just how varied they are.[1]

As described in the last chapter the QSM database is used in a commercial project management and estimation tool called SLIM. With data collected on such a broad range of projects, it becomes possible to compare the organization's overall productivity and effectiveness. One interesting study was performed in order to measure the return on investment from a multi-year tooling and process and improvement program. This illustrates the kind of studies I believe we will begin to see more and more of as industry-wide measurement databases mature.

The aim of the study was to evaluate the cost and benefit impact of a substantial multi-year tooling and training investment. Over a three-year period an investment of nearly $24 million was made on hardware and software tools and training to improve software engineering effectiveness (most of this involved a front-end CASE initiative). A simple survey was used to measure the use of this new technology in major projects completed in 1988 as compared to those completed in 1985.

Completed projects in each year were "scored" based on the survey results, with a maximum score of +10 signifying full adoption of the CASE technology and tooling that was introduced. As shown in Figure 8.8, the survey confirmed that the company was able to successfully put the new technology to use. Only one project was using it in 1985 (project #6), while all showed substantial use in 1988. The question was what was the payoff or benefit realized from this process change? Did the tools really result in making the company "better" and more productive?

To answer the cost/benefit question the company compared their projects completed in 1985 and 1988 *relative to the performance of other companies* reporting projects into the QSM database—i.e., to the average industry performance for the years in question. Figure 8.9 plots the companies' projects versus the industry average performance line.

---

[1]*Note:* Part of the variation is also caused by wide variations in the Lines of Code counting and reporting techniques between the different companies and organizations.

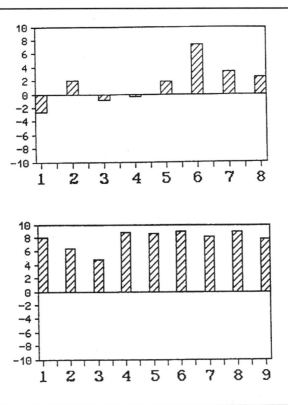

Figure 8.8.   Measured technology use—1985 vs. 1988 projects.

The three lines in each plot show the average and plus or minus one standard deviation for all projects reported to QSM for the year. The study company projects are plotted relative to these industry averages (denoted in the plots with + signs). In 1985 the company projects were average or a little above (two projects fell right on the average line, two fell above and two fell below) in terms of the number of thousands of source statements delivered per month of effort worked. In 1988 six of the seven completed projects fell above the average line, with three at or above one standard deviation from the mean (i.e., in the top 5 percent of all projects completed that year). This represented significant improvement relative to the rest of the industry over this three-year

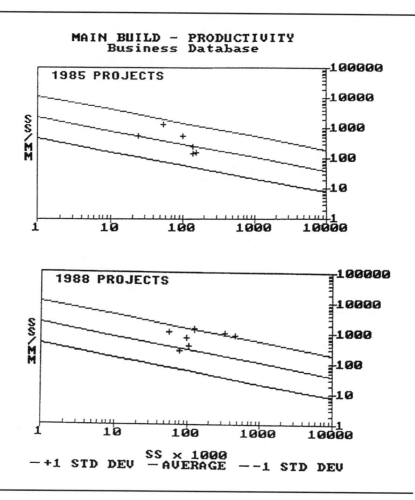

Figure 8.9.   Relative industry comparison.

period. The company was able to calculate how long the projects they completed in 1988 would have taken if they had not improved relative to the industry and compared this cost to the cost actually incurred. The result was a savings of $3 million a month! This was accepted as valid justification by the company comptroller and offers one of the best examples I am aware of where cross-project data was successfully utilized to analyze technology investment and benefit.

PROCESS ASSESSMENTS

The purpose of an "assessment" is to evaluate an organization's or project's software processes and practices to identify strengths and weaknesses. Process assessments have been conducted in many forms for many years ranging from the very informal (how are we doing self-check) to very formal independent reviews and audits. One common example is the project "post-mortem" conducted a few months after project completion. In a typical post-mortem, key members of the project team meet and analyze their project for lessons learned and changes that should be made on future projects. Another example would be in-process reviews conducted during a project that increasingly focus on process issues as well as project status. Over the years, post-mortems, as well as other types of audits and reviews that are conducted during a project, have become more and more quantitative and measurement based. Many now include the systematic capture and collection of standard project measures and provide baselines for comparison over time. All of this has helped spur a very active and evolving technology for software process assessment.

Use of the term "assessment" has become much more popular in recent years. Assessments are distinguished from other more informal evaluations by their emphasis on measurement and rigor in the specific steps and procedures used. One particular assessment approach has become highly visible and had substantial impact on industry practice. This is the Software Engineering Institute's (SEI) maturity model that was developed to provide guidance to the military services in the selection of software contractors. The framework for the model was initially outlined in Watts Humphrey's book *Managing the Software Process* [Humphrey 89]. Humphrey describes five evolutionary levels or layers of process maturity numbered for reference from 1 to 5. The levels are now used by many organizations within the DoD as well as in the private sector as a measure of overall software capability.

The SEI assessment was introduced just a few years ago, but since that time hundreds of organizations have been formally assessed, and hundreds, if not thousands, more have performed self-assessments and shaped their improvement efforts based on the maturity model principles. SEI has trained and licensed a number of vendors to work with organizations to conduct Software Process Assessments (SPAs) and also offers a self-assessment package and training support that allows organizations to informally determine their own maturity level. DoD contracting auditors have also been trained to perform Software Capability Evaluations (SCEs) that provide independent verification of process capability and maturity.

As this book is written the model is being refined. One of the improvements is the introduction of Key Process Areas" (KPAs) that are associated with and help to define levels 2 through 5 of the model. A key process area is a group of related practices that must be satisfied to attain the designated level of maturity. They may be thought of as building blocks in establishing a layer or level of process maturity. Figure 8.10 displays the five levels along with the key process areas specified in the revised model. (For example, the KPAs associated with level 2 are requirements management, project planning, project tracking and oversight, subcontract management, quality assurance, and configuration management.)

The levels and the key process areas are viewed like a series of hurdles. An organization can not be classified as level 2 until it fully satisfies all of the level 2 KPAs regardless of the extent to which any of the higher-level key processes are in place. Note also that there are no key processes associated with level 1. In the SEI model there are no criteria to be met to achieve level 1. Level 1 is the place you end up if you fail to satisfy one or more of the six level 2 key process areas. This is true whether you just miss on one key process or fail miserably on all six![2]

While the SEI assessment is the most visible, it should be emphasized that there are many alternative assessment approaches that enjoy significant following and usage. Several companies offer specialized proprietary process assessment services. (Examples include Computer Power Group, Software Productivity Research, most large consulting houses like Arthur Anderson, and my own company, Software Quality Engineering.) In addition, many large

---

[2]We might add that it is also the level most organizations who have been assessed end up at. The SEI reports that well over 80 percent of all the assessments performed fall at level 1.

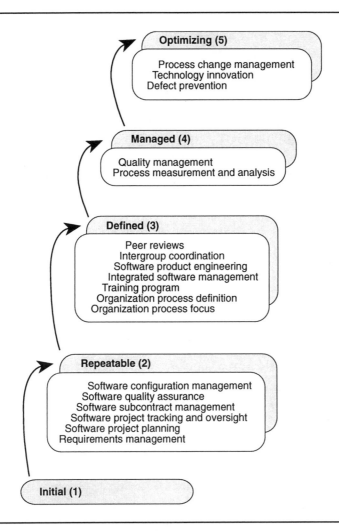

Figure 8.10.   CMM levels and key process areas.

companies have established their own in-house assessment capability and regularly evaluate many of their own projects using a combination of the SEI and other commercial approaches.

All of these assessments have the same basic goal of providing an objective appraisal of current software practices and support for continuing improvement. Nearly all involve the following basic steps:

Basic Assessment Steps

1. Planning and objective setting to define scope and plan out specific actions and tasks.
2. Survey to measure practices in use and identify candidate strengths and weaknesses.
3. On-site interviews and review of issues with selected team members.
4. Analysis of findings and discussion.
5. Recommendations and development of an action plan for improvement.

To start the assessment, the first step is to define the "scope" and put together a plan for the specifics of who, when, where, and so on. Determining scope is a key issue and an area of some controversy between SEI and most other commercially offered assessments. The SEI assessment was designed to measure an organization's maturity, not a single project or even a group of related projects. To assess an organization, SEI selects a small number (four to six is recommended) of representative projects and extrapolates the practices in use on those projects for the organization as a whole.

SQE also typically assesses a sampling of projects across the organization, but the results are not averaged or rolled up to obtain an organization-wide grade. For the SEI maturity assessment, it is critical that the projects selected be representative of the broad population of all projects. For many organizations that just doesn't make sense. There really is no organization-wide process to assess! My own experience in performing assessments has shown that key process characteristics are seldom shared across large organizations. SEI loses a lot of valuable insight by not reporting the assessment findings for each project individually.

I am convinced that the differences in practices between projects are important to highlight and that perhaps a good measure of organization maturity is the degree to which different projects use the same processes. That information and a record of how each project was assessed is not provided by the current SEI approach.

Step 2 in most assessments is some sort of objective survey or questionnaire. The purpose of the survey is to objectively characterize the practices in use. In an SEI assessment the survey is

SIZE ESTIMATING: Estimates for the size of software products are delivered according to a documented procedure.

1. Do you use a documented procedure to estimate software size (e.g., lines of code, function points, etc.)?
2. Do you use historical size data when available to help derive software size estimations?
3. Do you document the assumptions made in estimating software?
4. Do you review software size estimates?

Figure 8.11. Sample SEI assessment questions.

provided to the project leaders and managers of each of the representative projects. Their responses are used as a basis for discussion and review with selected functional area representatives (FARs) and are reviewed and confirmed on site by the assessment team.

As an example, one practice considered important for the level 2 project planning key process area is "size estimating." Sample questions SEI uses to determine use of this practice are illustrated in Figure 8.11. Each of these questions is answered Yes or No (or Not Applicable) by the project leader or manager in each of the representative projects.[3] In total, the survey contains about 100 such questions.

The SQE survey contains similar questions, but its approach and philosophy of data collection are entirely different. First, the survey is distributed to the full project team including managers, developers, testers, and any other support organizations heavily involved in the work. On a big project this will result in dozens and sometimes hundreds of completed surveys instead of just one from the SEI approach. Second, scaled responses from 0 to 3 are used instead of just a polar yes or no. The SQE scale was

---

[3]*Note:* It is the specifics of the questionnaire and how it is used that are being modified in the new model. Some consideration is being given to a graded response rather than just a simple yes or no. Readers will have to wait and see what the specifics of the new questionnaire look like after it has finished its current trial period. However, the framework for the five maturity levels and the basic assessment steps will remain unchanged.

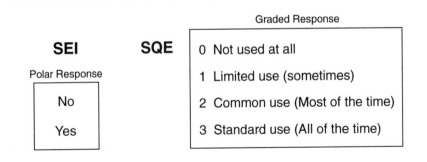

Figure 8.12. Survey question responses.

introduced earlier in the book when the results of the annual measurement practices survey were presented (see Chapter 1).

As shown in Figure 8.12, a 0 signifies a practice that is not used, while a 3 denotes standard use. Responses of 1 or 2 signal partial usage. While perhaps a minor point to some, using a scaled or graded response like this can have a big impact on the assessment results. How would you respond to the questions in Figure 8.11 if you use the practices only some of the time? Do you answer with a yes or a no? In most shops there are very few practices that are absolutes—either always used or never used. A polar choice of just yes or no forces the respondent to make a choice that doesn't reflect project reality and is likely to create significant bias in the resulting data.

The survey data is tabulated and made available to the assessment team prior to their on-site review. This enables the on-site visit to be focused on specific issues (strengths or weaknesses) brought out by the survey results. In an SEI assessment the focus is on the key process areas specified by the maturity model. SQE's assessments as well as most other commercial alternatives rely more on comparative evaluation with other project data. This difference in philosophy is important to understand and quite fundamental. In comparative evaluations what is important is being able to contrast your own practices with those of your competitors.

Consider the analogy of a salary survey. What a company wants to know is how do the salaries they pay (for comparable experience, skills, and responsibility) compare to what others are paying? This can be answered by gathering an industry-wide database of actual jobs and salaries from a broad cross-section of company's and then comparing a specific company's jobs to the database averages and ranges or percentiles. This is what companies like SQE offer for software practices and processes. They have accumulated a database of survey responses from many companies and can analyze data from one company by contrasting it to the norms and experiences of other projects in other companies. Figure 8.13 illustrates how such comparative survey data can be presented to provide a quick, high level picture of where the project stands relative to what has been observed on other projects.

Process scores are presented for seven areas. What each area score represents is the average of the 0 to 3 responses for a group of related questions—for example, all the questions related to coding and unit test practices. Three scores are shown for each of the areas. The heavy line at the top represents the highest score achieved (by any project that SQE has assessed). The dashed line is the average score, and the thin solid line is the score for the specific project being assessed.

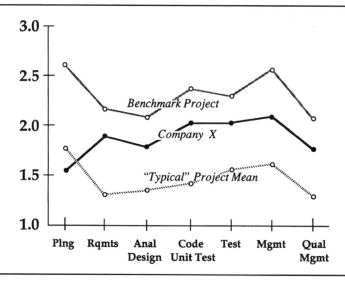

Figure 8.13.   Presenting comparative assessment data.

In the example, high (above average) scores were obtained in all areas except Planning. What a high score means is that more of the processes are in use. *It does not mean that the project is more effective or successful.* That is something that must be judged by the assessment team. The comparative picture helps the company and the team to evaluate where they stand in the use of processes and decide on priorities for improvement if needed.

A variety of other useful data may be drawn from the assessment survey. Analysis and comparison of individual practices (single questions instead of a group or area) and analysis of individual differences are common. Examples are shown in Figures 8.14 and 8.15.

Figure 8.14 displays box plots for each of the practices in the maintenance area (questions 61 to 69 on the SQE survey). We introduced box plots briefly in Chapter 2. Recall that the "box" graphically portrays the middle 50 percent of a distribution, and the line in the middle of the box is the median or 50th percentile score. These box plots show the variation in practices usage across a selected group of projects. In this case the projects are all from the medical products industry. The small boxes (practices 63, 64, and 68) indicate practices with similar usage in each of the different projects represented. Larger boxes (practices 62, 67, and 69) signify wide variation between projects. Practice 68 was the most used (median score of over 2.8), while practice 61 was little used (median score of 1.3). The dark circle in each box plot shows the score for the specific project under assessment. This provides a quick relative picture on the use of each of the individual practices and is very helpful in diagnosing specific improvement actions.

Figure 8.15 is a percentile plot showing the variation in process use between different individuals on the same project. Each of the small circles in the plot represents a single individual. This plot is *not* an unusual or extreme case. In fact it was taken from a rather excellent and well-managed project that was very successful. Note the extreme variation between the top 10 percent and bottom 10 percent. This is a pattern we see in virtually every project that we have assessed. A small number of individuals are doing (or at least reporting to be doing) nearly all of the practices on the survey, while another small group of individuals (in the

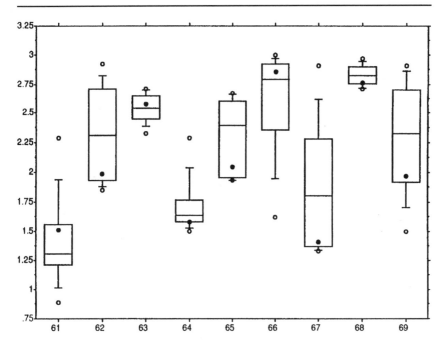

61. Design documentation is updated when changes are made during maintenance
62. Time from user call until "fix" is measured
63. Changes are implemented in priority order
64. Test cases are updated when changes are made during maintenance
65. Changes to software are implemented at scheduled intervals
66. Number of defects found after release is measured
67. Number of new defects introduced per "fix" is recorded
68. Number of open problems is tracked
69. Time to identify and correct defects is measured

Figure 8.14.   Individual practice box plots.

same project) are using just a few of them! The impact of these variations is something we are just beginning to understand. Unless you provide surveys to a broad cross-section of the project team, you can't measure it or even see it. The SQE survey approach does this and provides much more extensive information about the project practices, their variations, and how they compare to industry experience. I personally find it far superior to the SEI questionnaire in providing baseline assessment data.

We have discussed the first two steps of a typical assessment—planning and completing the baseline survey. Step 3 is an on-site visit and interviews with key project participants. No matter how thorough the survey, there is no substitute for an on-site visit by a trained review team. The on-site period need not be lengthy—a skilled and prepared team can typically complete its review in just a few days—but it is critical.

In the SEI assessment the focus of the on-site visit is on validating the project leaders' survey responses through interviews and meetings with key team members and functional area representatives. In SQE's assessment issues raised in the survey are

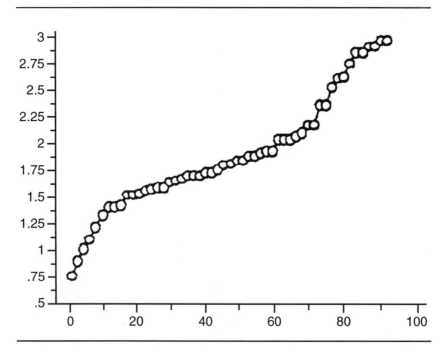

Figure 8.15.   Individual differences.

further reviewed in order to understand why certain practices are followed. Documents and deliverables are also reviewed and the project environment is profiled to understand constraints and special issues that might have had an impact.

Step 4 is an analysis of the findings from both the survey data and the on-site visit. In an SEI assessment the primary focus of the analysis is in deciding if the goals of the key process areas (KPAs) are met or satisfied for the organization. The eventual output is what is referred to in the revised model as the KPA profile (see Figure 8.16).

The profile displays the consensus finding for each key process area. A KPA can either be *Not Satisfied* (NS); *Partially Satisfied* (PS); or *Fully Satisfied* (FS). To decide that the review team first meets with the project leaders and decides on a "site" or organization answer to each of the survey questions. This is a judgment call when some projects are using a practice and others are not. Is the site answer a yes or a no? Rules for how the determination is made in that case have not been published by the SEI. The current guidelines emphasize the application of reasonable judgment and avoiding rigid rules.

The KPA is considered *Fully Satisfied* (FS) if there are no *no* questions at the site level and the team consensus is that the goals for the key process area are being met. The result is *Partially Satisfied* (PS) if there are more *yes* questions than *no* questions and *Not Satisfied* (NS) otherwise. As pointed out earlier, the maturity level is the highest level at which all KPAs up to and including that level are fully satisfied.

Analysis of findings in an SQE assessment focuses on identifying the primary strengths and weaknesses within each project. This is done jointly with the project based on the survey data as well as all the information gleaned from the on-site visit.

Step 5 of the assessment is the development of recommendations and an action plan for improvement. In the SEI case the recommendations tie directly to the underlying maturity model. The KPA profile shows which key processes are not being met. The improvement goal is always to get to the next level, so it is clear what must be addressed next. While easy to communicate and sell, I believe that this "cookie cutter" remedy approach is

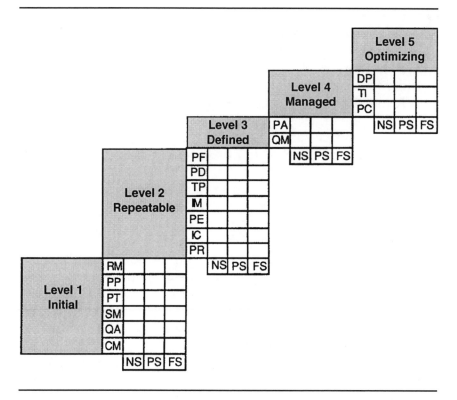

Figure 8.16. Sample KPA profile.

overly simplistic. Decisions about action plans must always address project constraints and real-world people and resource issues. Is this the right time to launch an improvement effort? Given several concern areas, which should be addressed first? Are the people available to support the required change? Is the organization ready? Such questions must be answered carefully and the action program must be tailored accordingly.

ASSESSING ASSESSMENTS

In the previous section we described the evolving and increasingly important technology of process assessments. How good is this technology and what can we say about it from' a measurement perspective? There are a number of basic questions we ought to be able to answer:

Some Questions About Assessments

1. Do "higher" assessments correlate with better, *higher quality* results?
2. Do "higher" assessments correlate with better, *more productive* results?
3. Are the assessments a "repeatable process"?
4. Do recommended changes lead to measurably more successful results when implemented?
5. Of the types of assessments described (SQE vs. SEI), which is more effective?

Unfortunately, and rather sadly, we can't answer any of these questions. No quantitative studies (even surveys) about the "accuracy" or "repeatability" of the assessment process have yet been published! We do know that most organizations view the assessment experience as positive and beneficial. They see it as helping their project to focus on process improvement and many have reported making substantial strides forward as a direct or indirect result. What we don't know is whether the maturity model is really valid and if what the assessments measure really correlates to project success. Do level 3 and 4 projects consistently produce better software than level 1 and 2 projects? This is something that could and should be measured but has not.

One of my personal soapboxes at the moment is that there should be measured justification for new technology and practices proposals. I believe that compelling measurement arguments should be required before a new practice or method is promoted and introduced. This is especially the case when the method is itself a means of measuring and evaluating other processes. Experiments and measured pilots should be the norm and validation should be expected as a routine matter, just as it is when new drugs or treatments are introduced into medicine. Why hasn't SEI correlated their assessment results with actual project results? Shouldn't we as an industry insist on knowing what the measured probabilities of success are for levels 1, 2, 3, and the few scattered 4s and 5s? Do higher levels deliver quality software on time and within budget more often? What would we think if we found out they didn't?

The previous section compared the SEI maturity model approach with SQE's industry database comparative evaluation approach. Is one "better" than the other? This, too, has sadly not been measured, but my personal bias is clear. I believe the maturity model-based assessment fares poorly as a measurement technology. After extensively measuring many projects we have found little evidence of "distinct plateaus of process capability." As I've already emphasized, we do not believe it is appropriate to extrapolate process maturity or the KPA profile across a site or a large organization. Differences in projects are extensive and should be visible, not covered up. We also believe all (or at least many) of the project participants need to be surveyed. Differences between individuals in the same project are also extensive and also need to be made visible. Most important, I am convinced that different projects achieve excellence in different ways and that a fixed model for a "good" process is inherently limiting. It is far better to use a model of goodness that is always in transition and based on what others in the industry are actually using and doing.

The good news is that as an industry we are doing much more process measurement and assessment. That has helped us focus on process improvement and led to more effective assessment approaches. The bad news is that we are not measuring how good our process measurements technologies are. This is something all of us must push for and make happen in the near future.

SUMMARY

The technology being used to measure software practices (surveys, studies, experiments, and assessments) is important and needs more attention and research.

Each of the technologies has distinct pros and cons:

Surveys have broad applicability, are easy and inexpensive to use, and excellent for measuring trends and perceptions. They are also seldom conducted "scientifically" and often biased or slanted.

Studies and experiments also have broad applicability and usually draw on "real" project data. They are time consuming and expensive, difficult to analyze and interpret, and are also often biased or slanted.

Assessments offer valuable process insight and support for process improvement but are still immature and have not themselves been measured or analyzed as to effectiveness.

All suffer from validation problems. All need better standards and discipline, more careful analysis, better peer review, better measurements of the measurements.

Our industry is not very rigorous when it comes to making process claims. We should be insisting on data that is available and accessible; independent, unbiased analysis; and a clear understanding of the criteria used for comparative "goodness."

Lots of good process comparisons have been made, and lots of poor and invalid comparisons have been made. What we publish should contain a much greater percentage of the former than it does.

Process management is fundamental to long-term, managed continuous improvement.

Bottom-up measurement engineering supports effective process measurement

CHAPTER 8 EXERCISES AND DISCUSSION POINTS

1. What does a higher "score" in Figure 8.2 mean? How might these results be validated?
2. Why is the QSM database data presented using log-log scales (Figure 8.7)? How would these plots look on regular scales?
3. Why do you suppose that the SEI assessment does not attempt to measure efficiency as part of process maturity?
4. Explain the significance of the high individual process variations found in even the best projects (see Figure 8.15). What does this say about the validity of process measurements in general?
5. List at least three reasons why SEI assessments might not be "repeatable" processes. What improvements could you suggest to overcome the potential variability?

6. Select a published experiment or study (use the bibliography in Appendix B if necessary) and critically evaluate it. Were the processes compared well defined? Were the criteria used to rank them clear and appropriate? Is the data available and accessible? Were the results analyzed by an unbiased, independent party? Summarize your findings and identify a list of questions you would like to have answered.

7. True or False—Process maturity is a prerequisite for measurement maturity. Explain.

Measuring Best Processes

"The most fundamental standard any software organization ought to heed is to base its important decisions on informed data .... If you don't collect data on your practices and measure the effort and results, then you can't meet this most basic standard."

Bill Hetzel

BENCHMARKING

Most surveys, studies, and assessments only provide *relative* comparison between various projects and processes. While it is useful to compare in relative terms, we also want to know what the best projects do—that is, we want a *benchmark value* or result to compare against. Knowing what is *best*, we can better gauge how far away we are and more efficiently plan or prioritize what we need to improve.

Benchmark values can be determined by two methods. One approach is statistical in nature. If we sample enough projects across a broad population spectrum, the "best" values (at least for practical engineering purposes) can be taken as the "top" percentile scores observed. (Indeed that is the approach of the historical database case studies discussed in the last chapter.) Alternately, we can choose a special population that we "decide" is representative of the "best" and measure only those—the limiting case being measuring just the one truly best project if only we knew how to identify it beforehand!

As an example, suppose we are seeking a benchmark value for height. We could approach the task by sampling a large number of people and finding the tallest among them. We could also isolate a much smaller group of individuals by publicizing our search and inviting anyone over seven feet tall to nominate themselves. Both approaches will produce reasonable benchmarks, but the second requires far fewer subjects to be analyzed, and in most cases is our only viable approach for software process benchmarking.

Many companies have established benchmark efforts. Often these are fairly informal—a small group of organizations is selected on the basis of perceived "excellence" in some process area or activity of interest. Exchange visits are arranged to visit these organizations and examine (measure) an area of interest. The benchmarking organization uses the data to identify improvements it can make to its own processes and is able to set realistic targets and criteria that its own people must strive for.

Benchmarks can also be obtained through the help of various third-party organizations that collect and distribute shared data. Use of an appropriate third party allows proprietary data to be shared while still providing confidentiality of the source.

Two years ago I had the privilege of leading a large-scale benchmarking study aimed at measuring the "best" software practices and gaining a better understanding of the role of measurement in software. The study derived from a joint initiative between Xerox and Software Quality Engineering. SQE had been seeking "centers of excellence" in various software practices for some time. Clients and students commonly asked questions like, "Who does the best job?," "Do companies really do the things that you are teaching?," "What do the best projects look like and how can I get my project to be one?" Xerox Corporation in El Segundo, California was looking for similar objective data they could use to compare themselves to the "best" companies and be able to set realistic internal goals.

After a series of planning discussions, a decision was made to pursue a joint study that was initiated in April 1990. The basic design consisted of a two-phase effort—an initial industry-wide survey to provide a preliminary assessment of typical practices and measures, and a second, more detailed survey to be given to participants in a small number of selected "best" projects. The intent was to seek out projects representative of the "best" software engineering work being performed and analyze those in detail to better understand them and establish meaningful industry performance benchmarks.

The key to the study was how to define "best." Depending on your viewpoint, a "best project" can mean many things (see Figure 9.1).

The approach taken was to use an initial survey to identify organizations using "more" of what industry generally considers to be "good" or "recommended" practices and then to invite those organizations to nominate their "best" project themselves. The three primary criteria in Figure 9.2 were provided.

Perception by the company as being representative of best engineering practices and high-quality results (budget, schedule, and project quality) was critical. To summarize, a small

---

Software Practitioner

". . . most fun and rewarding project I've ever worked on."

Software Project Manager

". . . ahead of schedule and budget with little or no frustration."

Project or Marketing Manager

". . . the top-selling product we've ever put out. Made more money than any other."

User or Customer

". . . the easiest to use, most functional software we've ever received."

Support Organization

". . . the least number of field problems and lowest support cost ever."

Figure 9.1. Varying perspectives on what "best" might mean.

1. Perceived as using the best practices and strong measurement—what you would wish all your projects to be like.

2. Perceived as producing high-quality results—a project the team and the user are proud of.

3. Implemented recently or in final test (so that the project team could be interviewed and some field experience was available to be able to assess quality.)

Figure 9.2.   Selection criteria for "best" projects.

group of companies were selected as candidates for participation in the study, and each of them chose a recent project (in a few cases, two projects) that they considered to be their best. A total of 10 "best" projects were selected and analyzed to obtain the benchmark data. Figure 9.3 summarizes the project size (KLOC and effort) characteristics.

The projects are all rather large-scale development efforts with generally moderate to high complexity and criticality. Project size (peak staffing) ranged from a low of 15 to 250. Durations (elapsed months) were generally a year or more, and in two cases exceeded two years. Code size delivered ranged from 88 to 1100 KLOC, and cost ranged from just under a million to over 15 million. Six of the projects involved software projects built for sale to the public marketplace; the other four were for internal business use. In total, the projects represent over ten thousand engineering months of effort and an expense of almost $80 million. Total code delivered was almost 3 million lines of code.

I believe that the projects were representative examples of outstanding, large-scale software engineering work. They were drawn from seven companies (GTE, AT&T, IBM, NCR, DuPont, Siemans, and Xerox), and each company made a concerted effort to put forward their "best" example. In several instances this was achieved through an internal competition. The IBM project was the AS400 development which had been selected for nomination for the Baldridge award and was subsequently chosen as a winner. Are these the best examples available anywhere? Almost

Proj	Application Type	Duration (months)	Effort (months)	Peak Staffing	Lines* (KLOC)	Cost* (Millions)
A	Financial Mgmt	9	86	15	140	.8
B	Customer Billing	27	2880	200	1100	15.0
C	Resource Mgmt	27	1560	26	250	15.3
D	Patient Monitoring	21	456	14	206	3.8
E	Network Mgmt	8	300	48	120	3.2
F	Operating System	16	800	63	100	5.0
G	Financial Mgmt	20	330	21	88	2.9
H	Operating System	23	3000	250	500	21.0
I	Network Mgmt	11	530	51	164	5.1
J	Operating System	16	570	89	200	5.9
	Totals	178	10512	777	2868	78.0

Figure 9.3.   Benchmark study project characteristics.[1]

certainly there are some better ones, but I am convinced these offer a meaningful benchmark for comparison.

Each of the 10 projects was "assessed" using SQE's process assessment methodology as described in the previous chapter. This included administering surveys to all of the project participants as well as on-site team interviews and visits to validate the survey data and understand why or how certain practices were employed. A Project Profile document providing project background, a description of the software processes in use, the survey data, and the review team observations was then completed for each project as a baseline record of the project practices.

---

[1]*Note:* Effort, cost, and KLOC figures in Figure 9.3 should be interpreted with some caution. The participating companies do not measure costs or even lines of code and effort in a uniform way. An attempt was made to normalize these numbers as accurately as possible for comparison purposes, but subtle differences remain and would alter the figures somewhat for a true "apples to apples" comparison.

BENCHMARK STUDY FINDINGS

An enormous amount of data was collected. What did we learn from the benchmark study? A special focus of the study related to measurement practices. Measures and measurement related practices found in common in the best projects are highlighted in Figure 9.4.

The use of measurement for both status and quality information is relied upon substantially in the best projects. In healthy projects, hundreds of small corrective actions are made every day, every week, and every month—all based on a large and diverse set of facts and understandings. Supporting this base of information is the job of the measurement infrastructure and process. *Good measurement was viewed as an essential element and prerequisite to effective engineering and software management.* Its role as an enabler to support practitioners and managers was recognized as a critical success factor in nearly all of the projects.

The best projects took the time at the beginning to prepare detailed plans and then used measurement from start to finish to track performance and assess task completion and effectiveness. All three measurement engineering building block systems were

Common Measures	*Common Measurement Related Practices*
Test defects	Past history is used to set schedules
Defects after release	Quality targets established in project plans
Open problems	Quality criteria required to be met at each phase
Open issues	Acceptance criteria clear and formally defined
Schedule performance	Quality measurement information fed back to
Plan and schedule changes	development
Test results	Defects traced back to requirements and code
Reliability	Design features traced to requirements and code
Time fixing problems	Tests traced to requirements
Defects from fixes	
Lines of code	
Process compliance	

Figure 9.4.   Measurement practices in best projects.

highly developed and effective. Resource Tracking, Work Product Tracking, and Problem Tracking had evolved over time and supported the basic IOR measurements that have been stressed throughout this book. This ensured management was aware of detailed project status and issues. These in turn were monitored and measured until resolved. There is nothing miraculous or magical about this formula for success, and it suggests that the measures of importance are basic but also undergoing constant evolution.

Key process characteristics found in common in the best projects are summarized in Figure 9.5.

Having led the study, I came away with a renewed apprecia-

---

1. Best projects make extensive use of nearly all of the surveyed practices and measures. Only a few of the practices were seldom used.

2. No one project was superior in all areas. The best projects excel in "different" ways and emphasize different techniques and phases of the life cycle.

3. Strong measurement and tracking of project status was evident in every project. The measurement of status to support management appears as a natural by-product of the good planning work and is a critical success factor.

4. Best projects emphasized quality control with regular reviews and inspections and very strong and independent high-level testing.

5. Industry's best projects are characterized by strong up-front planning (to define tasks and schedules) and close, careful tracking and reporting of status on an ongoing basis. A common theme is strong planning and control.

6. Best projects do not necessarily have state-of-the-art methodologies or extensive automation and tooling. They do rely on basic principles such as strong team work, project communication, and project controls. Good organization and management appears to be far more of a critical success factor than technology or methodology.

Figure 9.5. Best projects characterization.

tion for the importance of getting the basics right. Methods and practices are important and provide added insurance in the long run. However, no single practice is essential. The critical success factors are more primitive—good people, good management, good communications, good controls. Start off by taking whatever it takes to get well organized. Clearly define and specify the software to be built by breaking it up into manageable pieces and defining each in detail. Emphasize peer reviews and internal communications, and keep day-to-day status on everything that is done and all the issues and problems that arise. Then test the pieces and the parts and the whole in every way imaginable and make sure that changes and fixes and defects are rigorously tracked and retested. All of this is basic project management—but it is also the anatomy of best projects, and it works!

If there was one high-level finding that stood out, it is that *best projects get to be best based on fundamentals*. All of us know the fundamentals for good software—the difference is that most projects don't do them nearly so well and then get into trouble because they can't "see" the problems and don't have a good baseline!

I also learned again how hard it is to define and measure what "best" really means. In the study we compared projects by looking at the practices in use. We found strong bottom-up measurement engineering processes and support systems. But we also learned that "best" is much more than a checklist of good practices and techniques. The key to success lies in better understanding and management control over all project activities. For those who strive to be the best, our advice is to focus on the basic management, control, and measurement processes. The emphasis on methodology and technology that most of us pursue is important, but only after the fundamentals are solidly in place. We might like to conclude that the practices and technologies are the magic answer. They do provide insurance and are nice to have, but the truth is that these are never the silver bullet.

What did the managers of these projects feel were the reasons their projects were so successful? We asked each manager to identify practices of special value that in his or her opinion played a critical role in project success. Here are some of their responses:

"We keep the entire team aware of the big picture by having regular weekly meetings with everyone together."

"Each requirement was analyzed in detail to produce "work items," which were then assigned to individual contributors and tracked every week until completion."

"Requirements specifications were worked out in excruciating detail and reviewed extensively."

"Weekly program reviews to track progress against the plan, to identify exceptions and issues and assign actions and owners."

"Define key tasks within the project in detail, staff those tasks, and give the individuals the authority and support to execute them."

"Tracking of actual accomplishments is planned closely and regularly."

"Used structured techniques for thorough analysis and design that enabled us to communicate what we wanted to build easily to others."

"We make extensive use of electronic mail communications and have excellent interproject sharing of information."

"Project plans and stress on sharing dependencies—basic management stuff."

"A firm commitment to the "Quality Fanatic" concept with encouragement to the entire team to put quality first."

"Early prototypes with baseline software from each subsystem. This allowed us to examine design and performance issues and get feedback from customers, marketing and management."

"Testing, testing, and more testing. Thorough and intensive system level functional and stress testing conducted by the test group."

"Define in precise terms the expected operational profile and then build a test bed that simulates the profile and allows the developing system to be tested and measured in terms of performance and reliability."

"Very detailed and thorough review" of the requirements specs and high-level designs to remove all ambiguities and identify essential design goals and issues."

"The development process with tracking and formal reviews"

Common themes that stand out in these observations are strong planning, front-end definition, measurement, reviews and testing. Again, the point to emphasize is that the keys to success did not lie in high technology, fancy methods, advanced techniques or leading edge tools. The silver bullet (if there was such a thing) was good, fundamentally sound, project management and control from the outset.

PERSPECTIVE

Several other studies that sought to find out how the "best" organizations perform and better understand what it takes for successful measurement efforts have been completed recently. One example was a study conducted by Stan Rifkin and Charles Cox as a part of SEI's measurement project. [Rifken 1991] Eleven organizations were selected based on their "reputation" and personal knowledge of the researchers as being "leaders" in software measurement and having effective and successful software measurement programs in place. These organizations were visited and interviewed to identify the key factors they had in common that explained their success. Eight factors are highlighted in the report as having special importance (see Figure 9.6).

Most of these factors have been emphasized throughout this book as fundamental basics of bottom-up measurement engineering. Vision, definition, automated recording and reporting, and involvement of practitioners and managers have been reinforced over and over again.

The cultural and behavioral issues such as keeping data private and a nonjudgmental approach to quality problems have probably not been emphasized enough. The Measurement in Practice Report correctly focuses on these areas as critical to attend to. Reflecting on that key point, I remembered the following quote

1. Clear vision for how measures will be used
2. Rigorous definition
3. Automated data recording and reporting
4. Participation of stakeholders in implementation
5. Anonymity of data (each sees own data, averages of other data)
6. Training (users and implementors)
7. Motivation of managers to use measures
8. Decriminalization of problems

Figure 9.6.   Factors for successful measurement efforts.

from another study of the problems and challenges in setting up effective measurement efforts. [Spencer 1992]

> "What are you going to do with this stuff? You're going to hurt me. I can't control it, and if I can't control it, and you're going to measure my performance by it, I'm suspicious of it and I don't want to do it. I don't want to be measured."

The quote should emphasize for all of us how careful we have to be in implementing our measurement programs to be sensitive to people's needs, feelings, and uncertainties. This is just one of the major lessons learned by those who have been on the firing line and helped their companies achieve strong measurement efforts. Some other lessons taken from the same study that the quote came from are listed for us in Figure 9.7.

We agree wholeheartedly with all of these lessons learned, except for "driving it from the top." This book has emphasized that effective measurement engineering is dependent on the building block systems and really drives from the bottom. Management support and direction is important, but the trick is to get management to realize that good measurement is built on good engineering.

Programs built from the bottom up have continuity and staying power. They don't fall apart when a key manager leaves or gets promoted, or suffer fatal setbacks because an organiza-

1. Be committed for the long haul.
2. Drive it from the top.
3. Hire a vendor.
4. Formulate goals and objectives.
5. Secure buy in.
6. Appoint full-time resources.
7. Focus on relevance.
8. Start small and think big.
9. Educate everyone at every opportunity you have.
10. Provide feedback as soon as possible.
11. Be prepared to market and sell.
12. Persevere.
13. TRUST is everything. It must be earned and it will immediately be taken away if your customers suspect you are misusing their information

Figure 9.7. Some lessons learned [Spencer 92].

tion has been decentralized or reorganized. I have sadly (and rather helplessly) watched a number of established top-down measurement programs deteriorate when they lost continuity of management.

When a key manager changes, the new one brings different views, different directions, and different priorities. This is usually very disruptive to the metrics program and takes a lot of perseverance to get over. Some programs never recovered.

The whole idea of measurement engineering is to integrate the measurements with the engineering and technical work efforts. That insulates the program from management shifts and gives it staying power. A number of students in my measurement course have remarked that measurement programs are not all that hard to start. What is difficult is to nurture and sustain them! As Tom Gilb has observed, "Anything can be measured." We've learned throughout the book that what *should* be measured are the Inputs, Outputs, and Results of all software engineering work products. That in itself remains a tall challenge but one we hope we've made easier.

CHAPTER 9 EXERCISES AND DISCUSSION POINTS

1. What criteria would you suggest using in order to characterize a technique or activity as a "best" practice? (You may assume you have the benefit of hindsight.)
2. What criteria would you suggest using in order to characterize a project as a "best" project? (Again, you may assume you have the benefit of hindsight.)
3. Describe how you might evaluate an existing measurement program to assess its success. Assume you are given just a day or two to visit. What would you ask to see or look at? What criteria would you use?
4. True or False—Best projects are best because of the people assigned to them. Defend your position.
5. Explain the relationship between productivity and quality.
6. List a minimum set of I, O and R measures that you would recommend every organization collect, regardless of their process maturity or tools, techniques and expertise baseline.
7. Debate the central proposition of this book that measurement programs must be engineered in, bottom-up for long-term success.
8. Would it ever be appropriate to use measurement data to assess individual performance? Why or why not?
9. What role does (should) management play in shaping and directing measurement efforts?
10. What in your view are the most important questions (issues) we ought to be able to answer with measured data? Which of these is your company answering?

Appendices

The appendices contain reference information for the reader interested in further study. There are three separate appendices—A, B, and C.

A SOFTWARE MEASUREMENT BIBLIOGRAPHY

A list of several hundred sources that are either cited in the book or provide supplemental and background material for the topics and material covered. The list is in alphabetical order by the primary author's last name and in reverse chronological order in the case of multiple entries by the same author. References to this bibliography are made in the text by enclosing the author's last name and the year of publication in brackets. References published more than 10 years ago were generally excluded unless considered of significant value or not covered by more recent entries.

B ANNOTATED BIBLIOGRAPHY OF SELECTED PUBLICATIONS

A more selective list of key publications and reference resources viewed as especially significant and highly recommended for supplemental reading or study. The list is grouped by topical category, and each entry is annotated with a brief descriptive synopsis to help the reader locate or select further information on a topic or area of special interest. Anyone building their own library or wishing to obtain a deeper understanding of the rapidly growing and changing software measurement field should find the list helpful.

Most of the publications listed in this appendix may be obtained through SingleSource™, SQE's mail order service. SingleSource™ publishes an annual catalog including a listing of the 99 Best Software Engineering Books. They then contract with the publishers as a direct mail-order outlet to make the selections available. To obtain a free copy of the current catalog, or to order a book or special publication, call 800-423-8369.

C SOFTWARE MEASUREMENT TOOLS AND SERVICES

A list of major vendors offering measurement tools and services. The list is in alphabetical order by vendor name and includes contact information for the vendor along with a brief synopsis of what that vendor offers.

Software Measurement Bibliography

This section contains a traditional bibliography organized alphabetically by primary author. References published more than 10 years ago were generally excluded unless viewed as having significant value or not covered by more recent entries. Multiple entries for the same author are listed in reverse chronological order (newest reference first). References in the book are cross-referenced to this listing by enclosing the author's last name and the year of the publication in square brackets. As an example [Adams 84] would be a reference to the first entry in the list. A hyphen and a number after the year is used when there are multiple entries by the same author. For example [Basili 87-2] refers to the second Basili reference listed.

ALPHABETICAL LISTING BY AUTHOR

Adams, E., Optimizing Preventive Service of Software Products, *IBM Journal of Research & Development*, Vol. 28, No. 1, 1984, pp. 2–14.

Air Force Systems Command, Software Management Indicators, AFSCP 800-43, January 1986.

Air Force Systems Command, Software Quality Indicators, AFSCP 800-14, January 1987.

Albrecht, A.J., and Gaffney, J.E., Software Function, Source Lines of Code, and Development Effort Prediction: A Software Science Validation, *IEEE Trans. Software Engineering*, Vol. SE-9, No. 6 (November 1983), pp. 639–648.

Albrecht, A.J., Measuring Application Development Productivity, Proceedings of Joint SHARE/GUIDE Meeting, 1979, pp. 83–92.

Andersen, O., The Use of Software Engineering Data in Support of Project Manaement, *Software Engineering Journal*, November 1990, pp. 350–356.

Arthur, L.J., *Measuring Programmer Productivity and Software Quality*, John Wiley, 1985.

Arthur, L.J., *Programmer Productivity: Myths, Methods, and Murphology*, John Wiley, 1983.

Bache, R., and Neill, M., Validating Technologies for Software Certification, Proceedings Conf on Approving Software Products, Garmisch, W. Germany, 1990.

Bache, R., and Tinker, R., A Rigorous Approach to Metrication: A Field Trial Using KINDRA, *IEEE Trans. Software Engineering*, 1988, pp. 28–32.

Basili, V., and Rombach, H.D., TAME: Integrating Measurement into Software Environments, University of Maryland Computer Science Dept. TR-1764, 1987.

Basili, V.R., and Selby, R.W., Comparing the Effectiveness of Software Testing Strategies, *IEEE Trans. Software Engineering*, Vol. SE-13, No. 12 (December 1987), pp. 1278–1296.

Basili, V.R., Selby, R.W., and Hutchens, D.H., Experimentation in Software Engineering, *IEEE Trans. Software Engineering*, Vol. SE-12, No. 7, 1986, pp. 733–743.

Basili, V., and Weiss, D.M., A Methodology for Collecting Valid Software Engineering Data, *IEEE Trans. Software Engineering*, Vol. SE-10, No. 6 (November 1984), pp. 728–738.

Basili, V., and Weiss, D.M., Evaluation of a Software Requirements Document by Analysis of Change Data, *Proceedings Fifth Int. Conf. on Software Engineering*, New York: IEEE Computer Society, 1981, pp. 314–323.

Beane, J., Giddings, N., and Silverman, J., Quantifying Software Designs, *Proceedings 7th Intl. Conf. Software Engineering*, Washington, D.C.: IEEE Computer Society, 1984.

Behrens, C.A., Measuring the Productivity of Computer Systems Development Activities with Function Points, *IEEE Trans. Software Engineering*, SE-9, No. 6 (November 1983), pp. 648–652.

Bennatan, E.M., *On Time, Within Budget: Software Project Management Practices and Techniques*, QED, 1992.

Berns, G.M., Assessing Software Maintainability, *Communications of the ACM*, Vol. 27, No. 1, January 1984.

Betteridge, R., Fisher, D., and Goodman, P., Function Points vs. Lines of Code, *Systems Development*, August 1990.

Boehm, B.W., Improving Software Productivity, *Computer*, Vol. 20, No. 9 (September 1987), pp. 43–57.

Boehm, B.W., Industrial Metrics Top 10 List, *IEEE Software* (September 1987), pp. 84–85.

Boehm, B.W., Prototyping vs. Specifying: A Multi-Project Experiment, *IEEE Trans. Software Engineering*, May 1984, pp. 133–145.

Boehm, B.W., *Software Engineering Economics*, Prentice Hall, 1981.

Bollinger, T., and McGowan, C., A Critical Look at Software Capability Evaluations, *IEEE Software*, July 1991, pp. 25–41.

Bowen, T.P., Wigle, G.B., and Tsai, J.T., Specification of Software Quality Attributes, RADCTR-85-37 (three volumes), February 1985.

Bredero, R., Caracoglia, G., Jaggers, C., Kok, P., Tat, G., and Verner, J., Comparative Evaluation of Existing Cost Estimation Tools, MERMAID Report D7.1Y, 1989.

Brooks, F., *The Mythical Man Month*, Reading, MA: Addison-Wesley, 1975.

Buck, R.D., and Robbins, J.H., Application of Software Inspection Methodology in Design and Code, in *Software Validation* (Ed. H.L. Hausen), Elsevier Science, 1984, pp. 41–56.

Bush, M., and Fenton, N.E., Software Measurement: A Conceptual Framework, *Journal of Systems and Software*, Vol. 12 (July 1990), pp. 223–231.

Camp, R.C., *Benchmarking: The Search for Industry Best Practices That Lead to Superior Performance*, ASQC Quality Press, 1989.

Card, D.N., and Glass, R.L., *Measuring Software Design Quality*, Prentice Hall, 1990.

Carsana, L., Lancellotti, R., and Maiocchi, M., Software Metrics Measurement and Interpretation, Proc. EUROMETRICS '91, Paris, March 1991.

Cerino, D.A., Software Quality Measurement Tools and Techniques, Proceedings COMPSAC86, Washington, D.C.: IEEE Computer Society, Oct. 1986, pp. 160–167.

Collofello, J.S., and Buck, J.J., Software Quality Assurance for Maintenance, *IEEE Software*, September 1987, pp. 46–51.

Conte, S.D., and Dunsmore, H.E., *Software Engineering Metrics and Models*, Benjamin Cummings, 1986.

Cook, M., Software Metrics: An Introduction and Annotated Bibliography, ACM SIGSOFT Software Engineering Notes, Vol. 7, No. 2, 1982, pp. 41–60.

Coupal, D., and Robillard, P.N., Factor Analysis of Source Code Metrics, *Journal of Systems Software*, 1990, pp. 263–269.

Courger, J., and Colter, M.A., Maintenance Programming: Improved Productivity Through Motivation, Prentice Hall, 1985.

Curtis, B., Fifteen Years of Psychology in Software Engineering: Individual Differences and Cognitive Science, IEEE Proc. 8th Intl. Conf. on Software Engineering, London, August 1985, pp. 97–106.

Davis, J.S., Identification of Errors in Software Requirements Through Use of Automated Requirements Tools, Information, and Software Technology, 1989, pp. 472–476.

Davis, J.S., Investigation of Predictors of Failures and Debugging Effort for Large MIS, Information and Software Technology, Vol. 31, No. 4 (May 1989), pp. 170–174.

DeMarco, T., *Controlling Software Projects: Management, Measurement and Estimation*, Prentice Hall, 1982.

DeMarco, T., and Lister, T., *Peopleware*, Dorset House, 1987.

Dobbins, J.H., *Software Quality Assurance and Evaluation*, ASQC Quality Press, 1990.

Dreger, J.B., *Function Point Analysis*, Prentice Hall, 1989.

Drummond, S., Measuring Applications Development Performance, Datamation, Vol. 31, 1985, pp. 102–108.

Dyer, M., *The Cleanroom Approach to Quality Software Development*, John Wiley, 1992.

Ejiogu, L.O., *Software Engineering with Formal Metrics*, QED, 1991.

Evangelist, W.M., Complete Solution to the Software Measurement Problem, *IEEE Software*, January 1988, pp. 83–84.

Federal Software Management Support Center, Parallel Test and Evaluation of a Cobol Restructuring Tool, Office of Software Development and Information Technology Report, Falls Church, VA, September 1987.

Fenick, S., Implementing Management Metrics: An Army Program, *IEEE Software*, March 1990, pp. 65–72.

Fenton, N.E., *Software Metrics—A Rigorous Approach*, Van Nostrand Reinhold, 1991.

Fenton, N.E., Software Measurement: Theory, Tools and Validation, *Software Engineering Journal*, Vol. 5, No. 1, 1990, pp. 65–78.

Ferrari, D., Considerations on the Insularity of Performance Evaluation, *IEEE Trans. Software Engineering*, SE-12, No. 6 (June 1986), pp. 678–683.

Fetzer, J.H., Program Verification: The Very Idea, *CACM*, Vol. 31, No. 9, 1988, pp. 1048–1063.

Finkelstein, L., What Is Not Measurable, Make Measurable, *Measurement and Control*, Vol. 15, 1982, pp. 25–32.

Fitzsimmons, A., and Love, T., A Review and Evaluation of Software Science, *Computing Surveys*, Vol. 10, No. 1 (March 1978), pp. 3–18.

Freedman, D., and Weinberg, G.M., *Handbook of Walkthroughs, Inspections and Technical Reviews*, Dorset House, 1982.

Gibson, V.R., and Senn, J.A., System Structure and Software Maintenance Performance, *CACM*, Vol. 32, No. 3, 1989, pp. 347–358.

Gilb, T., *Principles of Software Engineering Management*, Reading, MA: Addison-Wesley, 1987.

Gilb, T., *Software Metrics*, Cambridge, MA: Winthrop, 1976.

Grady, R.B., *Practical Software Metrics for Project Management & Process Improvement*, Prentice Hall, 1992.

Grady, R.B., Dissecting Software Failures, *Hewlett-Packard Journal*, April 1989, pp. 57–63.

Grady, R.B., Measuring and Managing Software Maintenance, *IEEE Software*, September 1987, pp. 35–45.

Grady, R.B., and Caswell, D.L., *Software Metrics: Establishing a Company-Wide Program*, Prentice Hall, 1987.

Halstead, M., *Elements of Software Science*, Elsevier-North Holland, 1977.

Harrison, W.A., Software Complexity Metrics: A Bibliography and Category Index, SIGPLAN Notices, Vol. 19, No. 2, 1984, pp. 17–27.

Harrison, W., Magel, K., Kluczny, R., and DeKock, A., Applying Software Complexity Metrics to Software Maintenance., *Computer*, Vol. 15, No. 9 (September 1982).

Heitkoetter, U., Helling, B., Nolte, H., and Kelly, M., Design Metrics and Aids to Their Automatic Collection, *Information and Software Technology*, Vol. 32, No. 1, 1990, pp. 79–87.

Hetzel, B., *The Complete Guide to Software Testing*, QED, 1988.

Hetzel, B., and Craig, R., Software Measures and Practices Benchmark Study, Software Quality Engineering Technical Reports TR 900 through TR 904, June 1991.

Huff, D., and Geis, I., *How to Lie With Statistics*, New York: W.W. Norton, 1954.

Hollocker, C.P., *Software Reviews and Audits Handbook*, John Wiley, 1990.

Humphrey, W.S., *Managing the Software Process*, Reading, MA: Addison-Wesley, 1989.

Humphrey, W.S., and Sweet, W.L., A Method for Assessing the Software Engineering Capability of Contractors, Tech. Report CMU/SEI-87-TR-23, Software Engineering Institute, September 1987.

Ince, D., Software Metrics: Introduction, *Information and Software Technology*, Vol. 32, No. 4, May 1990, pp. 297–301.

Jain, R., *Art of Computer Systems Performance Analysis*, John Wiley, 1991.

Jeffery, D.R., and Low, G., Generic Estimation Tools in Management of Software Development, *Software Engineering Journal*, Vol. 5, No. 4, 1990.

Jensen, H.A., An Experimental Study of Software Metrics for Real Time Software, *IEEE Trans. Software Engineering*, SE-11 No. 2, 1985, pp. 231–234.

Jones, C., *Applied Software Measurement: Assuring Productivity and Quality*, McGraw Hill, 1991

Jones, C., *Programming Productivity*. McGraw Hill, 1986.

Jones, K., *Automated Software Quality Measurement*, Van Nostrand Reinhold, 1993.

Kafura, D., and Henry, S., Software Quality Metrics Based on Inter-connectivity, *Journal of Systems and Software*, Vol. 2, No. 2 (June 1981), pp. 121–131.

Kafura, D., and Canning, J., A Validation of Software Metrics Using Many Metrics and Two Resources, Proceedings 8th Intl. Conf. on Software Engineering, London, IEEE Computer Society, 1985, pp. 378–385.

Kafura, D., and Reddy, G.R., The Use of Software Complexity Metrics in Software Maintenance, *IEEE Trans. Software Engineering*, SE-13, No. 3 (March 1987), pp. 335–343.

Kan, S.H., Determining Phase Effectiveness of the AS/400 Development Process, Proc. 1st Intl. Conf. on Applications of Software Measurement (ASM'90), San Diego, November 1990.

Kemerer, C.F., An Empirical Validation of Software Cost Estimation Models, *Communications of the ACM* 30, No. 5 (May 1987), pp. 416–429.

Kitchenham, B.A., and Linkman, S.J., Design Metrics in Practice, *Information and Software Technology*, Vol. 32, No. 4, May 1990, pp. 304–309.

Kitchenham, B.A., and Taylor, N.R., Software Project Development Cost Estimation, *Journal of Systems Software*, Vol. 5, 1985.

Knafl, G.J., and Sacks, J., Software Development Effort Prediction Based on Function Points, Proceedings COMPSAC86, Washington, D.C.: IEEE Computer Society, October 1986, pp. 319–325.

Knight, J.C., and Leveson, N.G., An Empirical Study of Failure Probabilities in Multi-Version Software, Proc Intl. Symposium on Fault Tolerant Computing, IEEE Press, 1986.

Kusters, R.J., VanGenuchten, M.J., and Heemstra, F.J., Are Software Cost Estimation Models Accurate?, *Information and Software Technology*, Vol. 32, No. 3 (April 1990), pp. 187–190.

Landsbaum, J., and Glass, R.L., *Measuring and Motivating Mantenance Programmers*, Prentice Hall 1992.

Lauterbach, L., and Randell, W., Six Test Techniques Compared: The Test Process and Product, Proc of the NSIA Joint Conf. and Tutorial on Software Quality and Productivity, Washington, D.C., 1989.

Leintz, B.P., and Swanson, E.B., *Software Maintenance Management*, Reading, MA: Addison-Wesley, 1980.

Levitin, A.W., How to Measure Software Size, and How Not To, Proceedings COMPSAC86, Washington, D.C.: IEEE Computer Society, October 1986, pp. 314–318.

Li, H.F., and Cheung, W.K., An Empirical Study of Software Metrics, *IEEE Trans. Software Engineering*, SE-13, No. 6 (June 1987), pp. 697–708.

Lientz, B.P., and Swanson, E.B., *Software Maintenance Management*, Reading, MA: Addison-Wesley, 1980.

Lind, R.K., and Vairavan, K., An Experimental Investigation of Software Metrics and Their Relationship to Software Development Effort, *IEEE Trans. Software Engineering*, Vol. 15, No. 5 (May 1989), pp. 649–653.

Lister, A.M., Software Science—The Emperor's New Clothes?, *Australian Computer Journal*, Vol. 14, No. 2 (May 1982), pp. 66–70.

Lohse, J.B., and Zweben, S.H., Experimental Evaluation of Software Design Principles: An Investigation into the Effect of Module Coupling on System and Modifiability, *Journal Systems and Software*, Vol. 4, 1984, pp. 301–308.

Londeix, B., *Cost Estimation for Software Development*, Reading, MA: Addison-Wesley, 1988.

McCabe, J.J., and Butler, C.W., Design Complexity Measurement and Testing, *Communications of the ACM*, Vol. 32, No. 12, December 1989, pp. 1415–1424.

Mohanty, S.N., Software Cost Estimation: Present and Future, *Software Practice and Experience*, Vol. 11, No. 2 (February 1981), pp. 103–121.

Moller, K.H., and Paulish, D.J., *Software Metrics: A Practitioner's Guide to Improved Product Development*, IEEE Press and Chapman & Hall, 1993.

Murine, G.E., Integrating Software Quality Metrics with Software QA, *Quality Progress*, November 1988, pp. 38–43.

Musa, J.D., Iannino, A., and Okumoto, K., Software Reliability: Measurement, Prediction, Application, 1987.

Peercy, D.E., A Software Maintainability Evaluation Methodology, *IEEE Trans. Software Engineering*, Vol. SE-7, No. 4, July 1981, pp. 343–351.

Perlis, A., Sayword, F., and Shaw, M., *Software Metrics: An Analysis and Evaluation*, Cambridge, Mass.: MIT Press, 1981.

Perry, W.E., Measurement of the Customer's View of Information Systems Quality Characteristics, Quality Assurance Institute Research Report, 1989.

Peschel, A.H., Project Metrics and Corrective Action System Improvement, Proceedings 6th NSIA Joint Conference on Software Quality and Productivity, April 1990.

Putnam, L.H., and Myers, W., *Measures for Excellence: Reliable Software on Time, Within Budget*, Yourdon Press, 1992.

Putnam, L.H., Trends in Measurement, Estimation, and Control, *IEEE Software*, March 1991, pp. 105–107.

Putnam, L.H., and Wolverton, R.W., Quantitative Management: Software Cost Estimating, New York: IEEE Computer Society, 1977.

Rambo, R., Buckley, P., and Branyan, E., Establishment and Validation of Software Metric Factors, Proceedings of 7th Intl. Conf of Society of Parametric Analysts, May 1985, pp. 406–417.

Rifkin, S., and Cox, C., Measurement in Practice, Technical Report CMU/SEI-91-TR-16, Software Engineering Institute, July 1991.

Rook, P. (Editor), *Software Reliability Handbook*, Elsevier North Holland, 1990.

Rombach, H.D., A Controlled Experiment on the Impact of Software Structure on Maintainability, *IEEE Trans. Software Engineering*, SE-13, No. 3 (March 1987), pp. 344–354.

Ross, N., Using Metrics in Quality Management, *IEEE Software*, July 1990, pp. 80–85.

Rubin, H., *Software Engineer's Benchmark Handbook*, Applied Computer Research, 1992.

Rubin, H.A., A Comparison of Software Cost Estimation Tools, *System Development*, Vol. 17, No. 5 (May 1987), pp. 1–3.

Sackman, H., *Man Computer Problem Solving: Experimental Evaluation of Time Sharing and Batch Processing*, Princeton, NJ: Auerbach, 1970.

Schulmeyer, G.G., and McManus, J. (Editors), *Handbook of Software Quality Assurance*, Van Nostrand Reinhold, 1987.

Selby, R.W., Extensible Integration Frameworks for Measurement, *IEEE Software*, QualityTime, November 1990.

Selby, R.W., Basili, V.R., and Baker, F.T., Cleanroom Software Development: An Empirical Evaluation, *IEEE Trans. Software Engineering*, September 1987, pp. 1027–1037.

Shen, V.Y., Yu, T.J., Thebault, M., and Paulsen, L.R., Identifying Error-Prone Software—An Empirical Study, *IEEE Trans. Software Engineering*, SE-11, No. 4 (April 1985), pp. 317–324.

Sheppard, M.J., *Software Engineering Metrics*, McGraw Hill, 1992.

Sheppard, M.J., A Critique of Cyclomatic Complexity as a Software Metric, *Software Engineering Journal*, Vol. 3, No. 2, 1988, pp. 30–36.

Sheppard, M.J., and Ince, D.C., The Use of Metrics in the Early Detection of Design Errors, Proc. Software Engineering 90, 1990, pp. 67–85.

Shooman, M.L., *Software Engineering: Reliability, Development and Management*, McGraw Hill, 1983.

Siefert, D.M., Implementing Software Reliability Measures, *Quality Data Processing*, January 1990, pp. 12–21.

Silver, W., An Interview with Nathan Lowell, *Software Quality World*, Vol. 2, No. 2, 1990.

Silver, W., 3-D Scan Metamodel of the Software Life Cycle, *Software Quality World*, Vol. 2, No. 2, 1990, pp. 10–17.

Smith, W., Establishing an MIS Measurement Program to Measure Quality and Productivity, Quality Assurance Institute Research Report # 4, Quality Assurance Institute, 1990.

Spaulding, W.J., Selecting a Core Set of Management Metrics, Proc. 1st Intl. Conf. on Applications of Software Measurement (ASM'90), San Diego, November, 1990.

Spencer, N., METRICS Research Study Report, Northpoint Software Ventures, Framingham, MA, July 1992.

Symons, C. R., *Software Sizing & Estimating: Mark II Function Point Analysis*, John Wiley, 1991.

Troy, D.A., and Zweben, S.H., Measuring the Quality of Structured Designs, *Journal of Systems and Software*, Vol. 2, No. 2 (June 1981), pp. 113–120.

Tufte, E., *The Visual Display of Quantitative Information*, Graphics Press, 1993.

Tufte, E., *Envisioning Information*, Graphics Press, 1990.

United States Army, Software Test & Evaluation Guidelines, Dept. of the Army DA PAM 73-1, Vol. 6 draft dtd 15 June 1992.

United States General Accounting Office, Management Practices: US Companies Improve Performance Through Quality Efforts, GAO Report NSIAD-91-190, May 1991.

Vessey, I., and Weber, R., Some Factors Affecting Program Repair Maintenance: An Empirical Study, *Communications of the ACM*, Vol. 26, No. 2 (February 1983), pp. 128–134.

Vosburgh, J., et al., Productivity Factors and Programming Environments, IEEE 7th Intl. Conf on Software Engineering, March 1984, pp. 143–152.

Waguespack, L.J., and Badlani, S., Software Complexity Assessment: An Introduction and Annotated Bibliography, *Software Engineering Notes*, Vol. 12, No. 4 (October 1987), pp. 52–69.

Walston, C.E., and Felix, C.P., A Method of Programming Measurement and Estimation, *IBM Systems Journal*, Vol. 16, No. 1 (1977), pp. 54–73.

Ward, W.T., Software Defect Prevention Using McCabe's Complexity Metric, *Hewlett-Packard Journal*, April 1989, pp. 64–68.

Watts, R., *Measuring Software Quality*, National Computing Centre Booklet, Manchester, UK, 1987.

Weinberg, G., *The Psychology of Computer Programming*, Van Nostrand Rheinhold, 1971.

Weinberg, G., and Schulman, E., Goals and Performance in Computer Programming, *Human Factors*, Vol. 16, No. 1 (1974), pp. 70–77.

Weyuker, E.J., Evaluating Software Complexity Measures, *IEEE Trans. Software Engineering*, SE-14, No. 9, 1986, pp. 1357–1365.

Woodward, C., et al., Trends in Systems Development Among Productivity Enhancement Programme Members, Butler Cox PLC, London, 1989.

Yau, S.S., and Collofello, J.S., Design Stability Measures for Software Maintenance, *IEEE Trans. Software Engineering*, SE-11, No. 9 (September 1985), pp. 849–856.

Youll, D.P., *Making Software Development Visible: Effective Project Control*, John Wiley, 1990.

Zuse, H., *Software Complexity Measures and Models*, Walter deGruyter, 1990

Annotated Bibliography of Selected Publications

This section is a selective list of key publications and reference resources viewed as especially significant and highly recommended for supplemental reading or study. The list is grouped by topical category and each entry is annotated with a brief descriptive synopsis to help the reader locate or select further information on a topic or area of special interest. Anyone building their own library or wishing to obtain a deeper understanding of the rapidly growing and changing software measurement field should find the list helpful.

General Reference Materials

Applications of Software Measurement Conference Proceedings (ASM)

An annual conference held in November every year since 1990 (alternating between San Diego and Orlando). The conference emphasizes practical and pragmatic software measurement issues and applications. Proceedings are published by Software Quality Engineering and back sets may be ordered through SingleSource™. The proceedings typically include a one- or two-volume, large three-ring notebook with speaker presentation overheads; tutorial session notebooks; and a separately bound volume of any written papers supplied by the presenters.

Software Measurement Practices in Industry—Annual Survey Reports (1991 and up)

Annual surveys of industry practices covering usage and perceived value of most commonly cited or referenced measurements. Published as a technical report by Software Quality Engineering's Software Practices Research Center. May be ordered through SingleSource™.

American Programmer—Special Software Metrics Issue

The Vol. 4, No. 9 (September 1991) issue of *American Programmer* was dedicated to measurement. The issue contains four articles: "What Makes a Software Measure Successful?" (Card), "Measuring Rigor and Putting Measurement into Action" (Rubin), "Quality Metrics at AG Communication Systems" (Clay, Grzybowski, Webber, and Yourdon), and "Starting a Software Metrics Program: An Interview with Marilyn Bush" (Yourdon), plus a review of Capers Jones's book, *Applied Software Measurement*.

SEI Software Metrics Curriculum Module and Metrics Project

The Software Engineering Institute at Carnegie Mellon University provides a range of materials in support of measurement. Anyone considering offering a course should obtain the SEI Curriculum Module which includes a topical overview of the field and an annotated list of references.

AMI (Applications of Metrics in Industry) Handbook

AMI is an ESPRIT project providing a measurement program approach. The project has developed a handbook that offers a 12-step continuous improvement method (Assess, Analyze, Metricate, Improve) that was developed collaboratively using results from past ESPRIT projects . The project attempted to validate its method on 19 industrial projects, covering a spectrum of applications from commercial data processing to real-time control. The project also publishes a periodic newsletter called *De Facto*. For further information contact Robin Whitty at the Centre for Systems and Software Engineering, South Bank University, 103 Borough Road, London SE1 0AA.

International Standards—IEEE and ISO

Several software measurement-related standards have been developed under the sponsorship of the IEEE. This includes P1061 Standard for a Software Quality Metrics Methodology (May 1992) and P1045 Standard for Software Productivity Metrics (Sept 1988). Also of interest is Standard 1074 for Developing Life Cycle Processes which outlines a standard set of activity tasks. Some useful material related to measurement may also be found in the ISO 9000 series of quality management standards. ISO 9000-3 contains guidelines for the application of ISO 9001 to the development and maintenance of software.

IFPUG—International Function Point Users Group

The International Function Point Users Group provides a Function Point Counting Practices Manual and conducts an annual conference.

Measurement Books—Still in Print and Generally Available

This section includes all software measurement specific books known to the author that are still in print and generally available. *They are listed in reverse chronological order.* All may be ordered through SingleSource™.

Automated Software Quality Measurement—Keith Jones

A practical how-to with lots of examples covering automated monitoring and analysis of software quality within a large-scale mainframe environment. [Jones 93]

Practical Software Metrics for Project Management & Process Improvement—Bob Grady

A nifty book that lives up to its title in delivering practical and application-oriented advice for project and process managers. The book highlights Hewlett-Packard's experiences using software metrics; incorporates lots (over 70) of charts and graphs from real projects; and shows how the metrics can be rolled up into useful and workable organization indicators. Also includes a good bibliography. [Grady 92]

Measuring and Motivating Maintenance Programmers—Jerome Landsbaum and Bob Glass

A small paperback that describes Landsbaum's personal experience in information systems support at Monsanto. It deals with the frustrations and people issues of the software maintenance staff and how to go about elevating their professionalism. The book reports on what was done at Monsanto to improve the quality, productivity, and morale of the maintainers. It illustrates the metrics and tools they used and outlines the presentation they developed to explain (sell) the value of maintenance to management. [Landsbaum 92]

Measures for Excellence: Reliable Software on Time, Within Budget—
Larry Putnam, Ware Myers

Any organization using or thinking about employing automated size estimation and project tracking tools should take a look at this book. Putnam shares his experience with size estimation modelling and provides a lot of insight about what he and the industry have learned. The book describes a lot of what up until now had been proprietary QSM techniques for performing software estimations and measuring productivity, although most organizations who really want to use the techniques will probably still have to hire Putnam's company to help them. [Putnam 92]

Software Sizing & Estimating: Mk II Function Point Analysis—
Charles Symons

Organizations using or considering function points as a tool for project sizing and estimating should make sure they take a look at this book. Featuring case studies of actual applications, it provides a step-by-step guide for the new Mk II FP estimating method. [Symons 91]

Software Metrics — A Rigorous Approach—Norm Fenton

This was the first software metrics book to offer a philosophy and framework for how to approach the subject. It explains the common pitfalls of most measurement efforts and how to avoid them. The book is a must for measurement specialists trying to set up or revamp a new measurement program. It describes metrics strategies and how to set up experiments to validate metrics and models. [Fenton 91]

Software Engineering Metrics—Martin Sheppard

This book offers a collection of papers and original work from a group of experts in the field of software metrics. It also draws from non-software literature on measurement theory, statistical analysis, and experimental design. The result is a sourcebook on implementing code complexity measures, theoretical and empirical validation procedures, early life cycle metrics, automated measurement techniques, and a variety of software metric theories and methodologies. [Sheppard 91]

Applied Software Measurement—Capers Jones

The author describes "Applied Software Measurement" as the " . . . emerging discipline associated with the accurate and meaningful collection of information which has practical value to software management and staffs. The goal is to provide a set of useful, tangible data points for sizing, estimating, managing, and controlling software projects with rigor and precision." The book is organized into five major chapters plus an appendix providing an example of a measured project and annual baseline report. Chapters 1 and 2 are introductory and cover the history and evolution of metrics with a special emphasis on function points. Chapter 3 reports productivity and quality averages from a broad range of rather large U.S. projects completed between 1950 and 1990. While the data supplied in this chapter is extensive and informative, supporting validation and backup is lacking. Most readers will probably end up with more questions than actionable answers. Jones acknowledges this in his conclusion at the end of the chapter when he states that "the tables and data included are only provisional and many will no doubt be proved wrong in the future . . . it is hoped that at least the right set of curves and factors have been selected and that the general shapes and dimensions are correct." [Jones 91]

Software Complexity Measures & Models—Horst Zuse

This is a very difficult to read but comprehensive attempt to survey software complexity measures. We found it too detailed and in a few cases too theoretical to recommend for inclusion in SingleSource™, but it might be important for the measurement theorist or specialist to have on hand. Much of the information is drawn from Zuse's dissertation at the University of Berlin with several additional years of research at the IBM TJ Watson Research Center in Yorktown Heights. [Zuse 91]

Software Engineering with Formal Metrics—Lem Ejiogu

Ejiogu offers us a broad, integrated approach to the use of metrics in support of effective software engineering. The book offers a unified (albeit somewhat heavy and theoretical) view of how to assess complexity, appraise requirement definition, evaluate design, quantify quality, and validate products. [Ejiogu 91]

Art of Computer Systems Performance Analysis—Raj Jain

This is the best book available on the special topic of performance analysis. Jain has a considerable base of industry experience to draw on as he discusses modeling, simulation, and analysis methods for a variety of systems including networks, database management systems, and distributed systems. However, the book assumes substantial statistical background from the reader and can be pretty tough to plow through. Includes a good case study from Digital Equipment Corporation. [Jain 91]

Making Software Development Visible — Effective Project Control— David Youll

This management-oriented book focuses on the basics of project visibility — plans, schedule, deliverables, quality, and so forth. Many samples of plots and trend graphs covering these are included for illustration. The book does not contain hard measurement data but does provide the beginning project manager with good ideas for what should be measured and how to present it. [Youll 90]

Measuring Software Design Quality—David Card and Bob Glass

In this short but informative book on measuring software design quality, the authors have shown not only what to measure (as a starting point), but have given some useful insight on how to use the measurements once collected. The book is divided into three parts. The first of these begins with an obligatory discussion on the importance of software design and measurement. It continues with a proposed measurement approach based on a set of key measures. The focus is to limit one's efforts to a few quality characteristics rather than becoming mired in the details of trying to measure everything. Part 2 of this book was geared toward engineering applications of measurement. Initially, two models of complexity were examined: software science and cyclomatic complexity. The authors explain that while cyclomatic measurement of complexity has some practical applications, software science does not. Next in order was an examination of design modularization heuristics including module size, data coupling, span of control, and module strength/cohesion. A summary is given of the effect on cost and fault rate of each of the aforementioned concepts. This part ends with a discussion of the relationship between design complexity and the factors that contribute to that complexity. The third part of the book, and possibly the most useful, centers around management applications of design measurements. Project estimation (size, cost, schedule, and performance), quality control, and process analysis. The author concludes with a review (actually, almost a plea) as to the importance of measurement and its role in the future of software engineering. [Card 90]

Software Quality Assurance & Evaluation—James Dobbins

This book is aimed at practitioners actively involved in assessing and measuring the quality of software products. While not strictly a measurement book, it has enough emphasis and data in it to be included in this list. The foreword states that if there is one thing wrong with the book, it is the title, because developers and software engineers may pass it by. We recommend they don't. By gaining an understanding of what software activities can do, engineering and management can better appreciate quality assurance's roles and be better able to incorporate the quality discipline into their activities. Special topics and chapters covering initiation of the SQA activity including planning and budgeting, fairly extensive coverage of software inspections, government, military and industry quality standards, and an appendix with a variety of guides and checklists including sample SQA audit checklists and proposal scoring forms. [Dobbins 90]

Function Point Analysis—J. Dreger

This is a good introduction to function points and their use for measuring an application from an end user perspective. The book includes a good description of how to identify and "weigh" function points. A strong suit of the book is the frequent use of solid examples. [Dreger 89]

Managing the Software Process—Watts Humphrey

This book offers practical guidance for managing the software development and maintenance process. The approach is to provide a framework and technique for evaluating and improving the process of doing software, rather than presenting a specific set of solutions. This book grew out of work at the Software Engineering Institute at Carnegie Mellon University on a U.S. Air Force project. The objective was to help the military select capable software contractors. The method developed for evaluating their strengths and weaknesses has proven valuable in assessing other software organizations. [Humphrey 89]

Benchmarking: The Search for Industry Best Practices—Robert Camp

One important technique of measurement that is often overlooked by many companies is benchmarking. Benchmarking is the process of establishing a baseline of comparison within a company or with other companies. This book clearly spells out the process of conducting benchmarks based on the author's experience at the Xerox Corporation. [Camp 89]

Cost Estimation for Software Development—Bernard Londeix

This book surveys the role of estimation and presents a comparison of the Putnam-based approach versus Boehms COCOMO methods. Also includes coverage of supporting estimation tools. [Londeix 88]

Software Metrics: Establishing a Company-Wide Program—
Bob Grady and Deb Caswell

This book focuses on the efforts at Hewlett-Packard to establish a meaningful program to collect and analyze information to assist in the management and development of quality systems. Many papers and a few
books have previously addressed this subject, usually based upon isolated case studies conducted at several different companies. This book
examines the implementation of Hewlett-Packard's Software Metrics
Council, progress to date, and strategy for future effort. The authors have
taken special care to present all work in a professional, unbiased manner. Shortcomings as well as successes are explained in sufficient detail
to allow readers to draw their own conclusions and possibly develop a
similar model within their own organizations. [Grady 87]

Software Reliability: Measurement, Prediction, Application—
John Musa, et al.

This book grew out of an internal class taught at AT&T Bell Laborato-
ries. The authors also gained experience and insight by testing and refin-
ing the book's ideas on a large number of software projects at AT&T. It
offers the best coverage of reliability models and measurement we have
seen. Examples and case study problems are sprinkled liberally throughout and help the reader over some of the more theoretical spots. The
authors state that "... although much 'how-to-do-it' information is provided, the value of practically oriented insight is recognized." There has
been a conscious effort to avoid theoretical exuberance. The book is nicely
indexed so that it can serve as a reference, and a glossary of terms and
notations used are provided in the appendix. Another useful appendix
contains a summary of all the formulas needed. [Musa 87]

Programming Productivity—Capers Jones

This books is primarily a study of programmer productivity, especially
as it might be predicted by the Software Productivity, Quality, and
Reliability (SPQR) model developed by the author. A total of 20 major
and 25 other factors that influence productivity are enumerated, many
of which are input to the SPQR model. The book offers some illuminat-
ing discussions of some currently used metrics and problems associated
with them. [Jones 86]

Controlling Software Projects: Management, Measurement,
Estimation—Tom DeMarco

This is one of the first books to address measurement and estimation.
DeMarco shows in a nontechnical style how to effectively organize soft-

ware projects so they are objectively measurable and prescribes a number of helpful methods to forecast the costs of the future software projects and to track a project's progress with respect to its estimates. [DeMarco 82]

Software Engineering Economics—Barry Boehm

An excellent reference book on software measurements. Heavy emphasis on estimating including an in-depth explanation of the COCOMO model. Even though this book was published almost 10 years ago, it is still one of the most referenced and quoted books on the subject of software measurement. [Boehm 81]

Measurement Books—Out of Print But Important for Reference

This section includes significant software measurement specific books that are now out of print and generally unavailable. They are listed in reverse chronological order. Copies are available in most major research libraries.

Software Engineering Metrics & Models—S. Conte, H. Dunsmore

The authors have done a commendable job of collecting available material on measurements and metrics related to productivity and quality in the software development process. The result is a good reference text on the subject. There are good discussions of materials that have been applied in a practitioner's sense. The authors also show results from some of their own experiments to verify various metrics. The book is easy to read; the mathematics are nicely worked in without the need to refer to other publications. [Conte 86]

Measuring Programmer Productivity & Software Quality—L. Arthur

This book provides a look at the various aspects of how to measure productivity and complexity including a good explanation of McCabe's metrics. The author presents a set of 11 software quality metrics, including correctness, efficiency, maintainability, and reliability. These 11 metrics are then described as functions of a more basic set of some 22 different software quality criteria. The author then discusses these metrics in some detail, with specific references to various programming languages. [Arthur 85]

Software Metrics—A. Perlis, et al.

This book provides a review of the status of software metrics as of 1981 or slightly before. Specifically, it contains a number of state-of-the-art evaluations, as well as recommendations for research initiatives in related areas of software metrics. The papers were first presented to a cross-section of the computer science research community at the National Academy of Science in 1980. For reference purposes, it also contains an extensive annotated bibliography of more than 350 related references. [Perlis 81]

Elements of Software Science—M. Halstead

This book is a now a classic on the history of software metrics, the original book expounding the principles of the generally now refuted software science. Principal attractions of the theory presented was the notion of a unified theory of software metrics. [Halstead 77]

Software Metrics—Tom Gilb

The first metrics book—and fun to read if you can find an old copy. Gilb provides a lengthy list of interesting measures and shows how they can be used to predict and help manage the software efforts. [Gilb 77]

Other Books of Measurement Interest

This section includes several other books of special interest to software measurement. While not dedicated to measurement, they do contain key sections and are highly recommended. They are listed in reverse chronological order and most can be obtained through SingleSource™

Software Reviews & Audits Handbook—Charles Hollocker

This is a comprehensive book on reviews that incorporates the perspective of the IEEE standard (Hollocker was the chairman of the effort that produced the ANSI/IEEE Standard for Software Reviews and Audits). The book has some fresh material with good coverage of software audits and an emphasis on the use of audits for what Hollocker refers to as a "controlled process evolution." The human side of reviews is not emphasized. The books appendix is lengthy and contains 130 pages of sample checklists, forms, and report documents. [Hollocker 90]

Handbook of Walkthroughs, Inspections & Technical Reviews—
D. Freedman and G. Weinberg

A revised and updated version that provides full coverage of current trends, techniques, and methods of formal review. Practical and comprehensive in an interesting question and answer style. [Freedman 82]

The Mythical Man Month—Fred Brooks

This collection of thought-provoking essays on the management of computer programming projects is drawn from the author's own experience as a project manager for the IBM System/360 and for OS/360, its operating system. Although formulated as separate essays, the book expresses a central argument that large programming projects have different management problems from small projects due to the division of labor. [Brooks 75]

Studies, Experiments, and Special Publications

This section includes a selection of various studies and special publications (other than books) considered important as reference material to the software measurement field. The selections are listed in reverse chronological order (newest first). The Software Practices Research Center (a new unit within Software Quality Engineering) intends to maintain a library of these publications and will assist readers or researchers in obtaining copies. Write to the Center Director at 3000-2 Hartley Rd, Jacksonville, FL 32257 for assistance.

A Critical Look at Software Capability Evaluations—T. Bollinger, C. McGowan

A critique of the SEI process maturity model and the approach used for assessment (measurement) of an organizations maturity level. Points out many flaws and weaknesses and also highlights strengths. [Bollinger 91]

Are Software Cost Estimation Models Accurate?—R. Kusters, et al.

Reports on a very interesting experiment where a group of project managers were asked to estimate a project that had already been completed. Estimates were also developed using two commercial tools. The result was that the management estimates turned out better than the tools with all the estimates tending to overestimate the actual. The model estimates differed by a factor of two but participants found them helpful in drawing attention to issues that otherwise might have been overlooked. [Kusters 90]

Software Defect Prevention Using McCabe's Complexity Metric— J. Ward

Case study supporting the use of McCabe complexity, especially when module control flows were graphed. Engineers (Hewlett-Packard) were found to respond better to a visual image of complexity than to just numbers. [Ward 89]

Software Development Effort Prediction Based on Function Points—
G. Knafl and J. Sacks

An analysis of published function point data that concludes that they cannot be effectively used for predicting project schedules. [Knafl 86]

Measuring Applications Development Performance—S. Drummond

A description of the Hallmark Cards variation of function point counting and a successful case study of the use of function points. [Drummond 85]

Establishment and Validation of Software Metric Factors—
R. Rambo, et al.

An analysis of various static complexity measures and the threshold values that contributed to above-average error (defect) rates. Concludes the number of decision statements in a module should be under 15. [Rambo 85]

Fifteen Years of Psychology in Software Engineering: Individual
Differences and Cognitive Science—B. Curtis

Summarizes what we know and don't know about how programmers learn and solve problems. [Curtis 85]

Identifying Error-Prone Software—An Empirical Study—V. Shen

Analysis of data from five IBM program products showing that simple code measures can be useful in identifying error-prone modules early in development. Compares a variety of measures. [Shen 85]

Prototyping vs. Specifying: A Multi-Project Experiment—Barry
Boehm, et al.

An experiment with duplicate development of a small product by seven student teams. Four used traditional specifications and three used prototyping. Results showed certain measured advantages for both. [Boehm 84]

Productivity Factors and Programming Environments—
J. Vosburgh, et al.

Reports on a series of measurements made on a projects at ITT correlating productivity with various programming practices and environments. [Vosburgh 84]

Software Function, Source Lines of Code, and Development Effort Prediction: A Software Science Validation—Alan Albrecht and John Gaffney

This article explains function points and relates them to Halstead's metrics. It shows that they can be used effectively to estimate software size and effort. [Albrecht 83]

Some Factors Affecting Program Repair Maintenance: An Empirical Study—I. Vessey and R. Weber

Report on two studies that examined the relationship of various measures (factors) on maintenance effort and quality for a production Cobol shop. The effects of factors like complexity, structure, modularity, number of runs, and so on were unexpectedly small. [Vessey 83]

Evaluation of a Software Requirements Document by Analysis of Change Data—V. Basili, et al.

Case study of measures made on the changes to a large-scale baselined requirements document. [Basili 81]

Measuring the Quality of Structured Designs—D. Troy and S. Zweben

Various design measures of properties like cohesion, coupling, complexity, modularity, and size were compared on a single project. The coupling measures were viewed as most correlated to quality. [Troy 81]

Goals and Perfomance in Computer Programming—G. Weinberg and E. Schulman

Reports on the now 20-year-old but still famous experiment where six teams were given the same programming assignment but with different objectives. Each team optimized its own objectives. [Weinberg 74]

Measurement Tools and Services

This appendix contains a sampling of the primary vendors offering measurement tools and services. The list is ordered alphabetically by vendor name and includes contact information for the vendor along with a brief synopsis of what that vendor offers. The list includes large software houses with multiple measurement products and services available as well as smaller companies with just one or two products but who derive a large percentage of revenue from the measurement area. The intent is to help acquaint the reader with the services that are available and facilitate further follow-up or analysis.

WARNING! This list is not intended in any sense of the word to be a *complete* tools reference list. Not listed are the main hardware vendors (IBM, DEC, HP, etc., who also market a number of measurement products) or companies with small customer bases. Even defining a measurement tool is difficult as *any* good tool supports some of the basic input, output or results measures. Vendor products and the companies that offer them are in a state of constant development and change. Readers who are interested in selecting new tools should check with any of the reputable tool reference services that maintain tool availability information and publish reference guides and indexes. (See, for example, the Tools Reference Services available from Software Quality Engineering.)

Advanced Software Automation
3130 A Coronado Drive
Santa Clara, CA 95054
408-492-1668

Hindsight—An integrated software environment to describe existing program structure, logic flow, test coverage, performance, complexity, and productivity in a graphic, interactive format. Summarizes status of each system component on a colored structure chart graphically.

AGS Management Systems
880 First Avenue
King of Prussia, PA 19406
215-265-1550

Wings—Project management tool with planning, estimation, and tracking facilities. Supports distributed project management. Features include critical path analysis and float calculation, budgeting and cost management. Companion product provides graphic charts and reporting.

Applied Business Technology
361 Broadway, New York, NY 10013
212-219-8945

Metrics Manager—Measurement data collection and analysis repository. Provides for comparison with industry-wide means. Captures project characteristics and metrics including methodologies used, size (function points or KLOC), defect and failure rates, delivery rates, productivity statistics, performance statistics, and so forth. Provides many graphing and reporting options.

Project Workbench—Project scheduling, tracking, analyzing, and reporting tool.

Project Bridge—Front-end planning and estimating system to provide estimates and project task templates.

Applied Computer Research
PO Box 82266
Phoenix, AZ 85071
602-995-5929

ACR is not involved much with software measurement directly, but they do maintain a database of computing installations and market a variety of research publications including the *Software Engineer's Benchmark Handbook*.

Bullseye Software
5129 24th Ave. NE, Suite 9
Seattle, WA 98105
206-524-3575

C-Cover—Provides instrumentation-based test coverage analysis of C programs.

Cadre Technologies
2111 Wilson Blvd. Suite 700
Arlington, VA 22201
703-875-8670

CodeMap—Analyzes coverage for Ada and C without requiring instrumentation.

Computer Associates

Computer Associates is a large software house offering a broad set of software support packages including a number that directly support software measurement. Most of the companies' revenues come from the mainframe environment, but the company has a division located in San Jose that offers and supports PC-based products.

CA-METRICS—Project planning and metrics reposition support with comparison to industry norms and averages.

CA-FPXpert—Function Point Analysis and Counting Tool. Helps ensure consistency of counting and provides historical tracking. Also supports retro-counting for existing systems. Integrates with common front-end CASE tools.

CA-Tellaplan—Project planning and analysis, Gantt charts, critical path analysis.

Super Project Expert—Resource management, scheduling, and cost control

CA-PLANMACS—Project estimating and planning.

CA-ESTIMACS—Estimates for software projects.

Computer Power Group
823 Commerce Drive
Oak Brook, IL 60521
708-574-3030   FAX 708-574-3076

CPG as a company is best known for providing contract services staffing. They also support consulting in project management, quality, and metrics. The Applied Information Development division of CPG was the original developer of *MARS (Metric Analysis and Reporting System)* now marketed as Metrics Manager by Applied Business Technology. Provide overall support of measurement program implementation.

Compuware
31440 Northwestern Highway
Farmington Hills, MI 48018
313-737-7300

Compuware is a major software house offering a broad range of products focused on the IBM mainframe and CICS operating environment. Several specialized measurement products include:

PATHVU—Portfolio analysis for COBOL or Assembler programs providing static analysis of many common program measures like numbers of IF or looping statements, nesting level, percentage of control statements, verbs, data elements, element references, and so on. PATHVU categorizes programs into one of four categories or sectors that can help the organization baseline its status based on these basic measures. Also inserts comments in the Cobol source listing indicating branch paths and has a companion product called DATAVU that can provide a data dictionary indicating data attributes and where each is used or referenced.

Data & Analysis Center for Software
Rome Air Development Center
PO Box 120
Utica, NY 13503
315-336-0937

Quality Evaluation System (QUES)

EVB Software Engineering
5320 Spectrum Drive
Frederick, MD 21701
301-671-1475

CMT Complexity Measures Tool—Provides static analysis metrics to assist in Ada development.

Fleet Combat Direction Systems Support Activity
San Diego, CA
703-671-1475

CMS-2 Test Coverage Analyzer—Provides flow analysis of source code, inserts instrumentation code at branch points, and reports on coverage for VAX/VMS, MS-DOS, and CMS-2 environments.

CMS-2 Source Code Metrics Generator—Develops static metric reports including calltree hierarchy.

Howard Rubin Associates
Winterbottom Lane
Pound Ridge, NY 10576
914-764-4931

Rubin & Associates is a specialty company in the software measurement area. Their founder (Howard Rubin) is an active speaker and consultant and helped develop what used to be called RA-METRICS and FPXpert (now called CA-METRICS™ and CA-FPXpert™ and offered by Computer Associates). He is also associated with many other innovative measurement ideas (the "I/S measurement dashboard" and "readiness footprints" using a modified Kiviatt diagram are prime examples). The company offers consulting in installing new measurement programs as well as baselining and benchmarking services with comparison to its database of over 13,000 projects that have been measured by CA-METRICS users (claimed to be the world's largest). The company also offers training services and a variety of seminars and presentations on measurement related topics and authored the *Software Engineer's Benchmark Handbook* marketed by Applied Computer Research.

Marconi Systems Technology
1111 Jefferson Davis Highway
Arlington, VA 22202
703-920-7581

RTM—Strips requirements into a database for classification and keyword searching. Interfaces with Teamwork and Software Through Pictures CASE tools. Tracks requirements and design changes and provides traceability reporting. Operates on SUN, DEC, or HP systems.

McCabe & Associates
5501 Twin Knolls Road, Suite 111
Columbia, MD 21045
800-638-6316

McCabe & Associates is a services and software company with a special focus on software testing, validation and quality assurance. Its founder, Tom McCabe, developed the code-based structured testing methodology that led to the subsequent tool development. They offer consulting and seminars and are best known for two tool products—ACT and Battlemap.

ACT—Analysis of Complexity Tool to analyze source code and plot its control flow graphically. The tool provides basic complexity measures, quantifies the number of tests needed, and identifies test paths and conditions needed to achieve structural code coverage.

Battlemap—Analyzes existing code to identify modules (based on simple code measures) as candidates for maintenance or redesign.

Primavera Systems
Two Bala Plaza
Bala Cynwyd, PA 19004
215-677-8600

Primavera Project Planner—Project planning and scheduling. Highlights major review points, commitment dates, key constraints, and project dependencies. Supports entry of time sheet information and networking. Will import or export to Lotus, DBase, or Excel files.

Program Analyzers
56 Northbrook Street
Newbury, Berkshire
UK RG13 1AN
44-635-52-8828

TESTBED—Static and dynamic analysis to provide information on control flow, logical complexity, data flow, and variable usage. Provides coverage reporting and reports violations of assertions.

Programming Research Corporation
6401 Golden Triangle Drive, Suite 450
Greenbelt, MD 20770
410-982-2095

QA Manager—Checks for a broad range of reliability, portability, and maintainability standards and issues in C or Fortran code. Computes most of the normal static metrics and supports their analysis and reporting.

Protocol
500 International Drive
Mt. Olive, NJ 07828
201-347-7900

RTrace—A general requirements management tool that provides tracing and change reporting on SUN, VAX/VMS, and IBM RS6000 environments. Interfaces with Teamwork and Software Through Pictures CASE tools.

QualTrak
1250 Oakmead Parkway, Suite 210
Sunnyvale, CA 94088
617-273-0140

DDT—Distributed Defect Tracking—An incident-tracking and bug-reporting system with many graphical outputs and reports. Produces fault profiles.

Quantitative Software Management
McLean, VA

SLIM—Software Life Cycle Management—Project planning, tracking and cost analysis.

Programmers Planner—Project estimating.

Schemacode
89 Glenbrooke, Suite 100
Dollard Des Ormeaux
Qc, Canada H9A 2L7
514-683-8693

DATRIX—A comprehensive static analyzer with many graphical outputs to help profile code-based information. Produces program control graphs and analyzes relationships between units.

SET Laboratories
PO Box 868
Mulino, Oregon 97042
503-829-7123

PC-METRIC—Provides a range of static-code-based measurements including the major Halstead and McCabe complexity measures as well as Lines of Code and other common static measurements. Supporting products in the form of what is called a Professional Toolkit include PC-KIVIAT to generate a kiviat diagram and KB-QUERY to provide inter-active query reports that list modules exceeding or not meeting a given value range, create pie charts or histograms, produce scattergrams, and compute descriptive statistics.

Software Blacksmiths
6064 St. Ives Way
Mississauga, Ontario
Canada L5N 4M1
416-858-4466

C Metric—Calculates path complexity and counts lines of code, state-ments, and comments in C, C++, DOS, OS-2 environments.

Software Productivity Research
PO Box 1033
Massachusetts Avenue
Cambridge, MA 02140
617-495-0120

Checkpoint™—Software scheduling and estimation package. Provides comparison to standard norms based on data from over 3000 projects. Provides high-level analysis of project strengths and weaknesses, Gantt chart monitoring of project status, "What If" capabilities for evaluating alternative options, and built-in or user-definable charts of accounts. Provides estimates by activity of cost, effort, quality, schedules, and pro-ductivity with sizing for major deliverables of specifications, code, docu-mentation, test cases, and test runs. Normalizes between Function Points, Feature Points, and Lines of Code.

Software Quality Automation
1 Parker Street
Lawrence, MA 01843

SQA Manager—Overall tracking of test assets and incidents.

Robot—Capture playback tool for regression testing with automatic log files.

Software Quality Engineering
3000-2 Hartley Rd.
Jacksonville, FL 32257
904-268-8639

SQE manages the annual international ASM (Applications of Software Measurement) conference that was referenced frequently in the book and is the author's employer. SQE provides training and consulting in measurement and testing and annually surveys measurement practices. They maintain the SingleSource™ book service and a database of testing, evaluation, and measurement tools. They also provide baseline practices assessments and track software practices research.

Software Quality Tools Corporation
2000 West Park Drive, Suite 200
Westborough, MA 01581
508-366-5045

Software Quality Management System (SQMS)—A facility for a software project data repository and problem-tracking reporting. Using the tracking database SQMS provides reliability measurement and provides quality and volatility indexes on a module-by-module or subsystem basis.

Software Research
625 Third Street
San Francisco, CA 94107
415-957-1441

SRI has developed a series of specialized measurement tools focused on code coverage analysis and the measurement of the testing activity. They also offer consulting and training and sponsor the annual Quality Week conference held in San Francisco each spring.

TCAT/PATH—Path Test Coverage Analysis Tool—Provides dynamic analysis and code coverage reporting. Highlights "hit" and "not hit" areas of code segments and modules.

TSCOPE—Test Data Observation and Analysis System—Provides graphical analysis of source code flow and program structure or call trees.

Tiburon Systems
1290 Parkmoor Avenue
San Jose, CA 95126

Ferret—An automated testing product that supports requirements analysis imported as text. Tests are linked to the requirements with "buttons" for traceability. Writes and maintains defect reports. Predicts target quality level (reliability) using the Musa-Okumoto method.

Verilog
Beauregard Square, Suite 340
6303 Little River Turnpike
Alexandria, VA 22312

LOGISCOPE—Complexity analysis of software design and code as well as test coverage analysis is supported. Output in the form of Kiviat diagrams, control graphs, and call graphs is provided. Supports most common languages (Ada, Assembly, C, Cobol, Fortran, Pascal, PL/1, PL/M). The company also offers support and training services in the areas of quality management and software technology. Architecture and component results.

Veritas
4800 Great America Parkway, Suite 420
Santa Clara, CA 95054
408-727-1222

VistaTEST—Provides static and dynamic code measurement using a language independent preprocessor. The static report provides lines, segments, paths, interfaces, and function entry/exits as well as Halstead and McCabe measures. Dynamic data shows which parts of the code are reached by which test cases along with interface coverage for externally defined functions, code segments exercised, and test cases that duplicate coverage. Various plots are also available with a companion product VistaGRAPH.

VIASOFT
3033 North 44th Street
Phoenix, Arizona 85018
800-525-7775

VIA/SmartDoc—Provides documentation and measurement reporting for COBOL programs in MVS mainframe environment.

Index